A WALKING FLAME
SELECTED MAGICAL WRITINGS OF ITHELL COLQUHOUN

A Walking Flame: Selected Magical Writings of Ithell Colquhoun
Edited by Amy Hale

FIRST PUBLISHED by Strange Attractor Press in 2026, in a limited hardback and unlimited paperback edition.

DESIGN by Tihana Šare.
TYPESET in Alverata Regular & Irregular.

ISBN: 9781913689773

DISTRIBUTED by The MIT Press, Cambridge, Massachusetts. And London, England.

PRINTED AND BOUND in Estonia by Tallinna Raamatutrükikoda.

STRANGE ATTRACTOR PRESS
BM SAP, London, WC1N 3XX, UK
www.strangeattractor.co.uk

A WALKING FLAME

SELECTED MAGICAL WRITINGS OF ITHELL COLQUHOUN

Edited By

AMY HALE

CONTENTS

Introduction

After nearly sinking into obscurity, in the first decades of the twenty-first century, surrealist and occultist Ithell Colquhoun (1906-1988) is finally experiencing the glow of the spotlight on a life and uniquely powerful body of work that continues to shatter boundaries and expectations. Given the breadth and depth of her output, as evidenced in the vast archives of her work that remain, the woman was utterly tireless. I honestly doubt she ever slept. Although much of the recent interest in Colquhoun's work is focused on her painting and drawing, often within the context of her relationship to surrealism and the occult, she would have very likely perceived of herself as a writer as much as she was a visual artist. Colquhoun's written legacy includes eight book length manuscripts both published and unpublished, poems and prose poems, essays and observations and an unpublished autobiography of her youth. The subjects she addressed vacillated wildly, ranging from Celtic magic to alchemy, painting techniques, philosophy, aesthetics, a spiritual tour of Egypt, magical novels, and a truly weird and rambling account of the life of Aleister Crowley. She ranted about the discomfort and oppression of women's clothes and the needs to conform to the male gaze. She wrote about the ways in which women have to hide their light and be socially acceptable at all times. She described hiking her skirts and urinating behind a pyramid. One thing is very certain about Ithell Colquhoun: She was a woman who had something to say, yet it is only now, so many years after her death, that we can finally truly hear her.

In both her art and writing, Colquhoun greatly desired visibility, yet she was unwilling to water down her ideas to make them palatable or acceptable, and this uncompromising nature doubtlessly impacted her marketability. By most objective standards, Colquhoun's list of published works during her lifetime was impressive, yet even her consistent publishing record likely did not satisfy her desires to see public engagement with her work and ideas. Her archives show dogged determination at working to get published, yet despite the fact that she pushed manuscripts constantly to agents and publishers, a number of her novels, essays and short stories remained unpublished during her lifetime. Her quirky travelogues *Crying of the Wind: Ireland* and *The Living Stones: Cornwall*, both written in the 1950s, were likely her most popular and accessible publications during her lifetime and remain so to this day. Although her short surrealist novella *The Goose of Hermogenes* was critically acclaimed, it was hardly written for a mass audience. Most of her fictional writings were, frankly, not well organised, turgidly allegorical and simply challenging to read. Her characters were often poorly developed and seemed to stand in for higher allegorical concepts and archetypes rather than being developed and well rounded. Her attempts at nonfiction were often characterised by opinionated intrusion, which was a feature of many of her essays as well. *The Sword Of Wisdom*, published in 1975, one of the first historical accounts of Samuel "MacGregor" Mathers and the legacy of the Golden Dawn, has been frequently dismissed by later historians as unreliable as it recounted too many unsubstantiated stories and gossip. While that may be a somewhat unfair assessment that degrades the historical importance of that text, it is still very true that *Sword of Wisdom* suffers from many of the idiosyncratic features that afflicted Colquhoun's writing and kept her from being as widely read as she may have liked.

Despite Colquhoun's stylistic drawbacks, she wrote a great deal that was of value, and her command of her material and unique voice actually did resonate with many readers. Colquhoun found measured success in publishing smaller form pieces throughout her life, and could boast a not insignificant number of published poems, essays and even travel guides. Colquhoun scholar Richard Shillitoe has done the world a great service in posthumously publishing many of Colquhoun's unpublished and also some previously published works. His edited volumes *Medea's Charms*, an essential collection of essays, poems and prose poems and also his volume of *I Saw Water*, co-edited with Mark Morrisson, are exceptionally valuable in understanding Colquhoun's range. From the 1930s onward, Colquhoun aimed her publishing most successfully toward literary magazines, poetry journals, newspapers, popular occult magazines, and increasingly toward the end of her life specialist publications aimed at the growing occult and Pagan markets. Perhaps Colquhoun's widest audience for her shorter pieces was gained from 1968 to 1970 when she wrote short guides for budget travellers for the *Times Educational Supplement*, sharing her unique experiences of Ireland and Cornwall, but also Prague, Germany and Egypt. Yet throughout her life the one topic to which she always returned was magic.

Colquhoun wrote about all sorts of magical and esoteric subjects and her preferred format for doing so seemed to be the essay, which perhaps allowed for her to experiment with a wider variety of topics, and which frankly, gave her the most publishing opportunities. Colquhoun never wrote a full-length non-fiction instructional or theoretical text about her magic and she was far from unique as a woman occultist in this regard. With the exception of the highly influential magician Dion Fortune, full-length women's magical monographs in the twentieth century were rare. As a woman magician in early twentieth century Britain, Fortune was rather outstanding in her written legacy, even though her occult novels and magical writings about the Kabbalah are uncomfortably littered with classist and racist slurs which make for challenging reading today. Yet it is possible that Colquhoun's forays into book length esoteric fiction, such as *I Saw Water* and *Destination Limbo* were inspired by Fortune's successes in that genre. In earlier periods there were a number of well-known and successful woman occult writers of spiritual texts, of course Helena Blavatsky is a stand out, but Annie Besant and Alice Bailey are also notable. Yet in the early twentieth century post Golden Dawn flowering of British occultism, the majority of leading women practitioners of Hermeticism and magic did not produce full length texts, although they certainly did publish, mostly, like Colquhoun, in journals and magazines.

Although occult periodicals had a particular set of applications for women occult writers, Mark Morrisson has made an excellent argument about the wider role of the occult periodical from 1879 to 1920 as a form of discourse within the public sphere and also as exemplifying positions of occult modernity[1]. Occult periodicals were dynamic, often well circulated publications where debate and exchange could occur. As Morrisson notes, occult orders are generally portrayed as primarily concerned with esoteric hidden knowledge suitable only for initiates. However, in the late nineteenth and twentieth centuries these groups were often also concerned with wider cultural debates and were certainly invested in ideas of social reform that would emerge from a widespread recentring of spirituality, often with reference to principles of scientific progress and empiricism. Although Morrisson is focused on early publications emerging primarily from Spiritualism and Theosophy, I would argue that throughout the twentieth century and even into the internet era, occult publications are designed to not only develop community and conversation internally, they also have an externally facing legitimising function, and point to the desire of the building of a wider social movement advocating spiritual progress. Occult publications have historically intended, in fact, still intend to help build a better world by more widely disseminating esoteric teachings, and inspiring potential initiates. Despite a perception that occult periodicals are somewhat niche, on the contrary, many of them have historically enjoyed a significant readership.

For these reasons, occult periodicals had a unique functionality for women writers of the period, allowing their work to be more visible and also more influential with the general public. Of course, visibility and reach were of particular interest to Colquhoun. As historian Julia Phillips has noted in her biography of the British twentieth

---

1 Mark S. Morrison. "The Periodical Culture of the Occult Revival: Esoteric Wisdom, Modernity and Counter-Public Spheres" in *Journal of Modern Literature*, Volume 31, Number 2, Winter 2008, pp. 1-22.

century magician Madeline Montalban, many women esotericists were often primarily recognised for their writing in newspapers and periodicals[2]. This was certainly the case for the influential Montalban, as well as early American esotericist Eleanor Kirk, Doreen Valiente and Colquhoun. Helena Blavatsky, too, had early success writing for newspapers and periodicals. British based women occultists found outlets for their writing in periodicals such as *Prediction*, a popular magazine devoted to esoteric and occult topics marketing heavily to women readers, which started in 1936 and which was still published as late as 2020. Through this type of popular publishing strategy women occult writers found an audience and also, importantly, gained some sort of regular income. In the case of Montalban it allowed for her to also cultivate interest for her Order of the Morning Star through mail order lessons advertised in the back of the publication. But, like Colquhoun, although many of these women are considered key influencers in mid-century British occultism by insiders, they never attained the popular reach or name recognition of their male counterparts such as Crowley, Kenneth Grant or Gerald Gardner and as a result very wrongly have retained a status as merely supporting actors.

There may well have been other barriers to women's magical book publishing. Funds and marketing have always been factors in publishing decisions as they are today and of course many occult and esoteric publications were privately funded or were attached to spiritual organisations. It is possible that many women occultists didn't have the financial backing or organisational connections to attract a publisher, or they could not convince publishers that they could gain a readership that was worth the initial investment. This was certainly the case with Colquhoun, who found publishing very difficult in general. Although piles of rejection letters are common for most writers, Colquhoun also often faced feedback about her readability and the lack of a potential market for her work. Many of her early publishing efforts and her books were likely made possible

2 Julia Phillips. "Madeline Montalban: Magus of the Morning Star" in Amy Hale (ed). *Women in Western Esotericism: Beyond Seeresses and Sea Priestesses.* London: Palgrave, 2022. pp. 229-254.

by personal friendships emerging from her social network, people who believed in her and valued her voice, and who didn't mind taking a financial risk.

It may also be that, unlike Fortune, Colquhoun may have felt that she lacked the authority to produce a magical monograph. Although Colquhoun had no problems in challenging the top brass of any order with which she was associated, including Fortune's Society of the Inner Light, she never took an outward facing leadership position. In many ways she saw herself as a perpetual student and seeker, and was clearly more identified as a professional artist than a professional magician. It may have been that writing a book of that nature would have cut into her painting time in ways that she was not interested in.

About this Collection

As with everything about Colquhoun this is a very eclectic collection. Colquhoun had an exceptionally wide range of esoteric interests, yet they all seemed to converge in a perennialist vision where all genuine paths are part of a revelation of an ancient mystery school of adepts. In general, Colquhoun gravitated toward Hermetics and organisations that had historical links with the Golden Dawn, as she genuinely believed that she had been etherically selected as a potential initiate by the disincarnate astral plane-based Secret Chiefs of that order, despite being refused initiation in the 1930s[3]. For Colquhoun that current expressed itself in explorations of alchemy, Witchcraft, Kabbalah, Celtic Spirituality, esoteric heraldry, Co-Masonry, Theosophy, Druidry, Thelema, Tantra, Martinism and more. In all of her art and writing, Colquhoun was equally influenced by her own interest in dreams as much as she was ceremonial magic, and her dream life provided evidence of a complex cosmology of beings, dimensions and information that bridged subconscious and extradimensional realities.

3 See Colquhoun's account of her early encounters with the Alpha Omega lodge in the 1930s and her subsequent experiences of the "Secret Chiefs" in Colquhoun, *Sword of Wisdom* (1975).

There were a number of thematic and practical considerations in assembling this volume. Although the pieces are generally ordered chronologically by publication date, in some rare cases, such as with "The Openings of the Body", I have made the choice to place an essay where I believe it was likely first drafted because it helps to support thematic patterns and interests. Many of these manuscripts were unpublished and cannot at this time be reliably dated, so using internal evidence and consulting with other Colquhoun scholars I have simply made the best guess in terms of dating. Additionally, Colquhoun kept multiple versions of her drafts and sometimes would have them typed up long after they were initially written, which is another challenge to dating this material accurately.

In some ways the selections in this volume were simply a result of access to the manuscripts. Some texts in this collection were previously published in periodicals, others were early lectures and pieces perhaps intended for artistic or magical collections that never saw the light of day. A number of these essays have been reprinted by Richard Shillitoe in *Medea's Charms* or with the novel *I Saw Water*, and I acknowledge and am deeply grateful for Shillitoe's great help in providing me with a number of reliably transcribed manuscripts to which I had no previous access. In terms of subject matter, the essays chosen for this collection, and this is by no means a comprehensive collection, reflect her range of interests and also her general approach to magic. It is also meant to be primarily illustrative, showing Colquhoun's personal navigation through various cultural and subcultural contexts, and possibly even economies. They show the development of her own magical interests and her positions over time and the ways in which Colquhoun engaged with developing occult subcultures over the twentieth century in Britain. Some pieces I selected because I was interested in reproducing essays that were theoretically oriented or didactic rather than descriptive or poetic. There is in some cases a very fine line between Colquhoun's magical essays and her poetry or imaginative essays which reflect occult themes. In only a few cases a piece was selected not because it was explicitly occult, but because it reveals something about Colquhoun's values and approach, which may have been influencing or complementing her esoteric and magical directions. Her more journalistic pieces may not appear to reflect her practitioner perspectives on occult theory, but they say something important about her own development as an occult writer.

So, for the reader hoping to enjoy a coherent selection of Colquhoun's occult teachings, this is not the primary purpose of this book, although hopefully the reader will certainly appreciate Colquhoun's impressive depth that she brings to each topic. As a necessary caveat, the inclusion of an essay in this volume is in no way an endorsement of its quality. Colquhoun was a rather uneven writer. She often had trouble developing a point and articulating conclusions and she certainly had little restraint when it came to inserting herself into the text. Additionally, historical accuracy was not always a primary concern for Colquhoun, as she clearly favoured the mythic and archetypal over cold, hard fact. Readers of this volume are cautioned to read historical assertions critically. Without a doubt Colquhoun had mastery over the occult material she loved, but her frequent isolation as a writer and apparent lack of feedback on her writings did not always serve her well.

Yet her strong personality and commitment to her own vision is apparent in these works from the start. The earliest pieces in this volume were taken from lectures she gave at the Quest Society in 1928 and 1930 when she was 22 and 24 years old. The London Quest Society was founded by the esoteric Philosopher and Classicist G.R.S. (George) Mead. Mead was a Theosophist with a deep interest in Hermetic texts and Gnosticism and founded The Quest Society in 1909 with disaffected Theosophical Society members who left after the organisation found itself in scandal. The society had about 150 members, many luminaries from the occult and esoteric world at the time and held lectures and discussions, many of which likely seeded the publication *The Quest*. Colquhoun's engagement with this group gives us quite an indication of not only her mental horsepower but also her courage as even at this tender age she had no problem addressing a large group and sharing bold opinions. Imagine Colquhoun, a confident young 22-year-old in 1928, standing in front of a group of stuffy eccentric occultists, probably mostly male and likely just as feisty and difficult back then as they are today, delivering a blistering response to a previous speaker, a Reverend Ethelbert Goodchild who gave a lecture to the Quest Society on the nature of the divine. In her searing rejoinder, titled "In Search of the Divine" she basically accused Rev. Goodchild as offering no useful content and no practical advice for seekers. She came out swinging and pulled no punches, and this unwavering character never retreated throughout the entirety of her life.

Colquhoun's personal journey most certainly developed in tandem with changes and developments in British occult culture. The history of Colquhoun's essay publishing career provides some insight into the wider development of mid-century British magical subcultures, the increased popular interest in these topics and also the role of publishing in creating and cohering communities. Although the essays in this volume start in the late 1920s, as the century went on, Colquhoun's esoteric publishing opportunities increased. A number of her early esoteric pieces were written for literary journals such as *New Road* or *The Glass.* After World War Two, as her writing career developed, her writings about magic and the occult extended more clearly into a journalistic framework. In 1954 and 1955, she contributed ten pieces to *The London Broadsheet*, edited by her friend Antony Borrow. This was technically a literary publication and her contributions ranged from poems and short stories of a surrealist bent to proto-Fortean topics such as research into the paranormal and UFOs. However, she also produced interesting profile pieces on Gerald Gardner, Austin Osman Spare, Aleister Crowley and other esoteric topics, hoping, perhaps, to introduce midcentury British magical personalities to a wider audience. She later published a variety of essays and reviews for *Prediction* magazine in the 1950s, 60s and 70s that drew more on her expertise as a practitioner. Colquhoun's essays for *Prediction* magazine were among her most complex for a popular audience. It is clear that the audience for this journal was in her sweet spot for topics of interest to her, and she could write comfortably and authoritatively as a practitioner in this space. She published seventeen pieces for *Prediction* over a time span ranging from 1958 to 1973. The topics ranged from primers on Kabbalah, the Celtic Mysteries and sacred places, profiles of Aleister

Crowley and Samuel "MacGregor" Mathers, meditation techniques and esoteric heraldry. In 1958 she completed a four-part series titled *The Crown and the Kingdom* for *Prediction* which is clear that she had envisioned as an introduction to the topic. However, as was Colquhoun's way, she likely threw her readers into the deep end of the pool without a float.

Over the decades we see an overall increase in small publications devoted to people interested in Celtic Spirituality and modern Paganism, which intersected with the ecological and environmental movements of the 1970s, movements with which Colquhoun had some sympathy. Although Colquhoun had been interested in Druidry and emerging Celtic Spirituality since the 1950s, most of her publishing on these topics was likely propelled by the wider Celtic revival in the 1970s, inspired by a convergence of Celtic ethnonationalist politics, earth mysteries, and conservation movements. As Vivianne Crowley has noted, the wider cultural interest in both feminism and especially the growth of the environmental movement in Britain dovetailed with British Paganism expanding out from private initiatory orders toward a greater outward facing public presence[4]. The growth in occult and countercultural publications and magazines in the 1960s and 1970s, and wider access to the engines of publishing and distribution, provided Colquhoun further opportunities to find homes for essays and poems she had likely drafted much earlier, including a piece in the legendary *Man, Myth and Magic*. Some of her essays reflect very long-standing interests that were likely published long after their composition and which never would have had an appropriate readership in earlier decades. One example of this is "The Openings of the Body". This essay was published in 1970, but it reflects a body of work from the early 1940s about energy currents and ultimately her radical views about sex magic. What this tells us is that first, Colquhoun still believed in 1970 that this material was relevant and important to get out there. Second, there were actually publications supporting a literate occult readership that would publish it. Thus, in

4 Vivianne Crowley "Doreen Valiente: Unmotherly Mother of Modern Witchcraft" in Amy Hale (ed). *Women in Western Esotericism: Beyond Seeresses and Sea Priestesses*. London: Palgrave, 2022. pp. 173-200.

Colquhoun's writings from 1970 onward, we see an engagement with a variety of emerging magically oriented publications. Of course she continued her long-standing relationship with *Prediction* magazine, but she found many opportunities in the long running magical poetry journal *Ore* edited by longtime friend Eric Ratcliffe, Colin Murray's *New Celtic Review* stemming from his Golden Section Order, Adam McClean's *The Hermetic Journal* and in her final years *Wood and Water* focused on sacred landscape features and Goddess spirituality. Unfortunately, so many of these would be small run publications that resulted in these essays being ephemeral.

While Colquhoun definitely had themes and interests that captivated her throughout her life, such as esoteric uses of colour and sacred landscapes, we can also see how her own spiritual journey changed and developed over her lifetime. These essays also allow us to track how certain magical and occult themes and preoccupations appeared in Colquhoun's work across the disciplines in which she operated during different periods of her life. For instance, the recurrence of a single Spanish quote attributed to Fra Luis Ponce de Leon "Libro Primaro" found in a poem by Edgar Allan Poe that Colquhoun repeated over several texts in the early 1940s:

> Un no rompida sueno—
> Un dia puro—allegre—libre Quiera—
> Libre de amor—de celo
> De odio—de esperanza—de recelo.
>
> An unbroken dream
> A clear, joyous, free day
> I would love.
> Free of love, zeal
> Hate, hope and suspicion.

From the various pieces in which Colquhoun uses this quote as an illustration, we can more fully understand Colquhoun's esoteric readings of a state of liberty and true freedom, an idea that is key to both her surrealist and her occult contexts of the time, signalling the ideal state of humanity when finally freed from the agitations of desire in union with the divine.

We can also see a tendency in her writing over the decades to move toward a much more firmly nativist position with respect to her own spirituality, as she more heavily engages with groups focused on Celtic Spirituality. Although Colquhoun didn't often address issues of race or nativism directly, the connection between perceived race or ethnicity and esoteric practice was something she clearly considered and had views on that evidently changed over the course of her life. By the 1970s we see her starting to reject the inclusion of Asian and Indian material as perhaps not suitable for British people, who would have their own "native" esoteric systems to pursue. However, ironically, we see more references to Islam and especially Sufism cropping up incidentally in her writings later in life, possibly inspired by her interest in the writings of Idries Shah and René Guénon.

While Colquhoun's writings reflect the magical zeitgeists of mid-century British occultism, some of these pieces reflect odd snapshots in time, both in terms of Colquhoun's interests and also in terms of strange forgotten preoccupations of British esoteric culture. One short piece captures her interest in esoteric heraldry that likely emerged from her relationship with occultist and Traditionalist W.B. Crow. Colquhoun was fascinated by heraldry and its esoteric dimensions and there are many heraldic drafts among her papers. This makes sense as heraldry was one of the first places we find applications of esoteric and symbolic colour theory and even potentially may be the root of the magical motto. Perhaps the most impenetrable essay in this collection is "Dimensional Interrelation: A Meditation on the Platonic Solids" which chronicles her attempts to break through dimensional boundaries through experimenting with the cuttings of platonic shapes. Corresponding experiments in her archives indicate this was an important project to her, but the motives remain obscure.

My primary hope in assembling this collection of essays is that it will contribute to not only furthering our understanding of Colquhoun as an occult theorist and writer, but that it will also contribute to a wider understanding of women's participation in and negotiation of the occult subcultures of the mid-twentieth century. After two world wars, occult and spiritual orders as vehicles for social reform had receded, and in the middle of the twentieth century, the role of women as occult figureheads and leaders of movements such as Theosophy, Spiritualism and the Golden Dawn receded as well. Initiatory Wicca is, of course, an exception here. Many occult orders turned inward or faced schisms, until the social movements of the 1960s, 70s and 80s brought new intersections of the emerging post war counterculture with esotericism, and occultism, integrating contemporary Paganisms, magico-religious witchcraft, Goddess feminism, and earth mysteries with a new range of enchantments and social concerns. As a woman occultist, Colquhoun negotiated her own feminist sensibilities and desires for a better, more enlightened world within these unfolding and changing occult contexts. In some cases, Colquhoun's writings and publishing record reflects or even prefigures trends in the cultic milieu, such as the rise of the interest in earth mysteries. In other cases, Colquhoun appears to have resisted certain movements, seen in her quite careful relationship with Goddess spirituality, which she appears to have not fully embraced despite her lifelong commitment to the sacred feminine.

Despite Colquhoun's publishing challenges, I have always been amazed at Colquhoun's passion, utter brilliance, and depth and I have been deeply committed to helping her be seen, warts and all. When I read Colquhoun's writings, imagining her uncompromising voice in my head, I have a conflicted response. On the one hand I am frustrated that she continually sabotaged her own success and the visibility and position she was so evidently hungry for. Why couldn't she tone it down, find an editor, just rein it in a little bit, be more popular, more... likable? But what if she *had* reined it in, moderated her voice, compromised to be more marketable, made herself smaller, as so many women are socialised to do? Perhaps she could have had the success that she wanted, but that would have been its own tragedy, because today, in this moment, we have her unexpurgated words and her radical thoughts and we can appreciate how far ahead of her time she was.

Amy Hale, 2026

A Note On Spelling

Colquhoun often used archaic or idiosyncratic spelling, punctuation and formatting in her writings and she was not always consistent. For this volume we have kept her more unique spellings and usage when it was clear that this reflected some aspect of her belief. In other cases we have elected to bring certain spellings and usage into line with contemporary editorial practice. In general, while Colquhoun used the esoteric spelling Qabalah, editorial and framing material uses Kabbalah.

A Note On Colour Images

The essays in this book were selected to help demonstrate Colquhoun's range and competency in a variety of esoteric and magical topics. She brought the same sense of exploration to the visual components of her magical experimentation. The short colour section in this book provided an opportunity to present a few items from Colquhoun's archives which illustrate her engagement with magical theory, process and practice. Some images in this section are related to texts in the book, while others provide supplemental insight for the reader.

The Quest of the Divine: A paper read before members of the Quest Society, in criticism of an address by the Rev. Ethelbert Goodchild (c. 1928)

Reverend Ethelbert Goodchild MA was an eclectic man of letters with a bent toward social reform. He was an anti-vivisectionist and Fellow of the Society of Arts with a keen interest in esoteric matters and Spiritualism. He was especially concerned with the relationship between spirit, matter, and energy and delivered a series of popular lectures on this topic to the London Spiritualist Alliance in 1931. Colquhoun delivered this rebuttal to one of Goodchild's lectures to the Quest Society, a very popular occult organisation founded by the Classicist and esoteric scholar G. R. S. Mead (1863-1933) when she was only 22. In this early piece we can see that she is already developing an uncompromising critical voice in addition to demonstrating an early command of alchemy, Kabbalah and Gnosticism. Most notably perhaps, is the fact that this young woman was clearly unafraid of taking a position and engaging with the public.

Mr. Goodchild chose a title which suggests and summarises the main work of all transcendental research, but his speech gives no hint as to how that work was to be accomplished, or even begun, and no clear indication of the end in view. One would suppose that a speaker faced with such a heading would first attempt some definition of the word "divine" and then outline some system by which the defined objective might be reached, or at least essayed. From a practical point of view, therefore, Mr. Goodchild's address was vague and almost valueless. It was also very short; had he taken more thought, he might have added considerably to its stature.

His [opening] text was a passage from Browning, which implied that the quest of the Divine was like the pursuit of the *ignus fatuus*. He then narrated in his own words the story of Moses' journey through the wilderness, which he described as the "First Quest": and was subsequently carried away by Biblical legends and images, and his own rhetorical comments thereon; but failed to carry at least one member of his audience with him. He admitted these to be legends, however; but prefaced his remarks on the life of Christ by the words "now turning to history"; This must have surprised some of those present, for if he had cared to follow up the parallel between the lives of Moses and Christ, particularly with reference to the Samaritan versions he would perhaps have seen that both are such stuff as myths are made on. Still, he pointed out one important feature to both allegories, namely that the Quest seemed to fail at the moment of climax.

In these two myths there is much that is of use to the would-be initiate; and had they been less cursorily treated, they would have revealed a document showing the stages of the soul's progress: many alchemical writers have used them to illustrate the processes of the Great Work. In the legend of Moses, great significance is attached to the crossing of the Red Sea, the setting up of the Golden Calf, and the raising of the Brazen Serpent. "Learn, therefore to lift the Serpent up on high, which is called Nehustan, if thou wouldst cure infirm Natures after the example of Roses", says the *Aesch Metzareph*. Alas: these more profound aspects of the subject did not seem to have occurred to Mr. Goodchild; the only stage he emphasised was the apparent failure at the climax, the Dark Night of the Soul, and even this conception he did not see fit to amplify or explain.

Later on he mentioned that Christ was the supreme genius of the world; but it is impossible to criticise this statement, as Mr. Goodchild did not say whether he meant by it that the Logos was the moving principle of the universe and of man's soul, or that the supposedly historical Christ was the ablest man that the human race had produced.

Mr. Goodchild then went on to say that the "simian consciousness" must be supplemented by the "scientific consciousness", but did not explain either term. He seemed to think that the individual's reaction to the universe was of the first importance, and man's obligation was to supplement the primitive consciousness by progressively higher types of perception. A developed consciousness could perceive a consciousness of more than three dimensions. This development was to be achieved through alternate revelation and disillusionment. He did not say what form the revelation took, whether it was vouchsafed to all, nor whether it would continue everlastingly, but one gathered that this latter would be the case.

The idea of a progressive revelation continuing to eternity, setting the bounds of consciousness wider still and wider, and multiplying the dimensions of the universe indefinitely is wearying in the extreme. In contemplation of this dreary prospect, one turns with relief to the Buddhist conception of Nirvana. The divine is more likely to be reached by elimination than by multiplication of the modes of incidental life. Yeats somewhere writes of the soul as "imprisoned in the phases of manifested existence", which he symbolises as the phases of the moon and as finally liberated to escape into the sun, symbol of the eternal individuality, where "to sink into its own delight at last". This is a more satisfying doctrine, and one far removed from the "stagnation" which Mr. Goodchild offered as the only alternative to "progress".

Not until question time did he try to say what he meant by "the divine" or by "consciousness". Then he remarked that the divine was a combination of all ideals, which is almost meaningless. Again, the divine was a "tornado of energy" in sub-material existence. That is more likely to be true, but if it is the origin of the manifested universe, then it must be the Gnostic "second god" or "Demiurge", not the symbolic representation of the perfected soul, nor the forever unmanifest "Ain" of the Kabbalah.

As to consciousness, Mr. Goodchild indicated four types:

> The Simian, characterised by the obsession of substance, and transmitted by our Simian ancestors through the sense of grip.
>
> The Scientific, characterised by a perception of our dependence upon energies not immediately perceptible to the senses.
>
> The Aesthetic, characterised by the attempted application of these imperceptible forces to the maintenance of life. This evidently includes magic.
>
> The Ideal, which the speaker did not describe but which has presumably some connection to "the divine".

These divisions remind one of the classification in *The Cloud of Unknowing*[1], which partitions humanity into "the common, the particular, the singular, and the perfect". They are probably sound enough, as far as they go, but that is not very far. The perceptual question: what is the goal and how may it be attained? is left unanswered. The divine still seems so illusive (sic) that one is tempted to assume it is non-existent. †

1 A middle English mystical and contemplative text from the fourteenth century, translated by the wildly popular Anglo Catholic theologian Evelyn Underhill in 1922.

The Connection Between Mysticism and Blasphemy (c. 1930)

Colquhoun delivered this essay to the Search Society, which was formed by her cousin Edward Garstin in the wake of the demise of Mead's Quest Society in around 1930. This is a thoughtful and sophisticated analysis of "blasphemy" as defined by the sacred in the material, and by the idea that mysticism is blasphemous because it presupposes a merging of the mystic with the deity. This piece shows the significant influence on Colquhoun of Mead's writings on mysticism, along with those of the Christian mystic Evelyn Underhill. She also engages deeply with the works of William Blake here, both his poetry and also his Gnostic inspired mythologies. Union with deity through theurgy is a cornerstone of many of the occult practices Colquhoun embraced, and her visual art and writing often engage with taboo, blasphemy and transgression, perhaps as a way of expressing the divine within all things.

At first glance it appears as though the link between such seemingly opposed conceptions as mysticism and blasphemy can be slight, but there is not a little historical evidence to prove their close interrelation. At best, mysticism has always been a phenomenon "permitted but not requested" in organised religion. It would be easy to multiply instances of the suspicion, disapproval and persecution which have pursued the mystic in every age and clime. Small wonder that the adept is terrified of revealing all he knows, and is terrified lest he has said too much. Knowledge is only welcome among the knowledgeable and when the inquirer takes a road strange to orthodoxy, the authority which guards the established code is likely to be unsympathetic. The Church stigmatised as blasphemous such knowledge as was won by Galileo and Leonardo da Vinci, and one may also cite the burning of Giordano Bruno and the papal condemnation of Molinos'[1] writings. Leaving individuals and turning to sects, one may recall the Arian persecutions and the Albigensian massacres. Referring to non-Christian sects, the same reactions may be observed: a tendency toward Sufism has been by no means welcome in a Moslem community, nor has Kabalism (sic) among Jews, while the Confucian and the more mystical Taoist were often rivals.

The outer and inner teachings are not necessarily opposed to one another, but may very easily conflict in their practical aims. The outer church, usually in origin a fertility cult, exists primarily for the purpose of civic welfare. It can direct this welfare because it is, as it claims, in touch with the source of all goodness; but the individual mystic, or small group of mystics, also makes this claim and their respective interpretations of divine will are sometimes mutually exclusive. To deny or subvert the authority of a church is heresy; and the step from heresy to blasphemy is no long one, since the opinions of a heretic cannot seem but blasphemous to an orthodox believer. Therefore, the publication of esoteric teaching—property of a few individuals—tends to subvert, even if it does not actually deny, the authority of the exterior cult.

There are not wanting examples of a contrary theory, but the weight of evidence is against them: Evelyn Underhill even asserts that the greater mystics are all loyal and devoted children of their church. Some of the simpler-minded mystics themselves may have thought so, but their parent was not always of the same opinion: witness the case of such revered saints as Francis of Assisi and Joan of Arc, who frequently suffered from the strictures—to use the harsher term—laid on them by their church. The flaming soul of the mystic is not allowed to light the sanctuary: it might so easily burn down the whole edifice:

1 Miguel de Molinos, seventeenth century mystic whose advocacy of passive contemplation of God resulted in imprisonment by the Inquisition.

but once translated to another sphere it may safely shine down with remembered lustre. Passing from individuals to mystical orders, one notices that the Jesuits, though well established in a species of Yoga, have been more than suppressed, while of the order of the Knights Templar, it is unnecessary to speak. Dean Inge[2] deprecated "the dubious and dangerous mysticism of John of Parma and Joachim of Flora"; but all mysticism is by its very nature dubious to those who have no firsthand experience of it, and dangerous to those who prefer to rely on second hand information.

The grounds for the condemnation of mysticism by the orthodox are often merely those of expediency, and reference is not made to its ultimate value. There appears to be a general feeling that, unless it be kept strictly under control, it is liable to become something very much akin to heresy and blasphemy, which in their turn give rise to sects, schisms and ultimately to chaos. The seeming disparity between union with God and schism from God's earthly vehicle is only an appearance. The mental matrix out of which these two states is produced is identical. There is in fact a root idea, or state of consciousness, common to both desire for the unattainable and discontent with the already attained. One can neither blaspheme, nor reach any mystical intuition, without belief in a supreme being, or at least in some power higher than the individual self—in an essence which is not cognisable through the ordinary channels of sense, but which yet may be affected by human behaviour. Thus, faith and love are in some way pleasing to this being—are, indeed in an arcane sense, necessary to his existence: God needs man, as Eckhart says, "God can as little do without us as we without him." Similarly, man's hatred, contempt and ridicule are painful to him, even if they can afford him a sort of poisoned life. The state of mind which gives him no sustenance whatever is that of the indifferent agnostic, who is incapable of blasphemy as of mysticism. The invocation of the Devil and the worship of God are both equally tiresome and meaningless to a mind without belief in either. It is the fully-believing Christian who celebrates the Black Mass with the greatest devotion.

2 William Ralph Inge, Anglican priest and writer with interests in Christian mysticism and Neoplatonism.

One may assume, then, a common ground for both mysticism and blasphemy, namely faith in the reality of a "super being" whether to be attained to or rebelled against. Further, not only the existence but the nature of the deity is similar in the two conceptions, since both demand the doctrine of immanence and reject that of transcendence. By immanent deity, is meant deity which is accessible to human contact, difficult as it may be to establish much contact. Transcendent deity, on the other hand, is always completely unknown, unknowable and unmanifest—the "Ain" of the Kabbalah. Such deity is unapproached by the mystic, and undisturbed by the blasphemer. Not so the deity conceived as immanent, the idea from which springs pantheism and which imagines deity as almost completely manifest in visible nature. Thus, though the blasphemer may be said to lower the divine, while the mystic raises himself to meet his Lord, yet in fact both perform the same process—that of bringing the divine and the human into contact. Since any vehicle cannot be unworthy of divinity, the doctrine of the Incarnate God and the whole train of sacramental teaching that follows in its wake is in this sense blasphemous. Even the Athanasian creed admits that Christ is "equal to the Father, as touching his Godhead; and inferior to the Father as touching his Manhood."

If mysticism be defined briefly as the attempt to reach some exalted state of consciousness, and blasphemy as the outraging of anything sacred, there seems indeed little connection between the two; yet how often does the former process imply the latter! *The Book of the Holy Hierotheos*[3] says "Everything shall become one thing; for even God shall pass and Christ shall be done away, and the Spirit shall no more be called the Spirit... This is the limit of All and the end of Everything." There is a great gulf fixed between the human and the divine, and is not any attempt to bridge it a presumption comparable to that of Eve? The blasphemer would depose the tyrant and be a law unto himself, thus declaring his right to sole kingship, the mystic would share the throne, but likewise and with as little reason, asserts the godhead of his own being;

---

3 *The Book of Hierotheos* was a text of Syrian mysticism written by Stephen bar Sudaili. G. R. S. Mead devotes a chapter to this text in his 1913 book *Quests Old and New.*

If thou humblest thyself, thou humblest me.
Thou also dwell'st in Eternity
Thou art a man; God is no more
Thine own humanity learn to adore[4].

Both claim an unusual unwarrantable familiarity with things divine: "Him verily and seeing and fully feeling, Him spiritually hearing, Him delectably smelling and sweetly swallowing" is an instance from Julian of Norwich[5]. Since not only can nothing be known with certainty, but also any affirmation or negation limits in some way the One which is all, it is hardly possible to make a statement which is not partially untrue and therefore blasphemous about things which so far exceed the normal experience—to say nothing of the normal capabilities of language. Small wonder that such statements are often paradoxical, that there is an element of wildness in their familiarity—whether derogatory or adoring—which sets both blasphemy and mysticism apart from the ordinary motions of life, and links the two together. Perhaps the only successful way to take the kingdom of heaven is by force, but such maneuvers come near to profanation.

Another striking characteristic which both share is a fundamental nihilism. Their core is self-devastation, the breaking and defiling of the highest attained, since even that highest is low. Both "Turn to the East as symbol of the identity of Hope and Annihilation." "*Oporat himinem suas potentias anihilare*" says Molinos. There arises the strong conviction that all sense-impressions, all thought-activities, all known forms of being are poor, futile, worthless and without dignity or consequence—the "rotten rags of memory"[6] which recall by travesty some more exalted life. Legends of Lucifer, of the Fall of Man, and many other mythopaeic solutions of the problem of evil reflect some memory of a primal blessed state and this recollection causes impatience with the present imperfection. The mystic and the blasphemer would shatter to bits "this sorry scheme of things entire" and imagine sublime height after height won by some

4 This quote is from William Blake's "The Everlasting Gospel".
5 Julian of Norwich was a fourteenth century English woman mystic.
6 A line from William Blake's *Milton*.

destruction, until something is found which cannot be destroyed—some paranirvana of which one might say, were it possible to stammer aught, "where there is nothing, let there be God". And if All can be destroyed, why let there be destruction!

The connection between mysticism and heresy is easy to establish, if heresy be defined as the entertaining and disseminating of false opinions about God. But blasphemy has an added sense of profanation, whether thoughtless and irresponsible, as in common swearing, or deliberate, as in certain types of mystical or semi-mystical writing. With the pejorative forms of blasphemy, as with its legal definition, it is scarcely necessary to deal, except to remark that the word "imprecation" shows the nearness of the relation between a curse and a prayer. All cursing is praying of a sort: "The Devil too has his contemplatives" as the author of *The Cloud of Unknowing* remarks. Sometimes an utterance may be either mystical or blasphemous, according to the intention of the utterer, and the taste and creed of his audience; for example, if someone says that he is going to climb Mt. Sinai, a friend hearing him might remark that he would perhaps find at the top some new Tablets of the Law. This may be regarded either as irreverent fooling or as the ushering in of a newly revealed Dispensation. There is also a kind of unconscious blasphemy in many Christian hymns, of which the attempt to popularise the faith by emotional methods is a fruitful source. The refrain of a certain Salvation Army hymn ran as follows: "He sticks in my heart like a penny jam tart". One does not doubt the piety of the author, nevertheless the simile may well lead to mockery rather than to prayer.

Leaving comedy aside, a more serious consideration is that of deliberate blasphemy couched in mystical terms. Here, the author's object is to shock his readers into a reconsideration of orthodox belief which they presumably hold, especially when the beliefs clash with the author's own conception of reality. Such is Blake's long didactic poem "The Everlasting Gospel":

> Was Jesus born of a Virgin pure
> With narrow soul and looks demure?
> If he intended to take on sin

His mother should have a harlot been
Just such a one as Magdalen.

Swift's mockery of the Mass in *The Tale of a Tub* is another example of orthodoxy, blasé in the writer's opinion, attacked by blasphemy. So it may be said of the orthodox but uninspired believer and the fanatical prophet that:

Both read the Bible day and night
But thou read'st black where I read white[7].

In some writers the blasphemy is less deliberate than constitutional; they are unable to prevent its bursting forth at intervals though well aware of its nature. This gift, if such it may be called, is often accompanied by considerable mystical talent and a devotional temperament. Poets so endowed seem to suffer from a sort of dissociation or dual personality; a mood of devotion is indulged to excess, and reacts to the alternating mood of devastation. This combination is noticeable in many Symbolist writings, particularly in the poem where Verlaine ecstatically enumerates the various parts of his body with their appropriate sins, and imploring forgiveness, dedicates them to his Lord. The Symbolists were not without a following in England, and some of the fin de siècle poets here compare their own experiences with events in the life of Christ, in a fashion calculated to offend the conventionally pious. In certain Satanistic cults, the relation between mysticism and blasphemy is so obvious as scarcely to need indicating. In his work *Magick* Aleister Crowley, describing one of the more difficult and dangerous rituals, warns the magician performing it that it may even prove fatal to him, and adds "Blessed are the dead which die in the Lord": this certainly sounds as though the Devil were quoting scripture, but according to the ancient saying *Diabolus Deus Inversus*[8], so must be himself a God, or some aspect of God. Almost every religious system implies, if it does not assert, a Dualism, and as the two opposing forces are

7 From William Blake's "The Everlasting Gospel".

8 "The Devil is the Reverse of God". "*Demon est Deus Inversus*" was the magical motto of William Butler Yeats in the Hermetic Order of the Golden Dawn.

regarded in practice, if not in theory, as almost equally powerful, adoring approach of the one must imply contempt of the other. "But the Devil's account is, that the Messiah fell and formed a Heaven from what he stole from the Abyss"[9]. Blake's mythology descends in direct line from the Gnostic conception of the "Good God" and the "Just God", and he imagines the Universe to be the work, not of a beneficent Creator, but of a capricious and malicious Demiurge—"the Ancient Elf"—from whom Man is delivered by a Promethean Saviour. He names this demiurge "Urizen" a personification of Logic, to whom he opposes now "Enitharmon", the imaginative Intuition, now the fiery "Orc", and avatar of the Redeemer. Since all action, whether mental or physical, is a worship of the Gnostic "Second God", the mystical attainment of Negation must inevitably appear blasphemous to the adherents of his cult, and vice-versa:

> My spectre around me night and day
> Like a wild beast guards my way:
> My Emanation far within
> Weeps incessantly for my sin[10].

It will be useful also to point out where blasphemous tendencies appear in types of mysticism generally considered more reputable; since apart from what is irresponsibly profane on the one hand, or deliberately disturbing on the other, there is much high mysticism not untinged by a blasphemous element. One may include here many expressions of man's mythopaeic faculty; to look no further than the Bible, there is much recounted of Jehovah which would be libelous if written about a man. Again in Classical mythology, the stories of Jupiter's adventures outrun in scandal those of any other celestial being. To turn to literature more usually accepted as mystical, one notices four main types of what may be termed "blasphemous mysticism", our four typical characteristics of mystical writing which at least sail very near the wind. These are: the "pain of God", the "spiritual marriage", the "assuming of godhead" and "the transcending of deity".

9 From William Blake's *The Marriage of Heaven and Hell.*

10 From William Blake's poem "My Spectre Around Me".

To the "pain of God" and the "wound of love" one finds frequent references, yet such ideas are not only inapplicable to a supposedly All-wise and All-powerful deity, but a contradiction of the most praised human virtues. Since suffering cannot be endured without being inflicted, the desire for suffering and the delight in pain is a contradiction of human doctrine, and a blasphemy against the beneficent ruler. This accusation may be brought against St. John of the Cross, in spite of his poetic grace, when he sings:

> Ere the first morning air
> Blew from the tower and waved his locks aside
> His hand with gentle care,
> Did wound me in the side
> And in my body all my senses died[11].

This poem brings one to consider the "spiritual marriage"—a symbol which is open to misconstruction. It refers to the union of the soul with God, the soul being imagined as female; and many saints, St. Bernard among them, claim to have experienced this. St. Thérese of Lisieux even sent out an invitation to the other nuns of her convent, bidding them to her marriage with Christ. This class of metaphor may sometimes present a genuine supranormal state of the psyche, but it is easily comprehensible that both the metaphor and the state itself should not be encouraged by established churches. Incidentally, one is curious to know precisely what is meant by the term "spiritual wife", as used by the leaders of so many semi-mystical sects, and whether any peculiar supernormal power, inaccessible by other means, is obtainable through this relationship.

The "assuming of godhead" blasphemy is also common among schismatics and religious reformers. The *Toldoth Yeshu* relegates the exploits of Jesus to this category, and the subsequent claims of Manes, Simon Magus and Mahomet to fulfill the prophesies concerning the promised Paraclete are similarly treated by orthodox Christianity.

---

11 From "The Obscure Night of the Soul" (Also known as the "Dark Night of the Soul") By the sixteenth century Spanish mystic St. John of the Cross. This version was translated by English poet Arthur Symons in his 1899 collection *Images of Good and Evil.*

Today, the case—one among many—of the "World Teacher" Krishnamurti is comparable. The fact that these claims are patently untrue is alone sufficient to class them as blasphemous. Reason forbids belief that the whole of "the sum of things that are" could become manifest in a single human individual. If this were so, the rest of the universe would collapse. The idea, therefore, of a God-man is as blasphemous as the Man-god.

Nor can there be any doubt as to the blasphemous character of the idea that Deity is an illusion to be transcended, yet it is given very full expression in the *Book of the Holy Hierotheos* previously quoted: "Before the first beginning God was not God, and again, after the consummation of All, he is not God." And in the *Tibetan Book of the Dead* the soul is adjured, at the moment of bodily death, to deny existence or potency to the many gods that seem to throng around it, and through blaspheming them, to reach ultimate reality.

Though all blasphemy is not mystical, except in the sense that it attempts to deal with the transcendent, all mysticism is in a deep sense blasphemous—an intrusion upon the "Holiest of Holies". It may be that "the road of excess leads to the palace of wisdom", but it does not lead to the place of piety. The doctrine of *solve et coagula*—"dissolve to create"—which is closely connected with the conception of "mystical death", is one that may well alarm the timid. It is surprising, not that the secret tradition should be guarded with silence, but that it has not been more closely guarded. The imperfect must be burned on perfection, and what will escape the conflagration? Since the mystic must defy the churches, must rely on his own intuition rather than on the word of another, he must expect the pat reward; but the true contemplative will be neither seen nor heard, if he would escape impeachment of his sanity or curtailment of his freedom. This is the adept whom Éliphas Lévi has so finely described:

> He remembers the bereavement and murder of Orpheus, the exile and lonely death of Moses, the martyrdom of the Prophets, the tortures of Apollonius, the cross of the Saviour. He knows the desolation in which Agrippa died, whose

memory is even now slandered; he knows what labours overcame the great Paracelsus and all that Raymond Lully was condemned to undergo, that he might finish a violent death. He remembers Swedenborg simulating madness and even losing his reason in order to excuse his science; St. Martin and his hidden life, Cagliostro, who perished forsaken in the cells of the Inquisition, Cazotte who ascended the scaffold. Inheritor of so many victims, he does not dare the less, but he understands better the necessity for silence[12]. †

12 This passage concerning the trials and aims of the occult initiate is from nineteenth century French Occultist Éliphas Lévi's 1896 *Dogme et Rituel de la Haute Magie.*

Prose of Alchemy (1930)

This piece was published in G. R. S. Mead's esoteric journal *The Quest* in April of 1930. It demonstrates Colquhoun's deep familiarity with the manuscripts that guided and inspired her alchemically themed works such as *Goose of Hermogenes*, which may have been partially composed around this time. The particularly lovely thing about this piece, is that it focuses on the poetics, form and style of alchemical texts while still speaking to meaning. Much of her focus is on the alchemical writers' use of colour, which was a continuing preoccupation of Colquhoun's. In 1946 surrealist poet David Gascoyne wrote to Colquhoun and opined that "The Prose of Alchemy" was "one of the best, most stimulating short introductions to the subject of Alchemy considered as imaginative literature, i.e. a special department of poetry, that exists in English, I think." It seems likely that Colquhoun may have been inspired by J. E. Mercer's 1921 *Alchemy: Its Science and Romance*.

The Dark Ages lacked much that the twentieth century possesses, but they held one thing which this age may well envy: an imaginative unity of outlook on the universe. This unity appears, by contrast to the modern mind, variedly active. An oft-quoted saying of the times was the chief maxim inscribed upon the *Smaragdine Tablet* of Hermes: "That which is below is as that which is above, and that which is above is as that which is below." Under the Doctrine of Signatures, planet and herb, metal and deity, beast and precious stone, the months of the year and the parts of the human body were linked in subtle communion so that one could not indeed stir a flower without the troubling of a star.

One of the earliest authentic writers on alchemy was Zozimus the Panopolitan, who flourished in the fourth century and wrote *A Faithful Description of the Secret and Divine Art of Making Gold and Silver*, the paradoxical style of which may be judged from the following excerpt:

> Receive this stone which is not a stone, a precious thing which has no value, a thing of many shapes which has no shape, this unknown which is known of all.

And, again, marking its love of antithesis and repetition:

> Its kind is one, its species multiple. All comes from the one, and all returns to it... Here is the Mithraic mystery, the incommunicable mystery.

Fabulous antiquity was ascribed to some alchemical treatises, and Aristotle, Hermes Trismegistus, Moses, Solomon, Abraham even Adam, were claimed as authors. The practice of alchemy extends throughout the Middle Ages to recent times, when such as Strindberg have actually sought for the Philosopher's Stone. But the Middle Ages were its summertime, since hermetic art expressed the normal spirit of that epoch, ever seeking the One Thing, the *Magnum Bonum*, the basis of the cosmos. Though One Thing, this Grand Magisterium was nevertheless a twin conception: the eldest-born was the "*Lapis Philosophorum*", the "Corner-Stone", the "Pearl of Great Price", which would transmute not only base metals into gold and silver but every mortal thing into its immortal shape; the second, the Elixir of Life, which the Stone, once found, would become or procure. This double nature is conveyed in an anonymous essay, *The Sophic Hydrolith, or Water-Stone of the Wise*. The Stone was regarded as solid, tangible, the Elixir as liquid, potable, but they were, transcending reason, in essence One Thing. The quest of these was rather a poetical conception in the mind of a sage than a sober hypothesis in the mind of a scientific investigator.

Spagyric literature was usually in prose, though the strange *Book of Lambspring* was written in Latin verse by Nicholas Barnaud Delphinas and illustrated with engravings of allegorical beasts, and the small work *Atalanta Fugiens*[1] consisted entirely of emblematic pictures. The language of the writings varied with the culture and nationality of the author and included nearly every tongue of Europe and the Near East, but the writings, like the Magnificat, suffer little in translation. The prose is of the same type as that found in books of divination, herbals, lapidaries and bestiaries. which partook more of the nature of imaginative fiction than of scientific demonstration, for in them fancy triumphed over fact. The writers were not ingenuous. They did not set down their extravagant anecdotes of beasts and birds, stars and stones in scientific good faith but in conscious artistry. They were neither ignorant, foolish nor mendacious; they were poetic. Their concern was not with the accurate statement but with the imaginative treatment of a theme. No serious scientist of any age would propose an experiment to make "a white Milkie substance from the raies of the Moon," as did a certain John French: there is no physical connection between the two, but there is an imaginative link, which the literary artist will be quick to apprehend and utilise.

Hermetic prose claims consideration upon two grounds: first, it seems to be built of brightly-coloured stone like a Byzantine building and shows a quaint and individual beauty; and, secondly, this beauty is of its structure and not embossed upon it. The colour and decoration are not detachable; they proceed from the plan of spagyric thought. The alchemists personify the metals, calling Gold the King and Silver the Queen; they name substances after phantastic birds and beasts—calling Cinnabar the Red Lion—which have the same effect as the "Tyger" and the Lamb in Blake's poetry, they label their experiments by connecting each part with some striking object or incident. *An Open Entrance to the Closed Palace of the King* by Eirenaeus Philalethes describes one stage in the melting of gold with mercury when many colours appear as the "Peacock's tail" and likens another to the King stripping off his golden garments and descending into the fountain.

---

1 Referring to the 1617 Alchemical emblem book by Michael Maier.

A poet would not scorn their metaphors for chemical changes: they know black sulphides of mercury as the Crow and warn the experimenter that "the Black Crows will fly back to their nest," if the red sublimate disappears under insufficient heat. They do not allude to Classical myths merely to embroider their style, as the poets of the English Renaissance often do, but to explain the processes of their art more nicely, and infuse new meaning into ancient legends. The choice of the title *Atalanta Fugiens* is not accidental nor merely picturesque: the image of the running maiden stooping to pick up golden balls is in direct aspect to the philosophers' search for alchemical gold.

> I have a piece of Jason's fleece, too,
> Which was no other than a book of Alchemy
> Writ in large sheep-skin, with good fat ram-vellum.
> Such was Pythagoras' thigh, Pandora's tub,
> And all that fable of Medea's charms,
> The manner of our work; the bulls, our furnace,
> Still breathing fire; our argent-vive, the dragon;
> The dragon's teeth, mercury sublimate,
> That keeps the whiteness, hardness and the biting:
> And they are gather'd into Jason's helm
> The alembic, and then sow'd in Mars his field,
> And thence sublimed so often, till they're fix'd.
> Both this, the Hesperian garden, Cadmus' story.
> Jove's shower, the boon of Midas, Argus' eyes,
> Boccace his Demogorgon, thousands more,
> All abstract riddles of our stone[2].

There is an undercurrent of satire in this passage from Ben Jonson's comedy *The Alchemist*, for it is put into the mouth of an enthusiast duped by a sham philosopher, but it nevertheless shows the working of the alchemical mind. The precious stones and metals occur symbolically so often in old stories that the Hermetists are perhaps justified in their interpretations. Sometimes only a myth can enshrine a profound alchemical truth, since it has the double advantage of enlightening the adept while mystifying the uninitiated. The myth

2 This quote from Ben Jonson's 1610 play *The Alchemist.*

has frequently to be invented instead of adapted, as was the curious emblematical fairy-story called *The Chymical Marriage of Christian Rosenkreutz*, but it is seldom merely ornamental: it is indispensable in the interests of lucidity or obscuration. A fanciful panegyric on the Stone may be quoted from the *Brief Guide to the Celestial Ruby* of that enigmatic personality known as "the Cosmopolite," one of the greatest of English alchemists, who wrote under the name of Eirenaeus Philalethes:

> It is our door-keeper, our balm, our honey, oil, wine, maydew, mother, egg, secret furnace, oven, true fire, venomous dragon, theriac, ardent wine, Green Lion, bird of Hermes, goose of Hermogenes, two-edged sword in the hand of the Cherub that guards the Tree of Life. It is our true secret vessel, and the Garden of the Sages in which our sun rises and sets. It is our Royal Mineral, our Triumphant Vegetable Saturnia, and the magic rod in the hand of Hermes, by which he assumes any shape he likes.

Here the allusions possess great decorative value, but it is of a kind that springs naturally from essential content, since the adept must deal with such conceptions as the names signify. He is obliged to name metals and precious stones when writing of his work and so inevitably brings colour and brightness into his prose. Each of the seven metals known in early times was germane to one of the seven planets, which in turn had affinities each with its presiding deity, and thus the reader of alchemy passes, lit by the glimmer of heaven, through tunnels of meaning, faintly luminous, behind every word.

The style viewed in general, it may be well to examine more closely its characteristics of diction and imagery and explain its undeniable fascination. First of all, the alchemists are particularly happy in their choice of titles: *The Golden Tripod, The Brief Guide to the Celestial Ruby* already mentioned, *The Little Book of Pity* and *The Book of Royalty* by an Arabian alchemist, *The Triumphal Chariot of Antimony, A Golden and Blessed Casket of Precious Marvels, The Twelve Keys*. Some of these equal Böhme's *Aurora, or the Morning Redness*, and the names of the authors themselves, some of which were assumed, are scarcely less delightful than those of their works: Basil Valentine, Michael Sendivogius, Alain de L'Isle, Raymond Lully, Paracelsus, Arnold de Villeneuve, Delphinas. To see one of these below a book's title is to be immediately attracted.

A love of colour is one of their most pleasing traits of style, and their phrases are sometimes as pictorial as those of old Celtic romances like *The Dream of Rhonabwy*. In the Ninth Key of Basil Valentine's treatise, colour is combined with a sense of drama and pageantry:

> The King shares his royal dignity with noble Venus, and appears in splendid state, surrounded by all the dignitaries of his court. Before him is borne a beautiful crimson banner, in which there is an embroidered representation of Charity in green garments. Saturn is the prefect of the royal household, and in front of him Astronomy bears a black standard with a representation of faith in yellow and red garments.

There follows a description of the caparison and attendants of each planet, or rather metal, which might be a stage direction for a masque: this arises from the extreme use of allegory and personification. Instances of paradox have already been cited, and there is something paradoxical in the fact that realism is seldom found except in descriptions of the Stone, which was probably the least real part of the experiments. Van Helmont says:

> I have seen and handled the Stone. It had the colour of saffron in powder; it was heavy, and brilliant as glass broken into bits[3].

This style is clear enough for a modern book on chemistry; but though lucidity of style is common to most of these descriptions, the actual qualities set forth as belonging to the Stone alter with the varying imaginative taste of different authors. Bérigard de Pisa[4] says:

---

3 Notes from the fifteenth-sixteenth century Flemish chemist Jan Baptist van Helmont.

4 Claude Guillermet de Bérigard (1578-1663).

> *Colore non absimilis flore papaveris sylvestris, odore vero sal marinum adustum referentis.*

The names given to the Stone again show the fanciful turn of mind which would be out of place in a scientific treatise but accords well with poetical metaphysics: "stone of wisdom", "carbuncle of the sun", "old dragon", "basilisk", "phoenix"; and those by which the Elixir was known are not less marvellous: "virgin water", "divine water" and "heavenly balm". In these evocative phrases metaphor merges into symbol, figures of speech rise from mere imagery to statement of fact, albeit on the imaginative plane.

Metaphor is used more frequently than simile because it is more direct, more an indication, less a mere grace of style. Their imagery echoes the movements of nature, of planets and seasons with their attendant life of plant and animal, of all signified by the revolving circle, the serpent that bites her own tail. The vegetation metaphor in *The Philosophical Summary* of Nicholas Flamel is vital and satisfying, because of its link with recurring phenomena, yet piquant because of its suggestion of supernature:

> But in the Garden of the Sages, the Sun sheds its genial influence both morning and evening, day and night, unceasingly. There our tree is watered with rarest dew and the fruit which hangs upon the trees—gold and silver—swells and ripens and expands from day to day."

In George Ripley's *Twelve Gates of Alchemy,* metaphor has passed completely into symbolism and rises above the chemical directions which it professes to elucidate, to a state of pure emotion without subject or object, and consequentially almost incomprehensible to an ordinary mind:

> The work must be undertaken at sunset, when the husband, Red, and the wife, White, are united in the spirit of life to live in love and tranquility, in the exact proportion of water and earth. From the west, advance across the shadows

> towards the south: alter and dissolve the husband and the wife between winter and spring, change the water into a black earth, and raise thyself across the varied colours toward the East when the full moon shows itself. After the purgation, the sun appears white and radiant; it is summer after winter, day after night. The earth and water are transformed into air, the darkness is dispersed, light is made.

Little can be gathered from this but the author's love of contrast, and his dithyrambic triumph in the vanquishing of darkness by light, to which the paragraph works up. Both this and the ecstatic questions, exclamations and imperatives of the Arabian author of the *Book of Ostanes* are likely to bring the charge of obscurity against alchemical prose:

> O troop of seekers, take me, slay me. Then, having slain me, burn me; for I will after all revive, and enrich him who shall have slain and burnt me. If he come near me with fire, then I am alive. If I shall endure it all the night, even if he sublime me completely and enchain me absolutely, I am still alive. O marvel! How, being alive, can I bear ill-treatment?

The exulting in torture that informs this outburst brings one to consider a mode of feeling which occurs intermittently throughout hermetic literature. It is a reveling in the grotesque and macabre, even in the savage and violent. Thus Arnold de Villeneuve describes with Biblical ferocity the vicissitudes of a metallic solar Son who is born of a lunar Mother, and undergoes all kinds of torment in quest of the Essence:

> Then put him a second time on his bed and, when he has recovered his senses, seize him afresh to deliver him to be crucified of the Jews. The Sun being thus crucified you will not see the Moon, the veil of the Temple will be rent, and there will be a great earthquake. Then is the time to employ a hot fire.

Zozimus recounts a dream of his in a similar vein, and an elaborate panegyric in praise of the *margarita preciosa* in the *Third Book of Ostanes* ends with the words:

> It is a young man born in Egypt; it is a prince coming from Andalusia who seeks for the torment of the seekers.

The sharpness of these threatening sentences is not a fault; rather it is a virtue, since it relieves the over-sweetness which usually results from giving imagination too free a rein. It provides thorns for the fragrant briar.

Perhaps the word "exotic" best describes the prose of the Spagyrists. The colour, the allusions, the paradox, the grotesqueness, the symbolism and above all the fantastic subject of enquiry whose origin was the East, combine to produce a bizarre impression. Such a style fails of mature excellence because it is often too crudely gaudy, too extravagant and undisciplined. Its naïve transports and spark-like enthusiasms touch the reader as the sudden felicities of a child touch him, or the impossible splendours of a nursery-tale. But it is seldom flat or insipid, and even when monstrously obscure can sting with the thrill of adventure in a gloomy thick forest. †

Explanation of a Design for a Painting on Silk (1934)

This short piece is less of an essay and more of a narrative description of a painting. Nevertheless, it is important as it indicates a very early demonstration of Kabbalistic and Tantric themes and motifs in addition to a focus on an explicit concern with the material embodiment of the Divine Feminine. The piece to which this essay refers is currently held at the Penlee House Museum in Cornwall in the UK, where it is in a very delicate condition.

The design represents Malkuth ("the Kingdom"), tenth Emanation of the Sephirotic Decad, and lowest of the "Blossoms" on the Qabalistic Tree of Life. The magical image of Malkuth is said to be "a young woman crowned and veiled"; and she is called "the Daughter", "the Queen", "the Bride", and "the Virgin"; and again, "the Gate of the Garden of Eden". In the design—which in itself is suitable for the decoration of a Doorway—Eden is suggested by the tree against which the figure of the young woman stands, and by the "Four Rivers" that flow out of it. Here again one can trace the pattern of the "Tree of Life" with its ten "blossoms", the first of which, Kether ("the Crown") seems to rest above the girl's head. In the colour and treatment of the background is some hint of "Jannat al 'Adn", the Arab Garden of Eden and lowest of the Heavens, which is said to be made of red pearls; and perhaps some indication too of the tenth plague of Egypt, the "water-turned-to-blood".

As leader of the tenth Order of Qliphoth, Malkuth is called "the Evil Woman" or (simply) "the Woman". In the Egyptian hierarchy she corresponds to the unwedded Isis, to Isis as Virgin; in the Greek to Psyche and Persephone; in the Roman, to Proserpine and some aspects of Ceres; in the Christian, to "Ecclesia Christi", the Church imagined as the Bride of Christ. Among the phantastic animals of myth she corresponds to the enigmatic Sphinx; and in various systems of folk-lore she appears as the Corn-Maiden who presides over growth and vegetation. She is the tenth Heaven of Assiah, the "Sphere of the Elements"; and in the "Queen" scale of colour she is allotted the four colours which symbolise the elements. Her own particular element, however, is Earth, the "wet earth" in the classification of the "Ten Earths". In alchemical language she is the "Medicine of Metals" and the "Mercury of the Philosophers"; in the language of the Tarot she governs the "Tens" of each of the Four Suits—the "Empresses" or "Princesses". Of the ten virtues of the Adept she represents Scepticism. In the Qabalistic division of the soul into different parts, she is Nepheth, the Animal Soul that perceives and feels; and in the more complex division of the Hindu she is the almost-physical envelope, the "Sthula Sharira". From the Forty Buddhist meditations she evokes the meditation "on the body"; she symbolises manifested existence, the part of consciousness concerned with environment, the "body-of-fate". In Hindu legend she is Lakshmi or Kundalini, the mysterious "fire" that runs upward through the "Lotoses" (sic) or occult nerve-centres of the body.

In the design a suggestion of the Lotos-form is retained in the drawing of the "Blossoms", to trace the connection between the Tantrik and Qabalistic modes of thought. The body is divided according to that of the "Perfected Man" in the Egyptian, and coloured (for the sake of simplicity) in accordance with the Sephirotic attributions of the "King" ("Jod") scale of colour; though the "Empress" (Hé) scale would have been more appropriate, since the second "Hé" of the Tetragrammaton corresponds with "the Daughter". The "Blossoms" or Emanations of the Tree and the parts of the body over which they rule are coloured alike. Yellow being Malkuth's predominating colour, it is introduced into the Tree itself behind the figure, and in the gold with which both Tree and figure are outlined. †

The Two Creation-Myths in Genesis (c. 1930s, early 1940s)

This short essay may be Colquhoun's clearest characterisation of her convictions that both humans and the divine are essentially hermaphroditic and androgynous, containing both genders. This belief has a long history in Western esotericism and the modern occult, and was a fixation of Colquhoun's throughout much of her writing and magical experiments until the early 1940s. There is no firm date on this essay but it is consistent with the material Colquhoun was working on in the late 1930s to early 1940[1]. We also see her interest in the Divine Androgyne expressed in "The Water Stone of the Wise" connected with ideas of human spiritual development, but it may have also been an interest that was partially driven by her struggles with same sex attraction. Regardless, this essay serves to reposition and reestablish the Divine Feminine within Western esotericism and also within Abrahamic religions, where Colquhoun feels the Goddess has been erased by the patriarchy.

Not everyone realises that the first chapters of the book of Genesis are by no means a homogenous whole, but are, in fact, an attempt, only partially successful, at blending the different versions of the creation myths. These may be distinguished as the "Patriarchal" account on the one hand and the "Qabalistic" account on the other, the exoteric and the esoteric. The task of disentangling them is not made easier

1 Richard Shillitoe believes the essay to date to the 1930s based on the archival material with which it was found. Private communication, 22 May, 2024.

by the mistakes which the ignorance or willfulness of the English translators of the Hebrew original has caused them to make.

Taking the English Authorized Version of the "Bible", Genesis 1, 1-13 marks the beginning of the "Qabalistic" account; and in the first verse one is faced with a serious handicap to understanding, in a gross mistranslation of the word "Elohim" (אֱלֹהִימ). Why this word, feminine plural in form, is persistently translated as masculine singular, is incomprehensible, except on the supposition of the greater influence of the "Patriarchal" versions as will be shown later. However this may be, the word "Elohim", always rendered in English as "God", might more aptly be translated "The Goddesses", or rather "The twin Goddesses" since the form is the modified plural denoting not more than two. The section details, in the following order, with the creation: 1. Of the Heaven and Earth, and of Light; 2. Of a "firmament in the midst of the waters" (which is later said to be identical with "Heaven"; 3. Of the Earth (dry land), the Seas, the Vegetable Kingdom; 4. Of "Lights in the Firmament" (the Sun and Moon). (This seems strange since "light" had already been created on the first day, unless we interpret the first "light" as the "creative Lux" or "crystalline dew", the "Lux Occulta" of the Qabalah, the "Ain Soph Aur.")

With verses 14-25 begins the "Patriarchal" or "priestly" account, clumsily said to continue with the creation of the "fourth day", but stating "lights in the firmament", the sun and moon are now created. The inconsistency of this with verse 3, where light is created on the first day, is obvious, and makes apparent the attempted welding of two different stories. On the fifth day "moving creatures" to live in the water and air are created; and on the sixth "beasts of the earth" and "creeping things".

At verse 26 the Qabalistic account is resumed. The Creator says: "Let us make Man in our image". Elohim is at least here recognised as plural; but in the next verse confusion returns. "God created Man in his own image, in the image of God created he him; male and female created he them." (The translator evidently does not know how to cope with the passage; some scruple in using the singular of the plural form is troubling him; though not in using a masculine one for a feminine. He may have adopted the masculine, however, merely for the sake of convenience.) The sense, too, is unfamiliar, and may well, as it stands in the Hebrew, have appeared blasphemous to him. Hence his fumbling attempt to combine scholarship with orthodoxy.

To a student of the Qabalah, however, unhindered by allegiance to the Established Church, the sense is clear enough: it is the image of a hermaphrodite Creator extending and reflecting himself in the creature Man, also hermaphrodite. In the *Siphra Dtzenioutha*, the *Book of Concealed Mystery*, this process is expressly stated, and fully explained in the commentaries: "And Countenance beheld Countenance". There is no talk here of the sleep of Adam, or the rib from his side; male and female are co-equal and co-existent, and reflect equally the manifest aspect of the Divine. In the next verse, scholarship triumphs in the case of creature if not of Creator, and the new being is consistently referred to as "them".

The last three verses, which end the chapter, may be cited in support of any claim to divine authority which the cult of Vegetarianism may care to make: "Behold, I have given you every herb... to you it shall be meat." In the next verse, not only humanity but the animal, bird and reptile kingdoms were given solely "every green herb for meat." Thus end the labours of the sixth day.

With Chapter 2: 1-3 the rest of the seventh day is described, and in verse 4 the "Patriarchal" account is resumed. We are first made aware of a change of viewpoint by the consistent use of the name "the Lord God" as Javeh (Tetragrammaton) is translated, instead of "God" (Elohim). One is accustomed to think of Jehovah as indubitably masculine and singular, and for the purposes of the exoteric cult he certainly was so; but in the Tetragrammaton are hidden meanings which to the student present a deeper interpretation. "Jod" (י) the first letter is masculine, and represents in Qabalism "The King" or Father; "Hé" (ה) is feminine representing "The Queen" or Mother; "Vau" (ו) is masculine, symbolizing "The Son"; the second "Hé" is feminine and symbolises "the Daughter". Thus both hermaphrodite and plural elements appear in the name Jahveh.

Leaving esoteric tradition aside, the second version of the Creation-myth may now be studied. The work of creation is nowhere systematically divided between seven days, as in the Qabalistic account; but one gathers from verse 4 that the heavens and earth were formed on the first day and immediately after—whether on the same "day" or not is not stated—the vegetable kingdom. There was as yet no "rain", nor, presumably any "seas"; so there went up a mist from the earth, and watered the whole face of "the ground". Then Javeh formed Man "of the dust of the ground and breathed into his nostrils the Breath of Life"; and Man became a living soul. The word "Ruach" is used for both breath and soul, like the Greek.

The Qabalistic account is very slight: Man is "created" and nothing more is said. Here the process is described with greater detail. In verses 8-17 the planting of the Garden of Eden is described; and with verse 18 the account returns to created man—"Adam" as he is thenceforth called. The Lord God says "I will make a help meet for him", and so animals and birds are created and brought before Adam, "to see what he would call them", as is naively remarked. It is almost superfluous to point out the inconsistency of this passage with the Qabalistic account in Genesis I, where the animal kingdoms are created on the fifth "day" and the human not till the sixth. If any further proof were needed to decide that there are here two separate accounts to be dealt with, here it is. Adam, having named all the "cattle", "fowls of the air" and "beasts of the field" cannot find among them "an help meet for him"; thence follows the familiar account of the creation of Eve. How different in this Patriarchal account is the attitude to Woman, from the more ancient Qabalistic one. Here, woman is created some time after man, and expressly to minister to him; in fact, she only comes into existence at all, because Adam cannot find a suitable companion-help from amongst the animals; she is not even an independent creation, but formed from Adam's own flesh and bone. The story of the temptation of the Serpent, which follows in Chapter 3, lays the blame for the Fall on Eve, and punishes her more severely than Adam. (It is not too phantastic to trace in this influence of a Patriarchal civilization where women had few rights, and in the other, a more ancient civilization or Matriarchy, or perhaps a transition stage between the two, maintaining a just balance of the two sexes).

Not till Chapter 5 does the Qabalistic account again appear: "In that day God created Man, in the likeness of God made he him; male and female created he them; and blessed them, and called their name Adam." Here, even more clearly than in Chapter 1, Man the Hermaphrodite, reflecting a hermaphroditic Creator, is described, and though the interwinding of the two accounts continues throughout the Book of Genesis—and indeed throughout the Pentateuch, the creation-myths proper end with this paragraph. †

Dance of the Nine Opals (1941)

This is another commentary on one of Colquhoun's works, the *Dance of the Nine Opals.* This essay, and the accompanying painting, show some of Colquhoun's most developed thinking about the origin and function of what she considered to be sacred landscapes and megalithic antiquities. Although she claims this image arose from the unconscious, the essay indicates a number of layered and complex inspirations that help to explain the overall derivation of the piece.

When a picture comes directly from the unconscious, it is almost as difficult for the artist as it is for the spectator to say what it means. Imagine seeing a full-grown tree for the first time, without having any idea of its history or function! When unknown forms arise, they appear as any natural form might when seen for the first time; this is, in fact, what they are—forms from a super-nature which is only beginning to be explored. It is important to record these "rocks and stones and trees" of the supersensual life.

This painting, it seems to me, comes from some hinterland of the mind, some border-line region, since elements drawn from both "actual" and "potential" worlds are to be found in it. It is built from several impacted strata of material and meaning:

1) Various druidic stone-circles known to Cornish folk-lore as "Nine Maidens" (ni mên = "holy stones"). Legend says that the circle is

composed of girls turned to stone for dancing on (at) the Sabbat, and can be restored to natural shape if embraced at midnight when the moon is full. The monument is a petrified "Hexentanz"[1]; it is here seen as one of the "psychic zones" of the country-side, one of its "fountains out of Hecate"[2].

2) A Celtic solar festival or fertility-rite; the Maypole's streamers are replaced by coloured "lines-of-force" connecting the stones with the central fountain and with each other.

3) The nine planets of traditional astrology, including Pluto and Vulcan, revolving round the cohesive and dynamic force of the solar system.

4) Apollo, symbolised by the sun-burst in the centre of the ring, "leading his choir, the Nine."

5) The common chord, symbolised by the three tints—one of them basic—in each stone, carried through an octave, including the first two accidentals. The "music of the spheres."

6) Kether ("the crown") mitigating the nine lesser sephiroth—often represented in cabalistic tradition as a tree of life.

7) A supernatural flower with nine petals and fiery pistil.

8) The nine moons of pregnancy with perpetual solar impregnation.

9) The opal signifying by its combination of colours the animal, vegetable and mineral worlds. By its connection with the Zodiacal Libra, it links the whole morphological system with the idea of a balance between static and dynamic forces.

This is a list of the painting's inspirational starting-points, as far as I have been able to analyse them. Some of the interpretations of its

1 Witches' Dance.

2 This is a term from the Chaldean Oracles. Colquhoun uses it to refer to the idea that there are electromagnetic currents under the earth that can be accessed by humans.

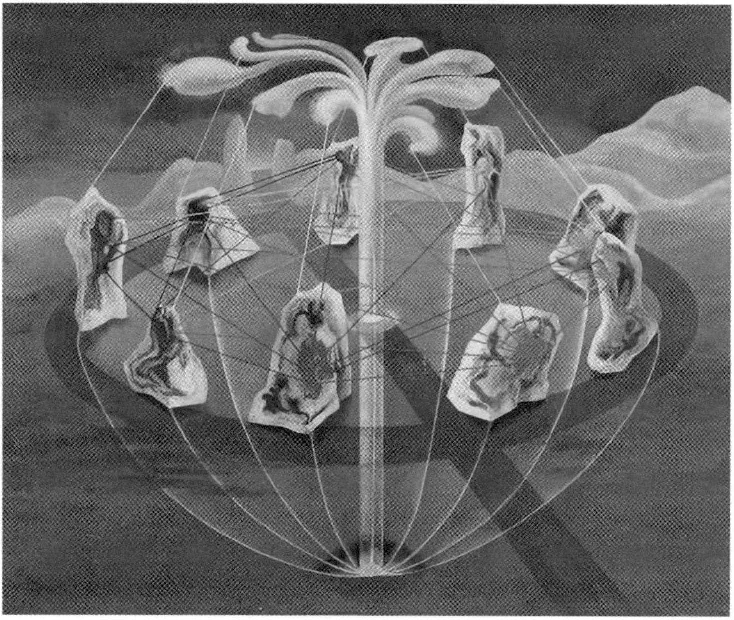

forms I noticed myself, others had been pointed out to me; others, still, doubtless remain to be discovered. But however much one may try to explain a painting, in the end it must carry its message direct to the unconscious of its spectator through his senses by means of its forms and colours. †

The Importance of *A Vision* (c. 1943)

Colquhoun considered W. B. Yeats to be a prophet, and she considered the text that he channeled with the help of his wife Georgie Hyde Lees, *A Vision*, to be one of the most important of his writings. Colquhoun was deeply influenced by this strange and complex work, almost psychedelic in nature, that theorised time in a cyclical manner, expressed by converging gyres and the phases of the moon and opined about the nature of the soul. Colquhoun was most certainly aware of the text by the early 1930s and it likely inspired both her alchemically driven erotic works and also her essay "The Water Stone of the Wise". Although Colquhoun held Spiritualist mediumship with the dead in disdain, this form of channeling suggesting information stemming from preternatural intelligences dovetailed with her growing interest in automatism and extradimensional planes in the late 1930s. She certainly would have been compelled by the idea that the nature of the universe could best be conveyed by shapes and abstractions. Based on correspondence related to this essay and internal dating, this was likely written in 1942, but as with many of her writings, she worked to promote it for many years after it was initially written. Colquhoun passionately believed that more people should work to understand this text and she delivered this as a presentation for many years, including to "Mrs. Nathaniel Levitt's Psychic Literary Luncheon" in 1957. Throughout her life Colquhoun was exceptionally engaged with scholarship about Yeats, and this essay demonstrates her deep readings of his *corpus*

and also shows that she was always seeking out the most recent critiques of his work.

Yeats was a philosophical poet, and wished to be understood as such; therefore his critics may be tested by their approach to *A Vision*, the work in which this poet-philosopher's basic ideas are given their clearest expression. Apart from an important cosmological theory, and the unique manner in which, as Yeats tells us, this was revealed—both of absorbing interest—the book contains, in the section "Dove or Swan", prose which he did not elsewhere surpass; and some of his finest poems, among them "Leda" and "All Soul's Night", here first appeared. The earlier edition contained also "The Gift of Haroun al Rashid", and the later one is the poorer for its exclusion; for this poem sets forth the romance of that automatic process by which the whole system was conveyed, and ends magnificently and characteristically with the lines:

A woman's beauty is a storm-tossed banner;
Under it wisdom stands and I alone—
Of all Arabia's lovers I alone—
Nor dazzled by the embroidery, nor lost
In the confusion of its night-dark folds,
Can hear the armed man speak.

It is the voice of this "armed man", metallic and resonant, speaking in geometric symbols, which many of Yeats' critics find antipathetic. Only one poet, Dante—to whom Yeats looked up as a "revered ancestor"—linked his imagery so closely to an abstract cosmological system. There can be few parallels in literary history—though several could be cited from the history of occultism—to the manner in which both system and imagery were crystallised.

No critic has as yet done justice to *A Vision*, though so far V. K. Narayana Menon, in *The Development of William Butler Yeats*, shows the most comprehension of the problems it raises. But the reading of such a study as Louis MacNeice's *The Poetry of W.B. Yeats*, begun perhaps with expectation, must be continued, if at all, with disappointment, once it is plain that yet another writer has failed in this appreciation.

Mr. MacNeice characterises *A Vision* as "arid", but to a sympathetic reader it is almost unbearably exciting; and one is reminded of the account which Yeats himself gives in one of his earlier essays of the excitement which, as he says, would "overbrim the page" and oblige him to stop reading, when he came upon some passage in the work of others which particularly struck his imagination. *A Vision* has the same effect on Yeats' own readers. G. W. Russell ("Æ"), his intimate friend for many years, showed more understanding than MacNeice when he foresaw that this book would "be discussed feverishly by commentators a century hence, as Blake's Prophetic Books—so ignored and so unintelligible a hundred years ago—are discussed by many editors in our time". In fact, to evaluate Yeats without close study of this fundamental work shows as little perception as to sum up Blake without reference to his Prophetic writings.

Mr. MacNeice is not alone in finding *A Vision* difficult; it is not an easy book and is still comparatively little read. Many who know Yeats' verse well are not equally familiar with his prose, and of those who admire his prose also, many have not yet approached *A Vision*. This is partly due to the method of publication which its author first adopted: a limited edition was privately printed by Werner Laurie in 1925. This was the only work which Yeats published in such a way; still influenced, perhaps, by hermetic precept, he may have felt that such writing should not be widely circulated. Not until twelve years later did a second edition, revised and enlarged, become available to the general public through MacMillans' [sic]. But this latter fact seems to have escaped the notice of another would-be assessor of Yeats' genius, the late George Orwell, who in a review in the January 1943 number of *Horizon* maintained that the work was never more than privately printed—an error which he repeated in the April 17/43 issue of *Time and Tide*. He at least, however, frankly admitted that he had never read *A Vision*.

Yeats, though not a philosopher in the strict sense, was a philosophical poet, even something of "prophet", and *A Vision* is the summing-up of his intuitions and convictions. In his preface to the second edition, he asserts that the system it sets forth was communicated to him through his wife at the dictation of "spirits". Whether or not this is the explanation of some very strange phenomena, it seems undeniable that the poet touched more nearly than he had done before the universal "unconscious"—*Anima Mundi* in the Neoplatonic terms he preferred to use—and that he penetrated to a particular region or stratum of it, for which a lifetime's study and speculation had prepared him. For this was by no means his first step on "the path of the Chameleon"[1]; in childhood even, the Celtic earth which was his home brought him continual intimations of a supersensual life; and in youth, before he left Dublin, he made conscious attempts to draw aside "the trembling veil"[2]. On settling in London, he was initiated into that Rosicrucian society known as "The Order of the Golden Dawn". How far this initiation was effective it is difficult to say, but it may well have given him an insight into little-known modes of consciousness. It influenced him in unsuspected ways; for instance, the title of one of his plays, *The Unicorn from the Stars*, is taken direct from the rituals of the Order, "Monokeros de Astris" being the title conferred on the initiate when he passed from the grade of Theoricus to that of Practicus. At a guess, one might say that this latter grade was the last the poet attained before his retirement from the order.

It is certain that afterwards the supernatural was his constant if sometime hidden preoccupation; and these "spirit-messages", therefore, were less the sudden onrush of another world, than the culmination of a special approach to reality which had long been his habit of mind. Premonitory hints of the spirits' main themes can be found throughout the verse of Yeats' middle period, that is, approximately, 1909/(1912?)-1920; certainly since the days of "the horn's sweet note and the tooth of the hound"[3]. There is evidence of them in his essays also, even as early as "Ideas of Good and Evil", though most strikingly, as he himself recognised, in *Per Amica Silentia Lunae*. Since the time when the actual messages closed, 1921,

1 This refers to the Golden Dawn Adeptus Minor 5=6 rite "The Path of the Chameleon" in which the colour symbolism of the Golden Dawn is explained. *Hodos Chameleonis,* referring to the path and the candidate, is also the name of a chapter in Yeats' 1922 *The Trembling of the Veil.*

2 An autobiographical volume from Yeats published in 1922, in which he recounts a predilection for esoteric and magical spirituality even in childhood.

3 From "Two Songs of a Fool" in *The Wild Swans at Coole* (1919).

his poetic thought worked unceasingly and almost exclusively the same inexhaustible-seeming mine. The spirits, if such they were, certainly did not palter with him in a double sense; on the contrary, they brought him a double gift. They were rather better than their word, for they gave him not only, as they said "metaphors for poetry", but a cosmology reaching back to epochs before Christianity, and stretching out to aeons far beyond it. Their promise is profoundly true; the poet's whole system of imagery is intimately connected, either by prophecy or by echo, with the ruling ideas of the system they revealed.

These ideas, summarily stated, are as follows:

> 1). The dependence of human life on cosmic processes, particularly sidereal time. This idea appears in Yeats' poetry whenever the great figures and epochs of history or myth are referred to, and its most frequent illustration is the change from the Graeco-Roman to the Christian era.

> Odour of blood when Christ was slain
> Made Plato's tolerance in vain
> And vain the Doric discipline[4].

The chief symbol for this cosmic movement is the closing and expanding gyre.

> 2). The achievement of human destiny through reincarnation, or rather by rhythm of incarnate and discarnate phases. The twenty-eight typical incarnations, two of which he calls "supernatural", are symbolised by the phases of the moon; and they chiefly absorb the poet through their connection with the attaining of beauty—"soul seeking itself"—and of wisdom—"soul seeking the world". This idea is outlined in the dialogue-poem called "The Phases of the Moon"; and when the moon appears in his poetry it is usually in this symbolic sense. The songs in

4 From "Two Songs from a Play" (1927).

"The Only Jealousy Of Emer" are particularly notable in this connection and "The Double Vision of Michael Robartes" may also be cited:

Although I saw it all in the mind's eye
There can be nothing solider till I die;
I saw by the moon's light
Now at its fifteenth night.

As regards the discarnate phases, almost any reference to "a haunting" in an attempt to explore them, the prose-play *The Words on the Window-pane*, with its preface, being a very complete example; while the long section of *A Vision* called "The Soul in Judgement" brings to a climax the poet's musings on this subject.

3) The doctrine of "antithesis" as applied to the individual soul. The "antithetical" side, or subjective nature, is contrasted with the "primary", or objective; these again are subdivided into other oppositions, the four "Faculties" and the four "Principles"; and a relationship with a "Daimon", a total opposition, is hinted at. This daimonic theme is reflected and magnified in the macrocosm where the whole universe humanly perceived is represented as "lunae" while the "utterly other", the unimaginable unchanging opposite of the person and aforementioned totality is characterised as 'solar'. This idea occurs in Yeats' poetry wherever he attempts to express the significance of the great personalities of myth or history:

That night and morning I may thrash
Greek Alexander from my flesh
Augustus and Ceasar, and after these
That great rogue Alcibiades.

or, in a more mundane fashion, when he makes a character-sketch of an acquaintance, such as William Morris, or of a literary figure, such as Landor.

It is unlikely that Yeats himself possessed the automatic faculty in any marked degree, but he was fortunate to meet in his wife with someone who did. *A Vision* seems to be the result of a mysterious collaboration, laid down in the unconscious of both, and subsequently elaborated with all the poet's fully-conscious ingenuity. Does one touch here that approach to wisdom, little known or little acknowledged in the West, through the impersonal use of sexual power? Was this co-operation a species of Laya Kriya[5]? If so, it was also perhaps an example of that relationship, described in many biographies of the occultists, in which the seer is dependent on the sybilline powers of a woman for his contact of the supernatural. Simon Magus and Helen, Cagliostro and Lorenza Feliciani, Dr. Pordage and Jane Lead, come to mind.

To appreciate the works of Yeats in any complete sense, it is necessary to stress a truth, the implications of which many will not wish to face, namely, that the basis of his thought is unchristian: "Homer is my example and his unchristened heart[6]." Christianity is not the only profound worldview; it is not even the most profound. There is something different from the Christian ethos implicit in the whole body of his work; and in certain passages this comes near to an explicit hostility. Or rather, it is less hostility than cold rejection, and the substitution for it of another mode of thought and feeling. This is expressed in "The Second Coming" and "Ribh Considers the Christian Love insufficient"—perhaps most clearly of all in that terrifying lyric "The Cold Heaven", which after opening rhythms which recall the menace of an approaching storm, continues

> And then I cried and trembled, and rocked to and fro
> Riddled with light! Ah, when the ghost begins to quicken
> Confusion of the death-bed over, is it sent
> Out naked on the roads, as the books say, and stricken
> By the injustice of the skies for punishment?

5 This refers to a type of yoga that activates the Kundalini. Here Colquhoun is likely referring to a practice of esoteric sexuality.

6 From "Vacillation" (1933).

The 'books' here mentioned can scarcely have been the Twopenny Catechism, nor even the Book of Common Prayer. In a note on 'Calvary', one of his haunting *Four Plays For Dancers*, the poet amplifies some of these ideas, though he does not indicate their source: "I have used my bird-symbolism in these songs to increase the objective loneliness of Christ by contrasting it with a loneliness opposite in kind, that unlike His can be, whether joyous or sorrowful, sufficient to itself. I have surrounded him with the images of those He cannot save, not only with the birds, who have served neither God nor Caesar, and await for none or for a different Saviour; but with Lazarus and Judas and the Roman soldiers, for whom He has died in vain... I have therefore represented in Lazarus and Judas types of that intellectual despair that lay beyond His sympathy, while in the Roman soldiers I suggest a form of objectivity that lay beyond His help." Ribh finds the Christian love insufficient indeed! Where else can be found so much disillusion in an unobtrusive footnote?

The truth is that Yeats drew his inspiration from a different spring. In the literature and philosophy of the European tradition, there is a vein, difficult to trace but easy to recognise, which cuts across the habitual distinction of Classical and Romantic, Catholic and Protestant, even of Christian and Pagan. It is an underground working that runs not only athwart them, but at a deeper level. This influence has been briefly studied by Professor Saurat, in *Literature and Occult Tradition*, and he has amplified some of his findings in his subsequent study of Blake. Spengler also recognised, in *The Decline of the West*, that the categories, at least, of Classical and Romantic were inadequate, and noted a third tendency which he called the 'Magian'[7].

Yeats had a 'Magian' mind; to see this one has only to read his description of the Byzantine epoch in "Dove or Swan", or the poignant "Sailing to Byzantium":

7 Oswald Spengler's 1918 *The Decline of the West* was a popular and decidedly unprogressive book. Spengler's notion of Western civilizational decline influenced Colquhoun's thinking about the decadence of modernity.

Once out of nature I shall never take
My bodily form from any natural thing;
But such a form as Grecian goldsmiths make
Of hammered gold and gold enameling
To keep a drowsy Emperor awake.

It is interesting to notice that 'Byzantium' is the title given by Mario Praz, in his study of *The Romantic Agony*, to the chapter which deals, not, it is true, with Yeats himself, but with many of his forerunners and contemporaries of the 'Decadent' school.

The Middle-Eastern parentage which Yeats imagined for his masterpiece may also be cited—that phantastic story with which he prefaced the first edition. He invented, as he admitted later, this rigmarole about old Cracow, the "Speculum" of one "Giraldus", and "Kusta ben Luki", sage of an obscure Arabian tribe, the "Judwalis". All this is, incidentally, in the general line of occult picaresque, and his affinities with the adventures of Dr. Dee and Edward Kelley, and even with those of Cagliostro.

Had Yeats lived, say, in Cyprus instead of Ireland, he might have found a form of Christianity which he could accept. His family was Protestant, but his outlook had nothing in common with Protestantism. It was more akin to Catholicism, and he must have seen much in the ritual and tradition of the Church to appeal to him. He had a hierarchic view of life, and shared the feudalistic leanings and anti-industrial protests of many modern Catholics. There is some evidence that he at least considered how far the philosophy revealed to him could be made to accord with the teachings of the Church; in "Wheels and Butterflies" he points out that Cardinal Mercier did not condemn as heretical the theory of reincarnation (on which a great part of *A Vision* is based). Lady Gerald Wellesley, in one of her conversations with Yeats, remarked on the likeness between the themes he developed in "The Soul in Judgment" and doctrines and beliefs connected with the idea of Purgatory, and tried to discover how far this resemblance went. But she could draw from him no definite reply. Not only did he not enter the Church which for the greater part of his life was literally at his door; but he was constantly and bitterly attacked by the more fanatical of the Catholics in Ireland, a result only to be expected on the propagating of unchristian ideas in a Christian country. Perhaps some of this tension is dramatised in the mysterious figures of "Michael Robartes" and "Owen Aherne", who represent two sides of his own nature, and about whom he wrote many stories and poems. Aherne is always represented as a devout Catholic, repelled yet fascinated by the "strange thought" and "barbarous words" of Robartes—the 'Magian' character par excellence—who usually takes the lead and imposes his will on the other.

Mr. MacNeice finds *A Vision* "unreadable", but admits that Yeats himself "attached vast importance to it". He also raises the question of Yeats' 'sincerity', and this is an unexpectedly difficult point, since the poet himself made some ambiguous remarks about his confidence in his own illuminations as a valid and tenable view of life. These must, however, be taken as the result of a mood, for there is little doubt that, apart from this one lapse, he considered the system revealed by his 'spirit-instructors' to be the most comprehensive he could arrive at. Such critics, as for instance Desmond MacCarthy in *The Sunday Times* of February 14, 1943, and Cyril Connolly in *The Observer* of the same date, seem to deprecate Yeats' magical studies and practices, while admitting that his greatest poetry could not have come into being without these. One feels tempted to apply to such people André Breton's doctrine of total consent or total refusal. Poetry cannot be made from mere superficial gestures and poses of the intellect; the question even goes beyond 'belief' as deliberate acceptance or rational conviction—it is a matter of obsession. Yeats was obsessed by a particular system of ideas and their clothing imagery, and could no more escape from these than the journeying Self, in "All Souls' Night", can plunge into the symbolic Sun and 'sink into its own delight' before its twenty-eight phases are accomplished.

Yeats' masterpiece has much in common with that of Spengler, *The Decline of the West*, though neither could have directly influenced the other, as Yeats points out by citing dates of publication[8]. But both authors chanced, as Yeats might have said, to tap the same immemorial sources. Yeats marks more strongly the dialectical basis of the cyclic theory; gives, indeed, life and colour to a system fundamentally Hegelian—in itself so extraordinary a feat as to suggest a supernatural habitat for his instructors. And while Spengler ends on a note of pessimism for the immediate future and can recommend nothing more vital than stoicism as an attitude, Yeats sees all as a series of gigantic gyres, and looks forward, once the two-thousand or so years of the Christian cycle have elapsed, to a new revelation. He outlines a monistic world-view, in which the Christian dualism is but a phase, and so avoids the tedious moralizing inseparable from a dualistic philosophy. He indicates a direction for research into the future; and the tendencies he predicts should be studied carefully and with perception.

That he hoped for students who would undertake this work is clear from several passages in the exposition; and for this study both editions of his chief work should be used, since, though the second has gained in coherence, it has lost some of the magic of the earlier. Yeats grew to lay more and more stress, as he said, on the "boney structure" of his writing; and in *A Vision* this structure is certainly hard, but the effort to grasp and to use it will not be wasted. †

8 Steven Borthwick argues that while Spengler's work did not influence Yeats' 1925 version of *A Vision*, he revised it to take into account Spengler's views. Spengler's "Magian" culture was derived from an imaginal early Arabic culture that was concerned primarily with good and evil and from which esoteric knowledge such as alchemy was derived.

The Divine Marquis and the Myth of Liberty (c. early 1940s)

Although this essay is not technically concerned in any explicit sense with magic or the occult, it does demonstrate a key value and focus of Colquhoun's during the early 1940s, that of liberty, a theme which we see surface in her critical essay "The Water Stone of the Wise" from 1943. This essay is primarily a response to the surrealist embrace of the Marquis de Sade, which Colquhoun found objectionable for a variety of reasons, but it also underpins some of her esoteric writings which are concerned with human (and especially women's) liberty as a goal of magical practice. Liberty is also a key feature of Aleister Crowley's Thelema, which Colquhoun appeared to have quite an ambivalent reaction to throughout her life. We also see here her use of a quote from Fra Luis Ponce de Leon's "Libro Primaro", a quote repeated in several essays and also in *The Goose of Hermogenes*, which point to her early ruminations on freedom as defined as being in a sleep like state, free from struggle or desire.

Any discussion of either myth or liberty—must, if it is to penetrate more profoundly than the catch-phrase, entail an examination of the nature and destiny of man and of the individual place in the community, indeed, of the purpose of life itself. But for the present, since five hundred words is inadequate for such an exploration, I must confine myself to the surrealist conception of liberty, as I understand it, in order to discover whether the ends to which it points, with such bright hope, are possible of realisation, and whether, if so, they constitute a genuinely desirable goal. Such an examination will show, I fear, that this conception is indeed a myth, or even a chimaera.

The Marquis de Sade is claimed in surrealist literature as the forerunner of freedom, the prophet of a new age—but, alas! Get with us—of liberty and love. Breton has declared himself "a moralist after the style of de Sade and Vauvenargues"; and other voices have echoed him. But what, in actual fact, does the "Divine Marquis" propose? He made many suggestions for the liberation of mankind, of which the following is not unfairly typical: each township should be provided with a municipal brothel, to which any man (or woman) might have a fellow citizen of either sex, who must submit without protest to whatever usages the summoner is pleased to adopt. This would mean, in practice, that one could not take two steps outside one's den without risking, at best, a loss of one's time, and, at worst, loss of one's health or even life. Is this the "poetry" that "should be made by all"? I do not myself think that life in such circumstances would be tolerable, let alone desirable continually at the mercy, (if that is the right word,) of these casual encounters. One might attain "estrangement of sensation", but could achieve little else, certainly not freedom.

If any disciple of the marquis feels I exaggerate the dangers of his doctrines, he would do well to remember that the final culmination of any sadistic practices, however seemingly innocuous, is the lust-murder, or 'slaughter' to quote the word used by Mario Praz[1]. All such practices symbolise this, to this they all point as to a complete consummation. That they do not always remain in the region of symbolism the words of forensic medicine abundantly prove. It may be objected that the milder forms of creating and typing, for example, cannot be compared with those extreme cases which can be best studied in the police-court or the clinic. But where is the line to be drawn? The answer is that de Sade drew it nowhere. He defended lust-murder as a mere rearrangement of molecules pleasing to its

1 Praz was the author of *The Romantic Agony* (1933), a study of the erotic and macabre in Decadent and Romantic literature. Praz was also known for his contributions to art criticism and interior design theory.

perpetuator. He defended in particular Gilles de Rais[2], whose case has since become a classic example of his theories. It is one which brings out most clearly the fact that, for their practice, any community must be divided into two classes: tyrants and victims. The tyrants would be free to act, it is true, and their victims must writhe in the most abject slavery. De Rais was free to indulge his whims, so long as they remained undiscovered (and in de Sade's utopia, concealment would be unnecessary) but his victims were not free. On the contrary, these children had to be captured and imprisoned, against their will, before they were tortured, raped and finally murdered.

Unless one is willing to risk a similar fate, I don't see how one can sincerely admire either the actions of de Rais, or the tenets of his defender. Do all surrealist theorists hope to find themselves permanently in the "tyrant-class"? Does their physique entitle them to such a hope? For what else is de Sade's gospel but a resuscitation of the ancient slogan "might is right"? If you are strong enough to disable another and have the desire to do so, "no preoccupation, aesthetic or moral", need hinder you. But your own skin is in danger for some more powerful experimenter. Surely there is no point in living so dangerously that you have to spend the greater part of your time in hospital, or (even) your whole time in the grave.

I cannot see in this type of suggestion a recipe for universal liberty. If it outlines a programme of freedom for the few—the powerful—it postulates also necessarily so, a "victim-class", the many and the weak. For the individual living in a community, no more liberty can be hoped for than that minimum of freedom to live, move and generally act without interference, simply on the grounds that he is a human individual (however this may be defended) and conditionally on his acceding similar rights to his fellow beings. As long as he does not injure the life, health or personal property of another, he should be free to live as he chooses. If this were carried out now, it would confer

2 De Rais was a medieval companion of Joan of Arc who was executed for the rape and murder of over 140 children in 1440. His guilt or innocence has been a matter of contention and debate since the Enlightenment. Figures such as Aleister Crowley and Georges Bataille famously embraced de Rais. Crowley believed he was innocent, while Bataille was fascinated by his transgression.

a greater of degree of liberty than is to be found at the present day in any state, totalitarian or bourgeois-democratic, though even they provide more of this desired commodity than the paradise of de Sade.

I have dealt only with civic liberty in the exterior sense; I will now deal with freedom in the psyche, and in this sphere also I can offer an alternative to The Divine Marquis. The entire sado-masochistic nexus, what pray designates 'algolagnia'[3], is not a comprehensive picture of the human psyche as it subsists at present, still less a creative aim for its future. It is a half-truth at best; it is coated in ambivalence, which in its truth is dependent upon the Oedipus complex remaining unresolved. If one of surrealism's express aims is to resolve the Oedipus, then it cannot at the same time encourage byproducts of the complex in its unresolved state.

In conclusion I would invite surrealists to consider the following lines an escape from the fevered alterations of algolagnia of Luis Ponce de Leon, which, express the desire for a different and, to me, more sympathetic ideal:

Un no rompido sueno
Un dia puro, allegre, libre
Quiera—
Libre de amor, de celo
De odio, de esperanza, de recelo—

[An unbroken dream
A clear, joyous, free day
I would love.
Free of love, zeal
Hate, Hope and Suspicion][4]. †

---

3 Generally a synonym for sadomasochism, defined by elements of lust or compulsion.

4 Colquhoun seems to have taken this fragment from Edgar Allan Poe's poem "Al Aaraaf" which includes these lines. This was attributed in a note on Poe's "Al Aaraaf" to Fra Luis Ponce de Leon "Libro Primaro". Poe notes this characterises a place in Islamic cosmology which is neither heaven or hell, where desire is quenched, where there are no extremes. It is repeated in "Water Stone of the Wise". She also uses this in *Goose of Hermogenes* as the frontspiece to "fermentation".

The Waterstone Of The Wise (1943)

"The Water Stone of the Wise", published in *New Road*, 1943 was both a response to Breton's concerns about the flagging surrealist movement during wartime and also an assertion of Colquhoun's esoteric ideas about social reform and the conditions for both individual internal and external liberation. Her vision is one of the Divine Androgyne, an end to gender, inequality, and, interestingly, an end to desire and the struggle that desire often brings. We see the quote which is repeated in "The Divine Marquis and the Myth of Liberty", also seen in *Goose of Hermogenes* attributed to Fra Luis Ponce de Leon in the notes to Poe's 1829 poem "Al Aaraaf". Poe's characterisation of the Muslim A'raf, a space of balance between Heaven and Hell, may also shed some light on Colquhoun's interest in a liminal space without suffering, a resolution of opposites. However, she seems to acknowledge that the attainment of liberty and freedom will require a paradigm shift of epic proportions. Richard Shillitoe has broken down many of the key references in this text in *Ithell Colquhoun: Magician Born of Nature*.

Myth is a volcanic force, liberty a perpetual stream, an ambiance that results from eruption.

Myth must break through the crust, scatter a thousand new comets in the void, illuminate the black sky with bengal-lights, decorate the day sky with vaporous plumes. What superhuman shapes may not burst from the next eruption, august yet tender beings, who evolve themselves in the light of gold! They borrow a wisp of substance from the earth, but their colour is from the purifying fire. We cannot have liberty without repeated explosions.

But we must have liberty. It is the clear stream, the embracing element without which we cannot move. Free air and free water! They are the interpenetrating silver-and-blue, they come from the gushing side of the mountain whose mouth yet steams. Freedom to move, to act, to speak, freedom to be still, to look, to be silent.

Myth comes from the region between sleeping and waking, the multitudinous abyss, the unceasing cauldron rimmed with pearls[1]. If we let it pour out unhindered, we shall be free to plunge into its depths. What shall we find there, far from "lordship and bondage?"[2]

Un no rompida sueno–
Un dia puro–allegre–libre Quiera–
Libre de amor–de celo
De odio–de esperanza–de recelo.

No more tyrants and victims, no more the fevered alternations of that demon star which sponsored the births of de Sade and von Sacher-Masoch–but the hermaphrodite whole, opposites bound together in mitigating embrace by a silkworm's thread. "And countenance once more beheld countenance." Oedipus will be king no longer but will return to Colonnus. The new myth, the myth of the Siamese Twins, will make of him a forgotten bogey.

In one of the planets' airy houses live the Twins, a boy and a girl, perpetually joined by an ectoplasmic substance which is warmed by

1 As Shillitoe notes, this is a reference to the regenerative cauldron of the Otherworld from the middle Welsh tale "The Spoils of Annwn" from the *Book of Taliesin*, manuscript dated to the fourteenth century.

2 From Hegel's *Phenomenology of Spirit*, also known as the "master-slave dialectic", the conditions under which one achieves self-consciousness both internally and in relation to others.

the solar and lunar currents of their bodies. They cannot part, nor do anything apart. They eat and breathe each other day and night.

They are united face to face, having passed forward to the condition of the androgynous egg. Their faculty is dream, their body-of-fate[3] the stream of images—sensual transpositions—induced by the incandescence of their own body and mind. They have no privacy from each other, and desire none, since theirs is a unity conscious of its own elements. They weigh down equally each scale of the Balance, and as the two Fishes, are held together in watery dance by a single cord. †

3 One of the four faculties described in Yeats' *A Vision* characterising one of the functions of the psyche. Body of Fate refers to a concreteness of internal reality and also to notions of attainment.

The Night Side of Nature (1944)

This essay was published in *The Glass* no. 8 in 1953, although she had been pitching it to literary publications from the early 1940s. The title was lifted from the 1848 book by Catherine Crowe, *The Night Side of Nature or Ghosts and Ghost Seers*, but Crowe admits that she also stole the title from some German publications of the same name. Crowe notes that the phrase was used to describe that which happens while a planet is turned away from the sun. Crowe's work, inspired by these German writers on the paranormal, argues that these phenomena are neither superstition nor supernatural, but indeed they are a function of nature. Colquhoun expands on this thesis suggesting that what are typically labelled as human psychological pathologies are actually reflected in other types of natural phenomena, forcing an early reconsideration of human exceptionalism. It shows her increasing engagement with psychology, but also indicates her belief that rhythms and patterns are universal. Here we also see her preoccupations with ideas of rupture and convulsion, also expressed in her art and writings featuring convulsive landscapes such as volcanoes, or even wells.

May not the same obscure forces impelling the depths of the human psyche operate also to shape certain phenomena of external nature? The investigation of this question is one of the chief problems which imaginative biology must set itself to solve. A genuine alchemical science of life must celebrate an extension, even to absurdity's limits, of that approach to nature known inaptly as the "pathetic fallacy"[1] and under this name already explored in part by Romantic poets.

Modern psychology finds that the type-qualities of the normal person are, in the neurotic, morbidly intensified: indeed, that neurosis consists in this intensification. Three main categories of the sick soul are indicated, and these agree, except in their undisguised vividness, with the chief normal character-patterns.

There is first the individual who may grow into the "manic-depressive" type of neurotic and finally plunge completely into some kind of "folie circulaire." Next there is the being whose inner life is thronged with phantasies of persecution and who may develop into a "paranoiac" and finally into the megalomaniac, or psychotic who is completely dominated by delusions, mainly of grandeur. Finally, there is the enclosed, self-regarding, narcissistic type who may become a 'schizophrene' and at last—the split between the claims of inner and outer life becoming complete—may reach a state that used to be called "dementia praecox." Needless to say, there are cases on the borderline between two of these typical categories, and others that show symptoms of all three; there is perhaps scarcely one pure example of any. The scheme should therefore be regarded simply as a diagram; and the same variety and lack of rigid definition must be expected, when the field of the human unconscious is compared with the corresponding manifestations of the external world.

If the mutual reflective power of microcosm and macrocosm may be assumed, and the sequence of like effect upon like cause, then the same forces which give rise to symptoms in the human psyche are the agents of equivalent effects in the larger nature. The "anima mundi" subsumes all human types, and sometimes it would seem itself to be a sick soul. An interesting line of research would be the predominance of one or other of the three chief forces in any given place or period of history, with its interaction between internal and external climatic conditions.

1 Referring to the literary tendency to give inanimate objects human emotions or characteristics.

The motto of the "manic-depressive" nexus is that figure of speech known as the *oxymoron*, the linking in a single phrase of two contraries, each containing the germ of its opposite. In nature it includes all cyclic manifestations; seasonal change and its cause in the duality of night and day; sleep and waking; the phases of the moon, recurring comets, tides and tidal waves; rut, menstruation and birth-pains; fevers and other recurrent maladies; the peristalsis of the intestines, the systolic action of the heart, breathing, growth in so far as it can be shown to proceed from alternate effort and calm.

Here too should be placed the idea of reincarnation, or rather of that rhythm of incarnate and discarnate periods which the psyche undergoes in its cycle of development. Such notions take their place as theories, even if they cannot be shown to connect with discoverable fact. And here must be assigned the idea common to several philosophers (Vico, Blake, Spengler, Gentile, Yeats) that the whole universe is cyclic in structure.

In the life of the emotions this phase is characterised by ambivalence, the psyche's alternating roles of lover and loved, tyrant and victim. It holds those aspects of life which are most feminine, all that ancient astrology symbolised by the moon; and this may make woman's traditional "fickleness" and "love of change" more comprehensible. In his work *Psychology*, Edward Glover[2] notes among his patients a preponderance of women, and of feminine men, in the "manic-depressive" group; and it is easy to see from woman's physical constitution why this should be so.

Observations, still of life though hardly of 'nature' in the narrow sense, may be added, as for instance the boom-and-slump of financial markets, and the fluctuations of trade, fashion and taste in general.

The motto of the 'paranoiac' group is *exaggeration* as a figure of speech.

> Why, man, he doth bestride the narrow world
> Like a colossus[3],

2 This may refer to Glover's 1928 book *The Technique of Psycho-Analysis.*

3 From Shakespeare's *Julius Caesar,* Act 1, scene 2.

and it may be surmised that the forces that urge the human 'paranoiac' towards his "folie de grandeur" impel corresponding phenomena in the macrocosm. The grandiose in nature—heroic or mock-heroic—shares the same category with the man who thinks he is Napoleon and the man who actually is Napoleon. Here belongs all gigantism whether natural, like that of the "Big Trees" of California, or freakish, like the effects of hyper-pituitary action.

Exterior power, whether real or fancied, can only be wielded and retained by force; there is no 'paranoia' without phantasies of persecution. This group therefore is concerned with aggression, and to it belong all structures with that objective, such as teeth, claws, predatory beaks, spines, prickles and piercing fins. It must also associate itself with defence and the prevention of attack, and so adopts various forms of natural camouflage and "protective colouring." And since it cannot be without the delusions that follow upon a swollen ego, whatever contributes to illusion must be classified with it, as mirage, "ignis fatuus," the double image. Indeed it is provided with little more than these by way of background; it tends to move away from seasons, weather and basic vegetation—mainly under the "manic-depressive" dominion—and to approach the animal kingdom and those parts of the vegetal realm which most resemble animals in structure and function, namely the parasites, symbiotics, fungi and carnivorous plants.

The 'paranoiac' must prey upon other beings and be in its turn preyed upon; profoundly, it concerns itself with the necessity for this kind of life. In the emotional life it is the sado-masochistic nexus. Glover notes among human 'paranoiacs' a preponderance of men; and, as can well be seen, the class includes every gradation of the hero-type, all that was anciently symbolised as solar.

In the body politic, it may be related to warfare and revolution; to politics in general, the sphere of leader and demagogue and of those upon whom such are imposed; to conspiracy and intrigue, the secret society or brotherhood felt as menace. It rules also the sublimated forms of combat such as the chase, sport and competitive games;

and all those tools and weapons, chiefly of metal, by which men substitute beak and claw. From this angle the universe is seen as an arena of perpetual struggle, as for instance in the Zoroastrian system.

The 'schizoid' takes for motto the figure of the *synecdoche*, the naming of the part for the whole. It is marked by that symptom of division which leads to every kind of fetishism. The 'schizoid' personality or thing is, as its name implies, notable for a splitting, superficial or deep, discovered either in the psyche itself or in its sense of separation from the rest of the cosmos and inability to make effective contact therewith. This separation is not an eminence *per se*, yet it tends to mark out the being from immediate surroundings and isolate it in a kind of vacuum. Here one finds riven rocks and blasted trees, all effects of landslides, earthquake, storm and volcanic eruption, of violences without apparent purpose. One thinks of Glover's "schizophrenic" patients with their intense yet pointless volubility, their "flight of ideas," so different from the logical and almost-convincing stories of conspiracy produced by his 'paranoiacs.' Or in gentler mood, budding and fruition may be found here, the infinitesimal splitting of cells to engender new life, and all in morphology that differentiates the part from the whole. Again, that which cuts off by concealment should be noted and hence the mists, clouds, fogs, vapours—whatever can form an occluding veil. The type expresses itself best through landscape, the fundamentals of life, the organic setting.

Its characteristic emotional life may be symbolised by any solitary figure, virgin or anchorite or Narcissus in contemplation, the seeming offspring of parthenogenesis. It is the type of hybrid and hermaphrodite—the split in the psyche is usually the division into male and female related as a discord. The task is to replace this unresolved duality by a genuinely androgynous whole, the fruitful relation of man and "daimon," "*conjunctio*": One remembers that "Mercury of the Sages" which is said to partake of the character of both sun and moon.

Socially considered, all pursuits demanding analysis should be included as 'schizoid,' as instance many branches of science and philosophy, literature and organisation. (Fully realised, as the perfected androgyne, it also embraces whatever demands the completest synthesis.) Here originate not only 'cataclysmic' theories, whether religious or scientific, of the beginning and end of the world, but myths such as the "Fall of man."

A duality is found in all these three fundamental types, so that in none can be found a true expression of Advaitin[4] philosophy. In the first the duality is cyclic, in the second algolagnic, in the third internal and continuous, so that all find their image in what is piebald or parti-coloured, in magpie and orchid, in alexandrite and tourmaline. †

4 Non dualism.

The Openings of the Body (c. 1944)

"The Openings of the Body" reflects Colquhoun's preoccupations in the late 1930s and early 1940s with energy circulations in the body, the origins of divine energy, and the way that people can exchange and transfer energy between them. Her 1940 painting, *The Thirteen Streams of Magnificent Oil*, reflects her inspiration from Samuel "MacGregor" Mathers' *The Kabbalah Unveiled*. Which shows the oil dripping from the beard of God, the "*Mezla*", entering the body through various openings. Although this was published later in her life, it is likely that much of this essay was composed earlier, perhaps in the early 1940s. Here Colquhoun opines that women are simply more suited than men to receive divine essence because they have more openings through which it can flow. This view puts her firmly in line with early nineteenth century esoteric feminists such as Frances Swiney who were convinced of the overall superiority of women.

In Madame Blavatsky's *The Secret Doctrine* there is a diagram showing the relationships and correspondences that exist between the various openings or "gates" of the human body. Seven of these openings are situated in the head; the remaining three situated below the waist, are related to three of the previous seven, but in this correlation the three openings of the upper body are inexplicably ignored. Only ten openings in all are mentioned—and these evidently with reference to the female body, as in the male there would be nine—and a symbolic connection with the Sephirotic Decad of the Qabalah is traced.

Madame Blavatsky nowhere defines what she means by an "opening", the eyes are not openings in the sense of "holes" so that by this definition two of the seven openings of the head would be excluded. One may mention also (while noting that it is excluded from Blavatsky's list) that the navel is only an opening before the birth of the embryo, after birth it is but the scar of the opening, though generally concave in form. Again, the nipples are openings only under certain conditions. But one may err on the side of caution if one does not mention various gland openings: for instance those of the glands of Bartholin in the female and of the Cowper in the male, and of the innumerable sweat ducts and sebaceous glands in both sexes. However, an opening might be defined rather as a "nerve centre" or "zone of sensitiveness", a passage for the giving and receiving of stimuli. Madame Blavatsky may have had something like this in mind, though her omission of the torso-openings is still unexplained. One must not be led away by the term "nerve centre" into any attempt to relate closely these visible The Openings of the Body with the *chakras* of Tantrik metaphysics.

In fact, there are thirteen main openings in the female and twelve in the male, and the greater number present in the female body may indicate a more highly-evolved and specialised structure than that of the male. It does not need much ingenuity to relate the twelve openings of the male to the signs of the Zodiac; the thirteen of the female may be adapted to receive that *Mezla* or 'influence' which is said to stream downward from the thirteen strands of the Beard of Macroprosopos.

The distribution of these openings needs much study in research and meditation. The first six are arranged in couples of two: the eyes, the ears, the nostrils; then there is a single opening, the mouth, completing the seven gates of the head. The next two are also a couple, the nipples, then follows the navel, completing the ternary of the torso or upper body. In the lower body there are three single and separate openings; the urethral and vaginal orifices and the anus, which make up the final ternary, complete only in the female.

The questions of the relative positions of these gates, the linking of their functions, the proportion of their distance from one another, and the duplication of certain among them, raises many problems. Since their diagram cannot be made to fit with any exactitude the pattern of the Sephirotic Tree of Life, the attribution of the Zodiac in the case of the male and to the "Magnanimity" in that of the female, seems more appropriate than Madame Blavatsky's theory.

How may the openings receive those "thirteen streams of magnificent Oil"? †

Children Of The Mantic Stain (1951)

This is Colquhoun's well-known essay setting out her views on surrealist automatism as both a spiritual and artistic practice. There was an earlier version of this essay, "The Mantic Stain", published in 1949, but this expanded version also addresses the pedagogical benefits of automatism as a method to unlock creativity. Of course, Colquhoun saw automatism not only as a way of connecting with the subconscious, but also with other dimensions.

The restless child who cries out to the teacher, "What shall I do?"; the inhibited patient who gazes with equal blankness at the paper before him and the art therapist's face. Indeed, all who find the actual beginning of a work of art a difficulty may be assisted by automatism. There is no doubt that many automatic processes can be used with stimulating effect in the teaching of art, whether to children or adults, to the healthy and "normal" or the sick in body and mind. The "play" aspect appeals to children of all ages, as I hope to show: to a beginner the fact that he is faced not with an empty white rectangle which he must somehow fill effectively but with a suggestive chiaroscuro or a colour combination with potentialities will give him confidence. This self-confidence is the first step towards revealing the mind's profound imaginative riches.

It must never be forgotten that it is chiefly to the surrealist movement that we owe the discovery and development of these automatic processes. So that no one need wonder what surrealism is, I here give the dictionary definition as propounded by André Breton, founder of the movement, in 1924:

> Pure psychic automatism, through which it is intended to express, either verbally, or in writing, or in any other way, the real working of thought. Dictation of thought, without any control exercised by reason, and beyond any preoccupation, aesthetic or moral.

It is obvious from the context that by "thought" and "the real working of thought" Breton means the unconscious. Thus, the exploration of the unconscious through automatism is, and has always been, at the very root of surrealism. It is that branch of surrealism known as psychomorphology[1] which concerns us here.

Psychomorphology is the discovery by various automatic processes of the hidden contents of the psyche and their expression through different media. The principle of all these processes is the making of a stain by chance, or "objective hazard" to use the surrealist term, the gazing at the stain in order to see what it suggests to the imagination and, finally, the developing of these suggestions in plastic terms. The method is at least as old as Leonardo da Vinci's example: we all know the story of his staring at the stains of damp in an ancient wall and seeing in these a hint of the mountains, ravines and fantastic foliage of a dream landscape. The homely, seeing pictures in the fire, or the cloud-images of childhood's visionary stare, show the same faculty in embryo.

Perhaps a personal anecdote will illustrate the process most vividly. At the time of a recent house removal I lay in bed looking at a plaster wall seamed with cracks. It was the day before I was due to move, and I thought after today I shall no longer see these marvellous cracks, indeed, no one will, because they will be obliterated by redecoration.

---

1 Psychological Morphology was a term coined by surrealist Roberto Matta in 1938 to characterise his approach to automatism. Colquhoun was likely deeply inspired by her time with Matta and Gordon Onslow Ford in Chemilieu, France in 1939, which is when she started seriously exploring automatism.

So, busy as I was, I sprang out of bed, glued some large sheets of tracing-paper together, fastened them to the wall and made a careful tracing of the cracks. This has since become a large mural, *Giantesses Undressing to Bathe*. Previously I had found the inspiration of another picture, *Autumnal Equinox*, in the artificial wood-graining of a painted door. In both these instances the basic stain was discovered and recorded but not directly made, by myself, so the process involved was a combination of automatism and the "found object". It is hardly necessary to point out that the same unconscious process which makes a mantic stain and recognises its pictorial scope also selects and illumines that morsel of external reality which constitutes a "found object".

The development of the initial stain may proceed along lines of complete abstraction, in which case the resulting shapes will not recall anything seen in nature. Or there may be a hint of natural objects which can be organised and intensified into a design. Or, again, a treasury of symbolic scenes or "mind pictures" may be dredged up from the depths of the fantasy life, that dreamworld of which many are hardly aware in waking consciousness. That is, in the first instance a "non-figurative" work will result; in the second and third, figurative works whose provenance is, respectively, external and internal reality. In *Le Profil Navigable* the Romanian surrealist Trost defines two different kinds of painting which he calls plastic and aplastic, or pictorial images and sign images. The first is built up from representational pictorial elements, however fantastic, and the second consists of the various automatic techniques without interpretation, left "in the raw", as it were. For myself, I do not see the classification quite in these terms. Trost does so because he will not admit of the interpretation of automatic deliverances. Indeed, in *La Connaissance des Temps* he stigmatises the interpretation of automatism almost as a deadly sin, calling it "equivalent to an absurd intervention in the mechanism of universal causality". For me the automatism may be significant in itself; but frequently it is no more, though also no less, than a basis upon which a work of art, figurative or non-figurative, may be built. And in regard to pupil or patient I am inclined to think that the best results will be obtained from interpreted automatism, though it is obvious that the mere making of the automatic stain will have an immensely liberating effect in many cases. Thus, the teacher will use what amounts almost to an inversion of the Rorschach method. In this, the psychologist has elaborated a series of cards marked with irregular patches of colour at which the patient is asked to look and note down what each suggests to him. Valuable as this may be as a preliminary aid to diagnosis, I feel that when a pupil or patient actually evolves his own "Rorschach cards" and interprets them, still better results may be hoped for.

I will now describe the actual automatisms in some detail. Perhaps the most promising of these is decalcomania, invented by the surrealist painter Óscar Domínguez, though the name is certainly much earlier. It was used to describe the decoration of furniture by transfer patterns and occurs in a family chronicle of about 1850:

> At Hexton House I amused myself painting, and Grandmama having seen some lovely designs—French—for the Decalcomania, then very fashionable, thought I might decorate four panels for her two "chiffonières" in the blue drawing-room.

The word, of course, comes from "décalquer" (to trace) and indicates the double image which is "traced" by pressure. One must not forget also that an almost identical practice was often used by Alexander Cozens as a beginning to his landscapes and called by him "blots". As for the surrealist handling of the process I cannot do better than translate the directions of Breton which he calls "How a window may be opened at will on the loveliest landscapes of this and other worlds":

> With a thick brush, spread black gouache on a sheet of white shiny paper, diluting the paint here and there with water. Cover it at once with a similar sheet and press them together fairly hard. Then, by the upper edge, slowly lift this second sheet... What you have before you is perhaps only the old paranoiac wall of da Vinci, but it is this wall carried to its own perfection. In fact, if you entitle the image thus

> obtained according to what you discover in it after looking at it from a little distance, you may be certain that you have expressed yourself in the most personal and valuable way.

Breton does not here deal with any development of the automatic image beyond conveying the possibility of this by an imaginative title. Several well-known painters, however, notably Max Ernst, have carried the process far beyond the automatic stage and used it as the inspiration for finished works. Again, the only medium indicated by Breton is gouache, but oil paint in black, black and white or several colours can be employed in the same way with equally striking effect. The pigment may be laid on prepared canvas or board instead of paper and must be diluted here and there with some appropriate medium such as linseed or poppy oil, turpentine or oil of spike lavender or with a mixture of any of these. Black or coloured inks may also be substituted for gouache but, of course, can only be diluted if not of the waterproof kind: if waterproof, variety of texture, one of the most characteristic beauties of decalcomania, must be obtained by varying the quantity of ink in different areas.

The stillomancy advocated by Trost is a more limited form of decalcomania; it consists in the folding of a piece of paper over a splash of ink and so producing a trace. The limitation is that the forms so produced are, owing to the fold, always more or less symmetrical in character; but in spite of this I have known remarkable suggestions to result. In any case, the procedure is already so well known to children under the title of "ghosts", where somebody's name is written thickly in ink and the paper folded over the writing, that stillomancy may be a good introduction for a class to decalcomania on a more extended scale. Incidentally the nursery "ghost" is frequently the rough sketch for a surrealist personnage.

Another painter who worked with the surrealist movement, Wolfgang Paalen, invented the automatism of fumage (named from the French fumée). The paper or board is held more or less horizontally just above the flame of a candle or oil lamp and passed rapidly to and fro without conscious direction. The resulting smoky trace is then sprayed with fixative like a charcoal drawing to prevent smudging, while the operator gazes into it to see what themes will emerge. The chosen forms are then stressed either in ink, watercolour or oil, and the irrelevant passages painted over with a background or otherwise erased. Breton wrote on the subject of Paalen and his discovery:

> "Man is fond of Society," said Lichtenberg, "even if it is only that of his lighted candle." But Paalen has done more than speculate upon the presence and luminous power of this candle... He [Paalen] has added a contribution of the first importance in fumage, tresses as far as the eye can reach of woman beloved in shadow.

Frottage is simply 'rubbing': it is the placing of canvas or paper over an uneven surface—stone, wood-graining, the thick weave of a carpet, for example and rubbing it over with charcoal, chalk, paint or carbon pencil on the principle of taking a brass-rubbing. The texture being recorded thus in the chosen medium, the resultant marking may be looked into and interpreted in the usual way. Ernst, beside working on decalcomania, has made great use of frottage in his paintings. It is recorded that he first became aware of its potentialities while staring at the rough boards in the floor of his bedroom at a small country inn.

Écrémage, initiated by Conroy Maddox, is "skimming"; the method is to cover the surface of water in a large bowl with some oily substance—oil paint or an ink with an oily base and to pass a board or stiff piece of paper just below. This is then lifted out of the water, which drains off it, leaving it marked by the skimmed-off oil. It may be of interest to note that the "marbling" of endpapers is produced in a very similar way. A variant of this method, developed by myself and named "parsemage" or "scattering", is to sprinkle powdered charcoal or the dust of coloured chalk on the water surface: this yields a somewhat different type of stain from that left by the trace of oil.

Collage is, of course, "sticking" or "gluing" and is, perhaps, the automatism best known to the general public on account of its adaptation to advertising and its wide use for display purposes.

It has also been already used by certain teachers as a basis for composition and a stimulus to children's expression of fantasy. It consists of the cutting out from their context of heterogeneous visual elements and the recombining them automatically to form a new synthesis without any rational intent. Once again it is to Max Ernst that we must look for a classic example, namely, the seven-volume masterpiece of illustrations without text *Une Semaine de Bonté*. To this we owe an offshoot, the cubomania of Gherasim Luca, a Romanian surrealist. Luca, like Max Ernst, takes an ordinary figurative engraving, often of the late Victorian period, but simply cuts it up into squares of equal size with a guillotine so that each square resembles one face of a child's brick. He then glues them together at hazard to form a picture the same size and shape as the original. Presumably he then "entitles the image thus obtained according to what he discovers in it, after looking at it from a little distance". Some of his titles are "Doubler le Réel" and "À la Moindre Impulsion Lycanthropique". The resulting booklet, *Les Orgies des Quanta*, is like the confused recollection of a nightmare with its fetishistic insistence on the part rather than the whole. This contrasts forcibly with the atmosphere of *Une Semaine de Bonté* which, though also horrific, reminds one of a seemingly coherent nightmare clearly recalled.

Trost has elaborated several more processes, one of which he calls "hypnagogic movements". This is begun by closing the eyes and allowing one's hand to draw or paint blindly using materials previously prepared. In this he tries to achieve by still one more method that synthesis of the states of dream and of waking which has been surrealism's chief aim since its inception. The images seen in this way are no doubt related to those classically termed "hypnagogic", which seem to pass before the eyes at the approach of sleep. Another automatism is to mark with a dot any slight irregularity of colour or change of surface on a blank sheet of paper and then to join the dots by lines. The specimens of this technique which Trost uses to illustrate his *Vision dans le Cristal* are all curvilinear, but my own experiments in this field, which Trost calls "entoptic graphomania", have straight lines only. He advocates the word "superautomatism" to describe drawing or painting completely at hazard, "letting a line go for a walk"; and makes the valuable point that the deeper layers of the unconscious consist of just such uninterpreted and perhaps uninterpretable images.

Finally, there is vaporisation in which a pool of ink or of diluted paint on a resistant surface is blown in all directions by means of a spray used for fixing chalk drawings or some similar instrument.

Perhaps the most significant quality common to all the processes I have described is their "morphologic constancy". In spite of the many vagaries of hazard each, in my own working at least, tends to produce its own characteristic forms and suggest its own peculiar themes. For example, decalcomania relates itself to landscape, with foliage, feathers, scales and marine life; *fumage* to semi-human figures or personnages, larval forms or imago-forms, *parsemage* often combines the two; while entoptic graphomania leads one towards the most austere kind of geometric abstraction. At the same time all processes are closely dependent upon the unconscious mood of the operator: if a number of experiments in a single process are undertaken in one day a great similarity of forms will be noticeable throughout. The same operator experimenting with the same process on another day will produce a quite different series of images, though these latter will be linked to one another by a certain "family likeness". It is for this reason that I feel these automatic stains to have a mantic or divinatory power, they may in some sort be compared with the practices of clairvoyants who use ink splashes, sand, pins thrown together by chance and the irregular patterns left by tea leaves and coffee grounds to set in motion their telepathic faculty. The famous crystal globe and the "scrying glass" have approximately the same function, and all have an august ancestry in that they are allied to the "great work" of alchemy. In many fascinating psychological studies Jung has shown how the alchemist would release the contents of his own fantasy world by intently watching the contents of the alembic. To quote from a seventeenth-century alchemical treatise *An Open Entrance to the Closed Palace of the King* by Eirenaeus Philalethes:

> The reign of the moon lasts just three weeks; but before it closes the substance exhibits a great variety of forms; it will become liquid, and again coagulate a hundred times a day; sometimes it will present the appearance of fishes' eyes, and then again of tiny silver trees, with twigs and leaves. Whenever you look at it you will have cause for astonishment, particularly when you see it all divided into beautiful but very minute grains of silver, like the rays of the sun.

This is nothing less than projection, a term pregnant in alchemical literature and one which might well be adopted to describe the imaginative interpretation of a "mantic" stain. Indeed, I wonder whether we may not take this analogy from our ancient inheritance still further and seek a correspondence between the four elements of earth, air, fire and water and some of the automatisms. *Fumage*, with flame as its chief agent, can easily be related to elemental fire; those processes, *écrémage* and its derivatives, which mainly employ water to this element; decalcomania with its basis of thick and solid impasto to the element of earth; and such techniques as vaporisation to air. We can go further and relate the varieties of "shut-eye" drawing to darkness while we ascribe Man Ray's rayogram and other automatisms connected with photography to light.

As with every method, successful results in class teaching based on automatism will largely depend on the personality of the teacher and the degree of understanding and enthusiasm he or she possesses. One consideration, however, is important: namely, that in encouraging the interpretations of the stain no censorship of any kind should be imposed, and each pupil or patient should feel entirely free to explore a new territory. The definition of Breton, "beyond any preoccupation, aesthetic or moral", should be taken to heart, and a considerable degree of freedom must have possessed the teacher before he can communicate it. If at the end of a lesson the classroom is disordered and the explorers splashed, so much the better. Does not all inspiration come from "the multitudinous abyss"? †

Essays from *The London Broadsheet* (1954-1955)

The following five essays were written for Antony Borrow's strange journalistic enterprise *The London Broadsheet* in 1954 and 1955. *The London Broadsheet* fancied itself to be a rather anarchic and subversive publication, proclaiming in an editorial its mission to fight censored speech, and oppression of thought. Many of its offerings were quite base and often misogynistic, and one wonders why Colquhoun was aligning herself with this publication. However, Colquhoun had her own column, called Heaven and Earth, and this was her opportunity to present to the public profiles of notable figures in contemporary magical culture, and strange phenomena such as UFOs or psychic research. She approaches most of these topics with a quite objective journalistic sensibility; they are nowhere nearly as personal as many of her later journalistic pieces. Despite this, it is clear that she rather took to Austin Osman Spare as both an artist and a magician. One wonders what would have happened had he not died shortly after their meeting.

Untitled Heaven and Earth Column, Profile of Gerald Gardner (1954)

This particular short piece is of interest because it was written shortly after Gardner published *Witchcraft Today* in 1954, very early on in Gardner's attempts to promote Wicca. The brief notes from this interview with Gerald Gardner still exist in Colquhoun's archives. It is not clear how many times they met after this first interview, but two letters in Colquhoun's archives from Doreen Valiente suggest they met several times.

Picturesquely situated beside an old windmill, associated with the witch-cult in local legend, stands Dr. Gardner's Museum of Witchcraft and Magic at Castletown, Isle of Man. Here are displayed the tools of the craft and much other cognate material, collected from various countries and fully documented. In summer Dr. Gardner shows people round and answers questions; he is himself a devotee of the "old religion," having entry to at least three covens in the British Isles. His account* contains information based on his own "field work".

Witchcraft is a Dionysiac cult of nature-mysticism, and what remains of it today is a genuine folk-survival from the Stone Age. It has no connection with the "Black Mass," which is obviously a post-Christian phenomenon; and little with Ritual Magic which evokes spirits to obey the operator's will. Rather, it is shamanistic, developing little-known powers of the human body and mind to achieve its effects.

Like Ritual Magic, Witchcraft uses the Circle; but whereas for the Magician this is a defence against hostile forces, for the Witch it is a psychic accumulator for conserving and directing the power raised by the coven. While the Magician often works alone or with a single assistant, the Witch, who may be of either sex, is gregarious, for the ritual demands a group of participants. The Magician in operation is appropriately and sometimes gorgeously robed, but in the coven nudity is insisted upon, because clothes inhibit the forces latent in the vitality-aura, from which "the power is raised."

There is, however, a certain overlap with Ritual Magic, since a sword after "the Lesser Key of Solomon" design appears among the accoutrements of the Southern coven at the Museum, and their unguent smells very like Aleister Crowley's "Ruthah"—though this was compounded of animal ingredients while the witches' perfume is said to be purely herbal. Crowley was a witch in his youth and was much influenced by the craft; its secrets were perhaps the only ones he guarded.

Two chief deities are worshipped—the Moon in her Hecate-aspect, the "Triple Goddess" or "White Goddess" of Robert Graves' study; and a Horned God who is Night, "Death-and-what-lies-Beyond," almost the "Baron Samedi" of Voudoun. Though each is allotted two yearly festivals, the Goddess is the favourite, as one might expect in a cult deriving from a matriarchal epoch; and all the monthly Sabbats take place at full moon.

Any power may be directed to ends socially useful or the reverse. Since witchcraft's aims are mainly positive, fertility and healing, persecution by the Church was unjustified, motivated as it was by jealousy of a rival religion's international hold.

**Witchcraft Today*, by G. B. Gardner. Rider. 1954. †

Divination Up-To-Date (1955)

For the past seven years a group of researchers in what they call "Advanced Study in Psychology" has been experimenting in new methods of pre-cognition. Led by a Harley Street specialist, they keep in touch with important universities in England and throughout the world. Their work is a logical extension of the field originally pioneered by Freud, continued by Jung, and enlarged upon by Rhine.

There is no link with "psychical research" as ordinarily understood. The group works by examining records of dreams, doodles, automatisms and other spontaneous material; and has made a number of accurate predictions from these. Upwards of sixty dreams occurring in one week have to be considered before a forecast is made: a single dream is seldom in itself clearly indicative. Rather it is an element in a general pattern, to be traced throughout the dreams of the different group-members. Any disturbance in this patterning must be carefully noted. Some dreams are realistic, many more symbolic; and the phenomenon of the "shared dream" has been observed between two or more members of the team. Material that would mean little to the layman yields up its message to the interpretation of an expert.

The group has been particularly successful in obtaining warning of disasters which are meaningful to the community in general. It seems that usually such incidents must be amenable to modification through human agency, as for instance, travel accidents by land, sea or air, or the explosion of thermo-nuclear weapons. Happenings which come into the legal category of "Act of God" tend not to be foreseen: for example, the typhoon in Japan this autumn which caused extensive floods and capsized a ferry with the loss of a number of American servicemen, besides many other casualties, did not appear in the premonitions. But there is no hard-and-fast rule—or if there is it has yet to be discovered—for the earthquake at Orleansville, Algeria, on the night of September 9th was indicated some days previously.

A tentative theory suggests that something akin to the instinct of self-preservation forces its way out of the collective unconscious and into the personal unconscious when danger threatens. Probably everyone receives the warning, but very few can understand it. Telepathic communication may also play a part, but this is by no means proved.

Oneiromancy is not new: it was already old in the days of the *Somnium Scipionis*, having been practised from the earliest times, though often in an "underground" manner. What is new is the scientific attention now paid to it. And almost anything, from coffee-grounds to the entrails of a beast, has in the past been used for divinatory purposes. Again, what is new is the careful recording of spontaneous material with its meaning and verification. University degrees are given in Psychological Medicine and Parapsychology by various faculties, and some members of the group hold such degrees. But one wonders whether, today as yesterday, the actual method is only important in so far as it excites the mantic capacities of an individual or a group?

Cassandra was fated always to prophesy truly and never to be believed; has her mantle now fallen upon a small group that meets in Harley Street? Let us hope that no means, however peripheral, of safe-guarding life and property (to say nothing of prestige) will be ignored by those responsible for public safety. †

Portrait of a Magician: Austin Osman Spare (1955)

Austin Spare, recluse, sensualist and mage as well as poet and draughtsman is true to his name, being spare of build. Under the tousled hair that may once have been golden his eyes peer out, a peculiar shade of peacock-green. He lives in a narrow terrace-house a long way south of the Thames, the hall-table heaped with small silver coins, the electric bulbs all broken.

This house is full of his drawings in various media. In one sense they look backward to the nineties, for some recall the reveries of Simeon Solomon, others the line of Beardsley—though Spare's is stronger and more pliable. But they also turn towards the induced hallucinations of surrealism: much of the territory explored by Dalí from 1927 onwards had already been opened up by Spare in 1909. He calls himself a "psycho-realist"; some of his work, particularly in pastel, is suggested by music, and a strong automatic element enters into most of it, as his speed of working shows. It celebrates the beauty and fascination of the horrible: such titles as *Satiated Succubae*, *Study for Schizogenesis*, *Aural Orgasm* and

Ghostly Combine hint at its preoccupations. Owing to the neglect of the West End, Spare usually exhibits at home or at his local.

Before 1920 he published six books, the text his own poetic prose, the illustrations his masterly drawings. All are now very rare. After years of silence, he is working on a new one epitomising his magical ideas. He uses a kind of literary *collage*—another unconscious link with surrealism: having written out a passage he cuts it up and reassembles the sentences at hazard, as Max Ernst did with engravings in *Une Semaine de Bonté*.

Spare is soon to give a radio talk on his magical ideas. The basic concept of *The Book of Pleasure (Self-Love): The Psychology of Ecstasy*, published in 1910, is "Kia," which the author equates with "freedom"; the conquest of duality; "Neither-Neither." Analogies are at once obvious with Hinduism's "neti-neti," the Great Extreme of Taoism and the Satori of Zen. The basic practice which it describes is to combine the letters that form a word or words so as to evolve a Sigil, then to attain vacuity "by exhausting mind and body through any pleasant means—a mantra, asana, sex, wine, games or walking" and finally to concentrate upon the Sigil as soon as thought returns. "...the mind, by Sigils, depending upon the intensity of desire, is illuminated or obsessed"—in other words, can obtain knowledge or power. "Sigils are monograms of thought for the government of energy." He also evolved his own alphabet of glyph-writing.

A natural psychic, Spare was taught divination as a boy by an old woman, and subsequently developed his own system of magic. But it was not until many years later that he came in contact with a witch-coven. He thinks that the witch-cult originated in the sex-starvation of elderly women who found release in the promiscuity of its rites: this is a different view from that of Dr. G. Gardner. Certainly Spare's most vivid and powerful line-drawings are those which take the Sabbat for theme; and one feels that he is himself part of that urban folk-lore which seethes unrecognised beneath the surface of city life. †

The Dying-Kick of the Dying-God (1955)

It is over seven years since the death of Aleister Crowley, but interest in his work and personality is by no means dead. Recently Kenneth Anger's colour film, *The Inauguration of the Pleasure Dome*, depicting a ritual enacted by a group of Crowley's followers in California, was shown to a club-audience in London. His books are still in process of publication. *The Gospel According to St Bernard Shaw* appeared in 1951, the annotated version of *The Vision and the Voice*—a record of experiments in the magical system of Dee and Kelley—in 1952, and *Magic Without Tears*—letters to a disciple—in 1954. A new and enlarged edition of that indispensable "prolegomena" to occultism, *Liber 777*, is in preparation.

One must try to disperse the smoke-screen put up around the name of Crowley by the sensational press, and to some extent densified by the man himself. Nor was it produced without a fire; but it is now time to examine calmly what contribution he made to esoteric theory and practice.

A thirteenth century Franciscan with Gnostic leanings, Joachim of Flora, proclaimed that the reign of the Father was past, that of the Son passing, and that of the Holy Ghost yet to come; and was sharply censured for so doing. Crowley said much the same thing in different terms. He declared that the Aeon of Isis—that of Matriarchy—was past, the Aeon of Osiris—that of Patriarchy, the saviour-gods, and sacrifice in general—had ended in 1904, and the Aeon of Horus—that of the "Crowned and Conquering Child" with its "word": "Do what thou wilt shall be the whole of the Law"—had then begun. His reception was no more encouraging than Joachim of Flora's.

The actual revelation came to him in 1904 at Cairo, after a series of rituals which culminated in a "direct-voice" communication dictating the script of *Liber AL vel Legis*. A qualitative change had come over the world-soul and all values were metamorphosed. This *Book of the Law* formed the basis of all his subsequent teaching; and he suffered throughout the remainder of his life in a struggle to spread its doctrine. He claimed that it predicted the world-cataclysms, spiritual, social and political, which have occurred since; and apart from questions of a cipher, its tone has adequately prefigured the flux, fatalism and violence characteristic of the century so far.

Crowley's system classified (conceivable) time into Four Aeons, comparable with the "Yugas" of Hinduism and the "Ages" of certain Classical writers in the West. The Aeon of Horus will be succeeded by that of Ma or Thmaist, the "Ageless Virgin-Harlot." (When he used the word "Harlot" or 'Whore' esoterically, he symbolised the "Utterly unbound"—perhaps what André Breton meant by the phrase "*Liberté, couleur d'homme*!")

To the collective unconscious of the present generation, Crowley's fascination lies in his being what he rejected: he was himself an embodiment of the Dying-God whose epoch he tirelessly proclaimed as finished. He was the Dying God's last avatar; this supplies a key to the ambivalences of his character, and explains why today he is "Old Crow" to people who never met him. For we look back, with some degree of nostalgia and self-identification, to the Aeon that has gone.

Crowley stated (perhaps this was a manifestation of his comic muse) that he was the world's greatest poet; but except for occasional flashes, notably in *The Book of Lies*, he was but an all-too-fluent versifier. In his prose-writings, however, many ideas made scientifically respectable by Freud and Jung are to be found, contemporaneously but in more colourful guise. For this reason, and because he was a link in the chain of initiates, he is worth studying. †

Unidentified Flying Objects (1955)

If Science-Fiction is always true, given time—and from Jules Verne onwards its prophecies have been fulfilled—then the reality of unknown aeroforms will soon be admitted.

Not all "unidentified flying objects" are saucer-shaped; cones, discs, globes, cigar-shapes, and others have been reported. Many seem to be directed by remote control or robot-mechanisms; the larger types may be manned by intelligent crews, but stories of "little men" or "monsters" must be treated with caution.

Those who claim to have seen these "objects"—and traced them, often simultaneously, on radarscopes—describe their speed, manoeuvrability and in some cases their immense size as precluding all possibility of their being "secret weapons" designed on this earth. The highest radar-checked speed is 9,000 m.p.h., but much higher estimates have been made by experienced pilots and navigators. "Objects" can stop or change course instantaneously, rise vertically, hover immobile for hours, or turn at an angle of 180°. "Saucers" can flip up on edge from horizontal flight and return at will to the horizontal. Size estimates vary from an eight-inch diameter to a length of 1,000 feet.

The sceptic's objection that there is no fuel capable of propelling a machine across inter stellar space seems outdated. If space-travel is a fact it must be achieved by some means which makes the word "fuel" sound old-fashioned possibly by the utilisation of electro-magnetic fields.

Since "saucers" hit the headlines in 1947, orthodox science has not been helpful in its explanations of these phenomena. If the "objects" in question are correctly described, many of them cannot be dismissed as reflected lights, temperature-inversions, mirages, meteors, comets, or research-balloons. Reflected lights do not appear on a radarscope, meteors do not maintain a horizontal course, nor balloons travel against the wind at supersonic speed.

Popular occultism is equally inept; "spiritualistic messages" from the stars are unconvincing; still more so the mushy idealism that hails the inhabitants of other worlds as necessarily wiser and more benevolent than we. If the "objects" exist, it is on the material plane and they should be investigated there, even though their "matter" may possess properties strange to us.

Worried Catholics, concluding that the "objects" imply the existence of intelligent beings who can scarcely share their faith, have feared to find the exclusiveness of its claims thus invalidated. But a transatlantic theologian has reassured them, stating that creatures from the demonic to the near-divine may inhabit other worlds with a different mode of salvation. It seems to "depend on what you mean by" a human being; the Universal Church evidently does not claim cosmic scope.

A few reports may be put down to mistakes, hallucinations, or hoaxes, the "saucers" news-value being too high to be resisted. But unless the whole affair is a gigantic hoax on the part of USA Intelligence Departments and the Press, engineered as a move in the cold-war, the only alternative is the interplanetary theory. One must choose the less unlikely.

Flying Saucers from the Moon, by H. J. Wilkins. (Peter Owen, 16/-.)

Flying Saucers from Outer Space, by D. E. Keyhoe. (Hutchinson, 10/6.)

Doubt, Vol. II, 40, ed. Tiffany Thayer. †

The Crown and the Kingdom series (1958)

This was an ostensibly introductory series on the Kabbalah that Colquhoun wrote for the popular British esoteric magazine *Prediction* over the course of four issues. Her spelling reflects a common spelling of the Hebrew term among the occultists of her day that distinguished it from both Jewish and Christian versions of these esoteric teachings. In the first of these essays, Colquhoun take a comparative approach, noting that the Qabalah, while emerging from Hebraic esotericism, has parallels in other wisdom traditions, including those of Hinduism, Sufism and Jainism. She introduces the reader to the glyph of the Tree of Life, noting the importance of this complex visual representation of emanation from Godhead into the material. In her second essay in the series Colquhoun describes the nature of the Sephiroth of the Tree of Life. In the third essay Colquhoun explains the role and nature of the paths that connect the Sephiroth, and in the fourth of these essays she examines the principle of the Four Worlds. These essays highlight a characteristic issue of Colquhoun's: she wanted to help distil this remarkably complex material for a popular audience, but in many ways leaves them drinking from a fire hose. She easily demonstrates her wide reading and command of the material, but her didactic sensibilities are perhaps a bit wanting.

The Qabalah

What is the Qabalah? Briefly, it is the esoteric tradition of the Hebrews; and it includes methods of gaining enlightenment that have caused it to be referred to as the Yoga of the West.

Many popular occult manuals owe whatever of value they possess to Qabalistic sources, though these seldom are acknowledged.

The exoteric cult of a religion frequently holds in suspicion its own hidden or esoteric aspects: thus orthodox Judaism today tends to regard the Qabalah as an unhealthy aberration.

Only a few sects, such as the Chassidim, founded in the eighteenth century by Baal Shem Tov, openly favour its teachings.

There are historical reasons for this; for instance, a Christianizing tendency in some Qabalistic commentators during the later Middle Ages antagonised Jews of the stricter type.

Another reason for suspicion was the feeling that occult knowledge should be passed on only to those few able to apply it wisely.

Understandable as such a viewpoint is, it is a difficult one to hold in its extreme form at the present time, since much that was once kept secret has been published.

But books alone will not inform the ignorant and, as with Yoga, a personal teacher is necessary to real progress.

Hebrew esotericism has affinities with that of Egypt, Chaldaea, Babylonia and Tyre, and with certain Greek Gnostic cults, notably Pythagoreanism. This does not necessarily mean it is derived from them—all may be derived from a common source, now unknown.

From time immemorial, reciprocal influences existed between the various cults of the Middle East. Moses was said to be "learned in all the wisdom of the Egyptians"; and it is likely that Jewish mystical thought took its Chaldean and Babylonian imprint during the Captivity.

The Qabalah has always been distinct, not only from the Law and Prophets, but from the Talmuds which are a commentary upon them.

Indeed, the Hebrew scriptures came to be divided into three categories: the Law and the Prophets for ordinary men, the Talmuds for the learned and the Qabalah for the spiritually enlightened.

A parallel with Hinduism may here be drawn, where the Brahmanas and Puranas embody the exoteric teaching, while the Upanishads enshrine the esoteric.

A tradition tells us that the Qabalah was taught by God to a group of angels, who then passed it on to Adam in order to provide humanity with a means to reinstate itself after the Fall.

The story should not surprise us, for legends ascribing a supernatural provenance to any kind of skill or learning are widespread.

Adam taught the Qabalah to Noah, who in turn revealed it to Abraham. And so the doctrine continued for centuries, passing "from mouth to ear" without being written down, much less published.

Whether or not we accept this version of Qabalistic origins, it is certain that esoteric "schools" existed from the most ancient times.

When texts mention "the Companions", they refer to the members of such a "school".

It was these "Companions of the Holy Assemblies" who received the hidden wisdom: the word *Qabalah* is derived from the root QBL, "to receive".

The oldest Qabalistic treatise extant is the brief *Sepher Ietzirah* or "Book of Formation", aphoristic in style and exceedingly cryptic in content, as may be judged from the following passage:

"Three Fathers and their generations, Seven conquerors and their armies, and Twelve bounds of the Universe. See now, of these words, the faithful witnesses are the Universe, the Year and Man."

Its authorship is uncertain, and has even been ascribed to the Patriarch Abraham; but an attribution to Rabbi Akiba, who flourished in the second century A.D. is more probable.

The earliest edition is written in the Neo-Hebraic language, but the ideas it perpetuates may be much more ancient than this fact suggests.

As has been said, centuries of oral transmission preceded the first manuscripts.

During the seventeenth century, about twenty Latin translations of the *Ietzirah* appeared at Lemburg, the best being that of John Stephen Rittangel or Rittangelius.

The most easily available translations into English are those made by W. Wynn Westcott last century and by Knut Stenring more recently.

It is in the *Sepher Ietzirah* that we can find the earliest indication of the famous cosmographic schema known as the "Tree of Life" or Otz Chiim (OTz ChIIM).

Next in importance is the *Zohar* or "Book of Splendour", which is indeed a literature rather than a book. It can thus scarcely be the work of one man, though frequently ascribed to the second-century Rabbi Shimeon ben Iochai.

It was edited some eleven hundred years later by Rabbi Moses de Leon, but not printed until the fourteenth century.

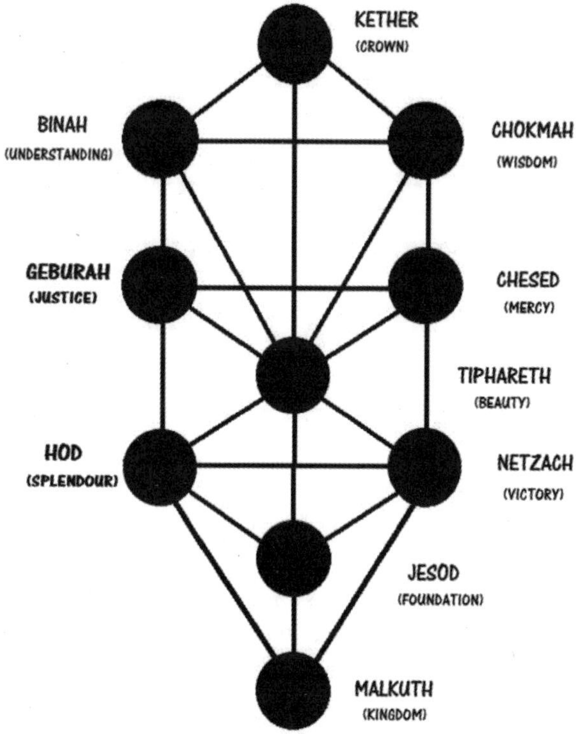

Again, this is not to deny that it contains ideas much more ancient. Its influence was immense, extending even to non-Jewish occultists.

The Literal Qabalah interprets the hidden meaning of words through numerical computation. As Sanskrit is the sacred language of the Yoga systems, so is Hebrew that of Western Occultism. Each letter of its alphabet is also a number. This, incidentally, is also true of the Chaldaean, Greek, Coptic and Arabic alphabets.

Thus the Literal Qabalah is, in effect, an attempt to apply the Jungian concept of synchronicity to interpretation.

To take a very simple instance, the Divine Name EL (AL) consists of the letters Aleph (1) and Lamed (30). If the digits of the total of 31 are again added, the "root-number" 4 is obtained.

Thus the word EL is linked with all other words of similar numeration, and its meaning extended. In fact it happens to be the Divine Name of the fourth *Sephirah* or "Emanation", *Chesed* (ChSD). Such links exist not by mere chance but by virtue of an essential connection, tenuous though this may appear, which is deeper than causality.

It is, however, the Doctrinal Qabalah with which we are mainly concerned[1].

Like many other esoteric systems, the Qabalah evolved a glyph by which it sought to symbolise cosmic relationships—the famous Tree of Life.

"As above, so below": this diagram, consisting as it does of ten *Sephiroth* or Divine Emanations, connected by twenty-two *Netibuth* or Paths, may be applied either macrocosmically or microcosmically.

In other words, it refers on the one hand to cosmogony and on the other to esoteric anatomy.

As the former, it is comparable to a "tree" in the genealogical sense, being a system of relationships.

As in the latter, it is to be seen rather as a "ghostly paradigm" of the human potential.

1 Besides the important treatises already named, one may mention the *Aesch Metzareph* or "Purifying Fire" which connects the Qabalah with Alchemy. There is a translation by W. Wynn Westcott.

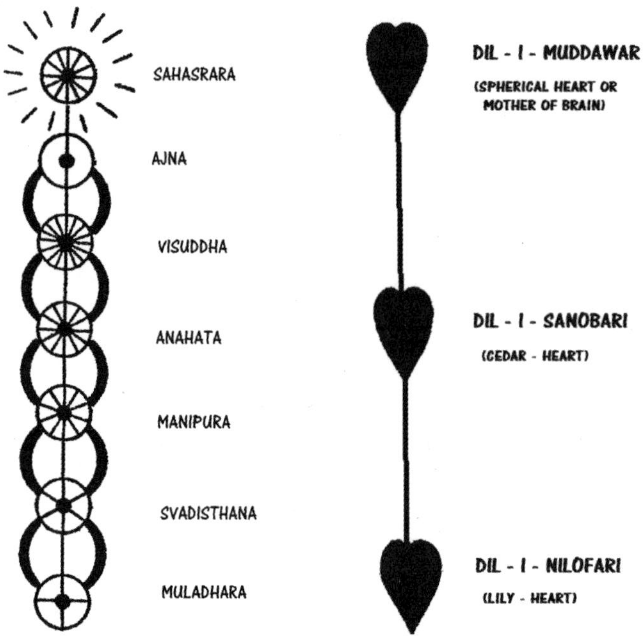

In both cases it is an attempt to map the unknown.

Taken in the microcosmic sense, the Tree has some resemblance to the diagram of the *Chakras* or Lotuses of the Laya-yoga systems now familiar in the West.

This is, of course, a simplified version. Sanskrit texts give many more than the usual seven centres, but the main point is that the *Sephiroth* are vortices comparable to the *Chakras*, while the *Netibuth* are currents comparable with the occult nerve-channels or *Nadis* of yogic thought.

Perhaps a closer parallel is to be found in the Shri Yantra of the Tantrik system, which would correspond fairly well with the Tree if this were drawn as a series of superimposed concentric circles.

A still closer parallel may be drawn from the literature of Sufism. Amin, a Dervish of the Naqshabend order, describes a symbolism which recalls, too vividly for coincidence, the upper part of the Tree.

Here the "centres" are related to various sages and each is assigned a colour; and these colours tally very well with those ascribed to the Tree as it appears on one of the planes of being.

Another Islamic writer, Prince Mohamed Dara Shikoh, indicates the following arrangement: where the "hearts" appear to be equivalent to the *Anja*, *Anahata* and *Muladhara* lotuses of the Hindu glyph, in which these three contain a *Trikoni* or *Yoni*, the shape of an inverted triangle, which is a "knot", through which the central column has to pass.

The Jains, too, have a glyph, more spatial in character, of the polarity underlying the universe and the concentration of its force into nuclei or "ganglia" connected by currents or channels.

Another example, better known to Western students, is the Caduceus of Hermes, which has obvious analogies with the diagram of the chakras.

All these, together with the Qabalah's Tree of Life, are attempts by the seer to record a vision of suprasensible realities. It is essentially the same vision; but having been perceived in each case through a different racial temperament and against a particular ethnic and cultural background, the records show dissimilarities as well as likenesses.

In so far as the vision is true, it relates to a sphere of timeless being; so it is not surprising to find it recorded at widely separated dates in human history.

The Ten Sephiroth (1958)

Plato thought nature but a spume that plays
Upon a ghostly paradigm of things

So sang W. B. Yeats in his poem "Among School Children". Through his early hermetic studies under MacGregor Mathers, Yeats was deeply imbued with Qabalistic thought; and the Qabalah's Tree of Life is just such a "ghostly paradigm". In *The Trembling of the Veil*, one of Yeats' autobiographical writings, he says:

> The Tree of Life is a geometrical figure made up of ten circles or spheres called Sephiroth and joined by straight lines. Once men must have thought of it as like some great tree covered with its fruit and its foliage, but at some period, in the thirteenth century perhaps, touched by the mathematical genius of Arabia in all likelihood, it had lost its natural form.

My introductory article presented the Tree as a cosmographic glyph, and compared it with similar diagrams from other systems. Among these, it is the one most appropriate to Western esotericism. I will now expound the nature of the Tree itself in greater detail.

The ten circles, centres or concentrations of force are the Sephiroth or Divine Emanations, sometimes called poetically "the diadems"; and they are connected by twenty-two channels or currents, the Netibuth or Paths. When the *Sepher Ietzirah* speaks of "thirty-two mysterious Paths of Wisdom", it includes both Sephiroth and Netibuth in the term "paths"; and this precedent is sometimes followed by other Qabalistic texts.

The Sephiroth are primarily the hidden aspect of the first numbers, one to ten; and the Netibuth the hidden aspect of the twenty-two letters of the Hebrew alphabet Aleph (A) through to Tau (Th). The doctrine is that it is by number and sound that the universe takes form.

AIN

AIN SOPH

AIN SOPH AUR

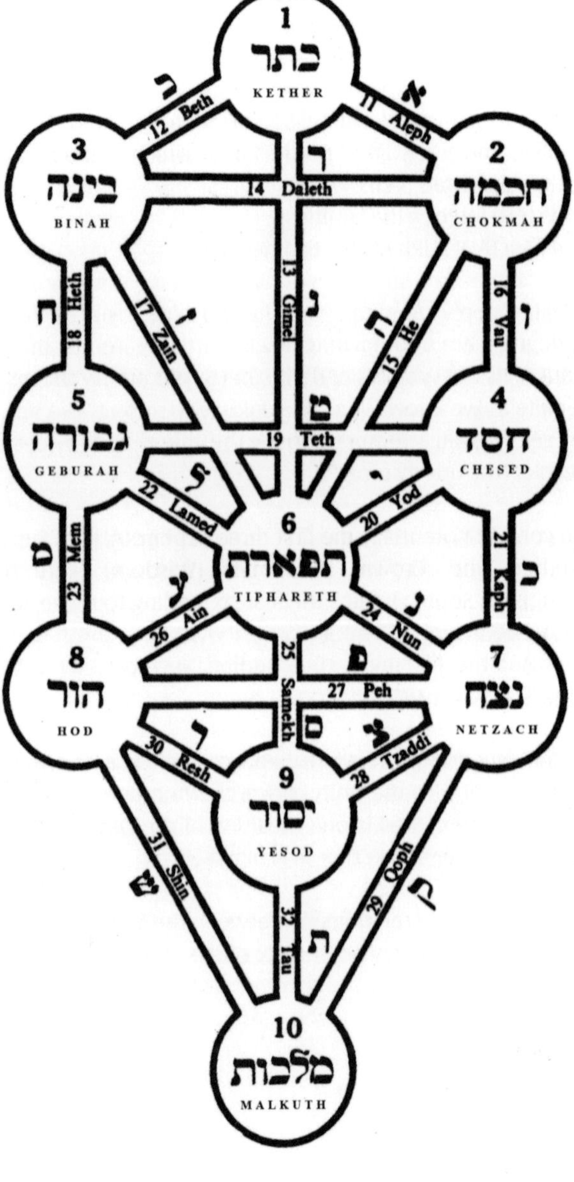

The Tree is the pattern of the process of this cosmic form-taking. It is a diagram of manifested existence; such existence being subject to conditions, cannot be absolute. Therefore, according to Qabalistic thought, an absolute existence precedes it. This Absolute is symbolised—it cannot, by definition, be expressed—as existing in three degrees:

1. *Ain* (AIN) = Negativity, No-thing; equivalent to the Void (Shunyata) of Buddhism and the AUM of Hinduism, in which syllable one can perhaps see the three "Veils" of Ain.
2. *Ain Soph* (AIN SUPh) = the Limitless.
3. *Ain Soph Aur* (AIN SUPh AUR) = Limitless Light.

Strictly speaking, only Ain can be the Absolute, since the two succeeding degrees are approaching, each a little nearer, to the point of manifestation. As the symbols of the higher Sephiroth try to cross the gulf between life as we know it and the unknown, so do these symbols of the three "Veils" of Ain attempt to bridge the chasm that divides from the unknowable, "the utterly other".

Ain is said to contain potentially the first three Sephiroth, the "Supernal Triangle"—Kether (the Crown), Chokmah (Wisdom) and Binah (Understanding). Ain Soph contains the first six, adding to those already mentioned Chesed (Mercy), Geburah (Severity) and Tiphareth (Beauty); and Ain Soph Aur the first nine, thus adding Netzach (Victory), Hod (Splendour) and Iesod (the Foundation).

In Malkuth (the Kingdom), the tenth Sephirah which is the material plane, a return is made to the unity, since, the number ten is a unity newly derived from zero. This is one meaning of the Qabalistic saying that "Malkuth is in Kether and Kether in Malkuth".

There seems to be a subtle relationship between the Sephiroth and the primordial letters in which they potentially subsist, thus:

Aleph, A, Kether.
Iod, I, Chokmah.
Nun, N, Binah.

Samek, S, Chesed.
Vau, U, Geburah.
Pé, Ph, Tiphareth.
Aleph, A, Netzach.
Vau, U, Hod.
Resh, R, Iesod.

Aleph is the first letter, not only of the word Ain but of the alphabet; and in its essence inheres Kether, the first Sephirah. Iod, pre-eminently the seminal letter, stands in a corresponding relation to the generating Chokmah. With Binah, Chesed, Geburah, Tiphareth and Hod, it is noticeable that the corresponding primordial letter occurs at or near the centre of the name. In the case of Binah, this is especially significant because central letter, Nun, has the numeration of fifty and symbolises the famous "Fifty Gates of Binah", the fifty properties of the understanding. Some editions of the *Ietzirah* have a short treatise added which gives details of these.

With Netzach a return is made to the initiating letter Aleph, while the parent of Iesod is the solar letter Resh. No doubt there are mysteries here for the advanced Qabalist to solve. Why the Absolute should need the Conditioned is a question which the Qabalah does not answer; nor, so far as I know, does any system answer it.

Rabbi Schimeon ben Iochai indeed asks: "How can we put water into a cup that is already full to the brim?" He might well have added: "Why should we want to?" Absolute existence is (obviously) its own purpose and needs no *raison d'être.* Conditioned existence implies purpose—but what purpose?

Those who are perplexed about the "problem of evil" have not delved deeply enough. The question is not, "Why should evil exist?", but "Why should the Absolute change into some lesser thing?" Such answers as that it is in order to gain experience, or to become conscious of itself, are so plainly inadequate that one would rather leave the question unanswered, accepting the fact of emanation, manifested existence, simply as "the way things are".

The process of manifestation is, as the Qabalah recognises, inseparable from potential evil; and below the Supernal Triangle, evil becomes more than merely potential. In dealing with the rarefied heights of Ain Soph Aur, it is hardly appropriate to use even the term "potential evil", but the *Zohar* does speak of contraction, constriction or concentration—*Tzimtzum* is the technical term. This contraction gives rise to the limiting factor of "rigour" or "severe judgement", *Din*, which is always associated with the emanative process. And contraction disturbs balance.

Kether

Thus Ain Soph Aur, the Limitless Light, contracts to a point which is Kether (the Crown), the first manifestation and the number 1. Kether is often called "the Small Point", "the Smooth Point" or "the Primordial Point". It is the Monad, and its function is demiurgic in the sense that from it the *Mezla* or 'creative influence', symbolised by the Lightning Flash, jets out to fill in turn the other Sephiroth, sometimes called *Kehlim* or "Vessels". (It must be understood that all language in relation to these states, forces and processes is necessarily metaphorical, and makes use of images.)

Chokmah

If Kether is the point, Chokmah (Wisdom), the number 2, is the point's extension, the line. It is called *Abba*, "the Father". The entire cosmos below the Monad, whether regarded objectively or subjectively, is the outcome of the interchange between two forces, positive and negative, male and female. Chokmah is the initiator of this interchange, the positive pole.

Binah

Opposite is Binah (Understanding); the number 3, the line directed to enclose a space. It is called *Aima*, the "Supernal Mother", the feminine principle and the negative pole. The perpetual conjunction of Chokmah and Binah, reflecting the hermaphrodite nature of immanent deity, sustains the totality of manifested life.

"When this Mother is conjoined with the King, all the worlds receive blessing, and the universe is found to be with joy," says *The Lesser Holy Assembly* in ch. XXII, 749. This is one of the books of the *Zohar* translated by MacGregor Mathers in *The Kabbalah Unveiled.* Analogies with Hinduism's doctrine of Shiva and Shakti are obvious, and a similar parallel could be drawn with systems originating still farther East.

Chesed

This union first produces Chesed (Mercy), the number 4, the square. It is noticeable that up till now there has been a progressive development in dimension; but with the number 4, a break in this occurs. The square, like the triangle, is a two-dimensional figure. We have already left the world of the Supernals, and are but echoing it.

Geburah

Next Geburah (Strength), the number 5 and the pentangle, is evolved. Chesed and Geburah, like the two Sephiroth preceding them, are respectively masculine and feminine, and reflect Chokmah and Binah in a sphere nearer to human consciousness.

Tiphareth

From them issues the number 6, Tiphareth (Beauty), the Son, a direct reflection of Kether and placed immediately below it on the diagram. One could perhaps say that Tiphareth is Kether comprehensible to the human mind. The point has become a hexangle.

Netzach, Hod, Iesod

The numbers 7, Netzach (Victory), the heptangle and 8, Hod (Splendour), the octangle, again reflect the Supernal Pair, and produce Iesod (the Foundation), the number 9 and the enneangle, a reflection of Tiphareth as the moon is of the sun.

Malkuth

Finally, from this, Malkuth (the Kingdom), the number 10, called "the Bride of the Son", is precipitated. Herein the universal stuff, which during the process of manifestation has been growing denser, crystallises into matter as we know it.

The emanative process symbolised by the Tree of Life not only produces the Heavens, the Earths and the Hells, as we shall later see; but also reflects itself in the psycho-physical constitution of the human being. In this sense it is both macrocosmic and microcosmic. †

The Twenty-Two Paths (1958)

In my last essay I described the Ten Sephiroth or "Emanations" which appear as circles on the diagram of the Tree of Life. They symbolise the stages through which manifested life evolves from the unmanifest before it reaches complete exteriorisation in Malkuth, which is life as we know it.

But the Sephiroth subsist by a series of connecting currents which link them one with another; these are the Netibuth or "Paths", and it is they which make the whole glyph a picture of cosmic relationships.

For a detailed grasp of the elements of the Qabalah, even when the texts are studied in translation, it is necessary to know at least the Hebrew alphabet. This is a "Garland of Letters" comparable with the Sanskrit alphabet in the Tantrik schools of Hinduism. Not only is the numerical aspect of the Hebrew alphabet important, every letter being in itself a number; but the actual shape of each holds secrets for the dedicated student. However, not everyone will wish to master them; so in this series I have adopted for Hebrew words their usual transliteration into Roman letters.

The alphabet has few vowels—Aleph (A), Vau (U or O) and Iod (I)—which are also used as consonants—and finally A'ain, which is usually O but may also be Aa or a consonantal Gn. Other vowels are indicated by the "pointing"—marks on the nearest consonant—or in unpointed Hebrew, are omitted, being left to the understanding of the reader.

The letters are twenty-two in number: Aleph (A), Beth (B), Gimel (G), Daleth (D), He (H), Vau (V or O), Zain (Z), Cheth (Ch), Teth (T), Iod (I),

THE QABALAH

AIN

AIN SOPH

AIN SOPH AUR

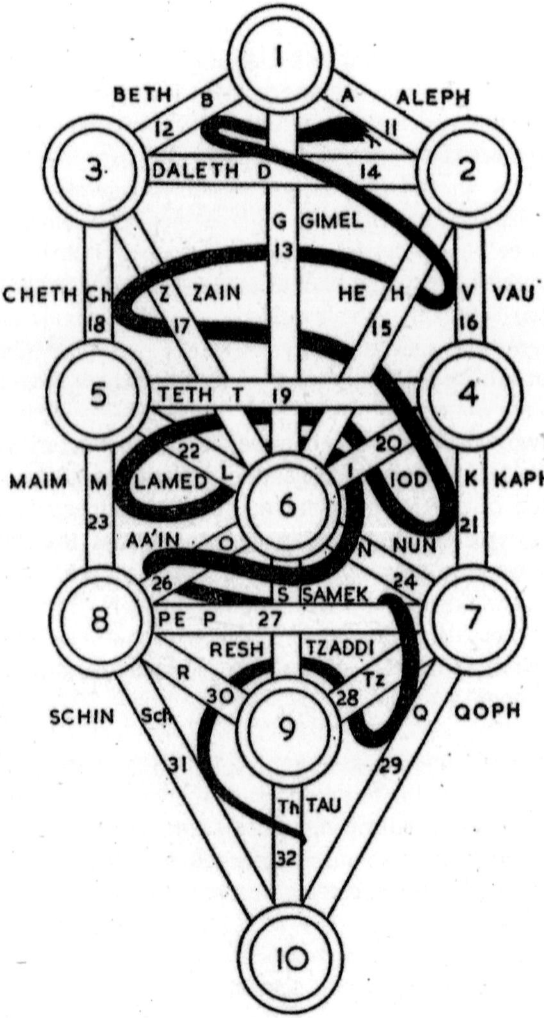

Kaph (K), Lamed (L), Maim (M), Nun (N), Samek (S), A'ain (O, Aa or Gn), Pé (P, Ph), Qoph (Q), Resh (R), Schin (Sch), Tau (Th), Tzaddi (Ts).

According to the *Sepher Ietzirah*, both Number and Letter are one with Sound. In the Sephiroth, Number is emphasised; in the Netibuth, it is Letter. Each letter of this alphabet is a creative agent, since each consists in a special force which provides a medium, a channel of connexion, between the unmanifest essence of life and some aspect of manifestation. Thus the doctrine is, that the alphabet produces the twenty-two Paths, not that the paths are self-subsistent and are merely distinguished each by a letter of the alphabet.

But before expressing itself in the Paths as such, the alphabet defines primarily three "Mother-Letters", so called because it is from the interplay of their currents of force that all else depends. They are Aleph (A), Maim (M) and Schin (Sch), and they give rise to what the *Ietzirah* calls the 'Three Fathers", namely the Elements of Air, Water and Fire. Air, proceeding as it does directly from Kether by the eleventh Path of Aleph, is the element nearest to the unmanifest; and it acts as a balancing force between the other two. One is reminded of alchemical symbolism, in which the Philosophical Mercury bears a similar role in relation to Sulphur and Salt. The first ten of the Netibuth are numerically connected with the Sephiroth: the eleventh path is, like Kether, an aspect of unity, since Aleph is not only a letter but the number 1.

It will be noticed that the numbering of the Netibuth begins with eleven, thus classifying the Ten Sephiroth as "Paths"—"the Thirty-two mysterious Paths of Wisdom," in the words of the *Ietzirah*.

The other Elemental Paths are Maim (M), Water, the twenty-third Path and Schin (Sch), Fire, the thirty-first. Tau (Th), Earth, shares the thirty-second path with the earthy planet Saturn. It therefore clearly does not participate in the demiurgic function ascribed to the first three elements, but is rather regarded as the receptive ground of their operation, and so is not included among the "Three Fathers". It is the last of the paths, that which joins Iesod with Malkuth the material world, and is thus very near to life as perceived by the physical senses.

After the three Mother-Letters, seven double letters are described—those having both a "hard" and a "soft" sound in pronunciation. From these emanated the Seven Planets—as did the elements from the Mother-Letters—and the paths which are their expression. They are Beth (B), Gimel (G), Daleth (D), Kaph (K), Pé (P), Resh (R) and Tau (Th).

The twelfth path, Beth (B) is an aspect of the number 2, as are the thirteenth and fourteenth paths, Gimel (G) and Daleth (D) which follow it, of the numbers 3 and 4. All are planetary paths, Beth conveying the force of Mercury, Gimel that of Luna and Daleth of Venus. The *Sepher Ietzirah* does not say exactly which letter produced each planet; commentators have tried to clarify this point, but neither Kircher, Kalisch, Mayer Lambert nor Knut Stenring gives a correct list. It is only by considering the attribution of the twenty-two Trumps Major of the Tarot to the paths that one arrives at the true consonances.

The remaining double letters are Kaph (K), conveying the twenty-first path and the forces of Jupiter; Pé (P), the twenty-seventh path and that of Mars; Resh (R), the thirtieth path and that of Sol; and Tau (Th) the thirty-second path and that of Saturn.

The *Ietzirah* further equates these planetary paths with a list of "pairs of opposites" which vary with different translators; I suggest the following as the correct one:

Mercury	Beth	Wisdom and Folly
Moon	Gimel	Riches and Poverty
Venus	Daleth	Fertility and Sterility
Jupiter	Kaph	Life and Death
Mars	Pé	Power and Servitude
Sol	Resh	Peace and War
Saturn	Tau	Grace and Abomination.

These are no doubt the "right" and "averse" aspects of each planetary path, their dual nature being hinted at in the double letters.

The remaining paths arose from the twelve Simple Letters, which produced the Zodiacal Signs. They continue the expression of the first numbers. The fifteenth belongs to Aries, which arose through the letter He (H), and has affinities with Geburah through the number 5; the sixteenth to Taurus through Vau (U), and is allied to Tiphareth or 6; the seventeenth to Gemini through Zain (Z), and is connected with Netzach and the number 7; the eighteenth to Cancer through Cheth (Ch) and with Hod and the number 8; the nineteenth to Leo through Teth (T) and with Iesod and the number 9; and the twentieth to Virgo through Iod (I), and with Malkuth as the number 10.

Libra as the twenty-second is breathed forth by the letter Lamed (L); Scorpio the twenty-fourth by Nun (N); Sagittarius the twenty-fifth by Samek (S); Capricorn the twenty-sixth by A'ain (O); Aquarius the twenty-eighth by Tzaddi (Tz) and lastly Pisces the twenty-ninth by Qoph (Q).

All the Netibuth are in a sense mutations of the same force. Being placed higher on the Tree than Malkuth, they subsist in a non-material medium; but all have as well their material counterparts or reflections, and on this fact the Doctrine of Signatures is based.

As the Lightning-Flash of the Mezla or creative "influence" connects the Sephiroth in the order in which they were evolved, so the coils of the Serpent *Theli*, while evading the Sephiroth, bind together the Netibuth.

In spite of the well-known ambivalence of the serpent-symbol, there is nothing in the *Ietzirah* to identify Theli with the Serpent of Genesis, with Job's Leviathan or with the sinister *Thenanim* of the Psalms. On the contrary, it is expressly called "the Celestial Dragon". It is therefore the Serpent of Wisdom who twines about the Tree of Life, and is distinct from the tempter associated with the Tree of Knowledge or the malevolent water-dragons.

Microcosmically, Theli may be compared with Kundalini, the serpent-fire which lies coiled "three times and a half" at the base of the spine, below the Muladhara Chakra; and which, when woken into activity, may ascend to the Kether or "crown" of the head.

Some writers stress the Sephiroth at the expense of the Netibuth: Dion Fortune, for example, in *The Mystical Qabalah*, describes the former in detail but only mentions the latter cursorily. In this they are certainly not following the lead of the *Ietzirah* and its dependent texts, which are mainly concerned with the twenty-two paths. Reference is made to the Sephiroth in the first chapter only, and even then their names are not given. Since the paths are so fully described in this, the oldest Qabalistic treatise, one must assume that they have an equal importance with the Sephiroth for the understanding of the complete symbol.

One reason for their importance lies in the fact that they link the Sephiroth one with another, relating them together in a delicate equilibrium. Thus, the thirteenth path, Gimel, provides a medium—the planet Venus—through which Chokmah, the second Sephiroth, acts upon Binah, the third. It is Aphrodite-Urania uniting the Supernal Pair.

Other commentators have stated that the Sephiroth refer to the Universe and the paths to humanity or, in other words, that the former have a cosmographic application and the latter a psycho-physiological one. This also is an error: the *Ietzirah* distinctly states that the twenty-two paths refer to "the Universe, the Year and Man", The glyph of the Tree of Life is meaningless for either except in its entirety.

There is, however, some teaching to the effect that by a diagram of the Paths alone, omitting the Sephiroth, the constitution of the animal-world, as distinct from man, may be represented.

Here the animal-glyph is drawn horizontally, though in each case the combination of the central paths forms the spinal column. How the diagram should be modified so as to apply to invertebrates, and to the plant-and mineral-kingdoms, must be left to students more advanced than myself.

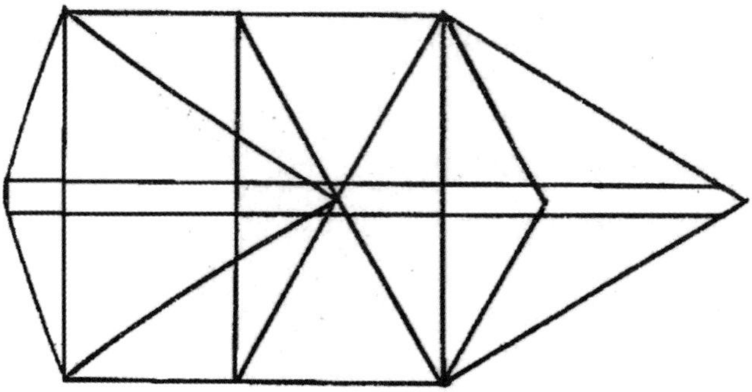

ANIMAL GLYPH

If the Qabalistic scheme has any validity, it can no doubt adapt itself to the more detailed factual information of later ages. Modern astrologers who may have wondered about its "seven" planets will be interested to know that attempts have been made to accommodate such recent acquisitions as Uranus, Neptune, Pluto and Isis upon the Tree. It has been suggested that, since five letters of the Hebrew alphabet—Kaph (K), Maim (M), Nun (N), Pé (P) and Tzaddi (Tz)—take a different form and carry a different numeration when they occur at the end of a word, the "latent" planets may be referred to them. These "final" letters still leave us with one more planet to be discovered—or is it re-discovered?

The 400 Desirable Worlds (1958)

The two main components of the Tree of Life, namely, the ten Sephiroth or Emanations, and the twenty-two Netibuth or paths, have been briefly described in the previous essays of this series.

Such a description does not, however, nearly exhaust the properties of the glyph, nor of the qualities which it symbolises. The Qabalah teaches that manifested existence is divisible into four worlds—or "planes", to use the familiar theosophical term.

If the three higher worlds of the Qabalistic order are sub-divided each into two, one "abstract" and the other "concrete", the four-fold scheme is converted into a seven-fold one, and a close approximation to cosmologies derived from Hinduism will become apparent.

The four worlds are:

Olam Atziluth (OULM ATzILUTh)—the Archetypal world.
Olam-ha-Briah (OULM H-BRIAH)—the Creative world.
Olam-Ietzirah (OULM H-ITzIRH)—the Formative world.
Olam ha-Assiah (OULM H-OSchIH)—the Material world.

Atziluth proceeds directly from Ain Soph Aur, the limitless light of unmanifest existence; next in the scale, Briah depends from it; then Ietzirah, and finally Assiah, the material cosmos, including those aspects of it which are not generally cognizable by humanity today.

It will thus be seen that the four worlds, like the ten Sephiroth themselves, represent degrees of densification between what is unmanifest, and the solidified cosmos which presents itself to our senses, and in its turn is moulded by our "common sense".

As the Tree of Life is projected downwards through all four worlds, each world has its own tree, for the Malkuth of the previous world gives rise to the Kether of the world following. (See Diagram I.)

For example, in representing diagrammatically the emergence of Briah from Atziluth, that is, of active creation from potential archetype, one may place the circle symbolizing the Kether of Briah immediately below, but contiguous to, the circle symbolizing the Malkuth of Atziluth; and so on down the worlds.

Another method is to impose one circle upon the other; or to cut a single circle transversely in half, in which case the upper half would be the Malkuth of Atziluth, and the lower the Kether of Briah. "Kether is in Malkuth and Malkuth in Kether", particularly at the pivot where the qualitative change from world to world takes place.

Each Sephirah, while predominantly either masculine or feminine, is also androgynous in essence: it not only receives the Mezla, or creative influence, from the Sephirah next above it, but also transmits it to the Sephirah next below.

Even the Kether of Atziluth is receptive, or feminine, to a ray from the limitless light.

Thus the glyph is developed from a tree of ten Sephiroth to one of forty, the projection of the ten Emanations in the four worlds. Though they exist primarily as pure number, the Sephiroth manifest themselves through a different mode in each world.

In Atziluth, it is through the divine names, each of which expresses an aspect of divinity. In Briah, it is through the archangels, to each of which is delegated a function of the divine power.

In Ietzirah, this power is sub-divided into the ten angelic choirs, each of which extends, on the plane of formation, the scope of one of the archangelic rulers in the world of Briah above.

One may remark in passing that though Christianity has retained a few shreds of this angelology, the full hierarchy of the ten archangels has disappeared from its orthodox teaching.

Traces remain of those guarding the four quarters—Michael, Raphael, Gabriel and Uriel—of which Michael is definitely the favourite, while Uriel seems, for some reason, to be more than a little suspect.

A treatise by the fifth-century "pseudo-Dionysius", which had a great influence on mediaeval thought, gives a list of nine angelic orders.

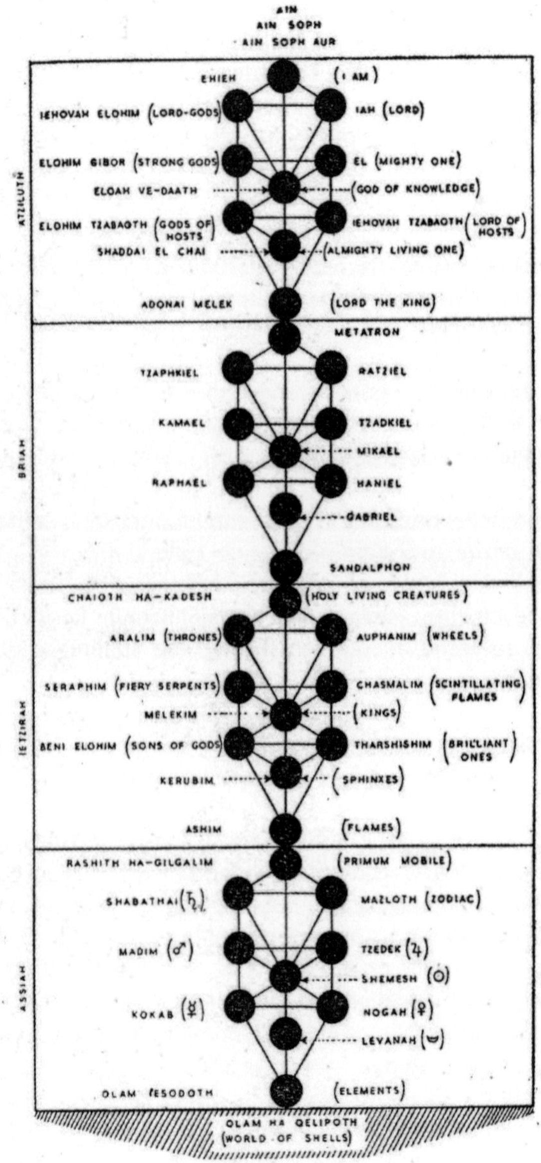
AIN
AIN SOPH
AIN SOPH AUR
ATZILUTH
EHIEH
(I AM)
IEHOVAH ELOHIM (LORD-GODS)
IAH (LORD)
ELOHIM GIBOR (STRONG GODS)
EL (MIGHTY ONE)
ELOAH VE-DAATH
(GOD OF KNOWLEDGE)
ELOHIM TZABAOTH (GODS OF HOSTS)
IEHOVAH TZABAOTH (LORD OF HOSTS)
SHADDAI EL CHAI
(ALMIGHTY LIVING ONE)
ADONAI MELEK
(LORD THE KING)
BRIAH
METATRON
TZAPHKIEL
RATZIEL
KAMAEL
TZADKIEL
MIKAEL
RAPHAEL
HANIEL
GABRIEL
SANDALPHON
IETZIRAH
CHAIOTH HA-KADESH
(HOLY LIVING CREATURES)
ARALIM (THRONES)
AUPHANIM (WHEELS)
SERAPHIM (FIERY SERPENTS)
CHASMALIM (SCINTILLATING FLAMES)
MELEKIM
(KINGS)
BENI ELOHIM (SONS OF GODS)
THARSHISHIM (BRILLIANT ONES)
KERUBIM
(SPHINXES)
ASHIM
(FLAMES)
ASSIAH
RASHITH HA-GILGALIM
(PRIMUM MOBILE)
SHABATHAI (♄)
MAZLOTH (ZODIAC)
MADIM (♂)
TZEDEK (♃)
SHEMESH (☉)
KOKAB (☿)
NOGAH (♀)
LEVANAH (☽)
OLAM IESODOTH
(ELEMENTS)
OLAM HA QELIPOTH
(WORLD OF SHELLS)

Diagram 1.

These are plainly related to the angelic choirs of the Qabalah, the tenth of which, attributed to Malkuth, being the *Aschim* or "Souls" and therefore not strictly an "angelic" order.

The fact that, in the doctrine and ritual of any Christian church, the place of the angels is but a small one, may well be felt as an impoverishment.

In the world of Assiah, the Sephiroth manifest themselves primarily as the heavenly spheres—the very words "Sephirah" and "Sphere" are etymologically akin.

The first of these spheres, reflecting Kether, is the *Rashith ha-Gilgalim* (RASchITh H-GLGLIM) or "Beginning of Whirling Motion", the Primum Mobile of Ptolemaic astronomy.

The second, reflecting Chokmah, is *Mazloth* (MZLUTh), the Sphere of the Zodiac or the fixed stars.

The next seven, from Binah as *Shabathai* (ShBThAI), "Rest" the sphere of Saturn, to Iesod as *Levanah* (LBNH), the sphere of the Moon, are planetary.

The tenth and last, representing Malkuth, is *Olam ha-Iesodoth* (OULM H-ISUDUTh) or "World of Foundations"; by which is meant the four elements.

Since the discovery of the "new" planets it has been suggested that, the Sphere of Neptune should represent Kether; that of Uranus, Chokmah and that of Pluto, Malkuth.

It must in any case be emphasised that these spheres are not to be understood as identical with the material planets, but rather with their etheric counterpart or their "sphere of influence".

They are also the spheres through which Beatrice guides Dante in the *Paradiso*. The poet may simply have taken them from the Ptolemaic system, but there are indications that he knew the Qabalah or some esoteric teaching consonant with it.

The order of his paradisal spheres certainly agrees with that of the Tree of Life; but when he and Beatrice enter the heaven of the Moon (Iesod) they call it the "first" instead of the "ninth", since they are ascending from Malkuth upwards.

They go on through Mercury (Hod), Venus (Netzach), the Sun (Tiphareth), Mars (Geburah), Jupiter (Chesed) and Saturn (Binah).

They then enter the heaven of the fixed stars or the Zodiac (Chokmah) through the sign Gemini; and later pass on to the Primum Mobile (Kether itself). Beatrice tells Dante:

> Here is the goal, whence motion in his race
> Starts; motionless the centre, and the rest
> All moved around...
> The vase wherein time's roots are plunged thou seest:
> Look elsewhere for the leaves...

This latter image is curious in that some drawings of the Tree show it as growing "downwards" with roots in Kether and branches extending to the lower Sephiroth.

From this Kether of Assiah, Dante looks upward to the next World (that of Ietzirah) and sees a vision of the blessed souls and beyond, of the angelic choirs; in this description, the work of the seer "Dionysius" is actually referred to.

As to the Netibuth in the four worlds, they must of necessity exist, or the Tree would not be workable. But information about them is less accessible than about the Sephiroth.

In Atziluth only the planetary and elemental paths are dignified by divine names, the Zodiacal paths being nameless. As regards Briah, there are individual Zodiacal angels ruling the appropriate paths, so one may speculate that there are probably angelic cohorts similarly occupied in Ietzirah.

In Assiah, the planetary paths take the names of the planetary spheres, the Zodiacal ones the Hebrew names of the Zodiacal months; while the elemental paths each takes the Hebrew name of its appropriate element.

But for the sake of simplicity, the names of all Netibuth have been omitted from the accompanying diagrams.

The workings of the Sephiroth and Paths in different modes through the four worlds form the basis of the practical Qabalah, or transcendental magic. In the West, nearly all ritual magic of a sophisticated type is thence derived.

Therefore is the magician instructed to memorise the divine and angelic names, that he may use them as words of power to control the impalpable realms, and to deck his temple with such material objects as are, by their very nature, in harmony with the type of force he intends to manipulate.

The subject of the practical Qabalah, fascinating though it is, would take us far beyond the scope of these essays. Suffice it to say that scraps of its lore have filtered down from the magician's "high lonely tower", and may to this day be found mixed with the shamanistic magic of the countryside which stems from a different source.

To return to the doctrinal Qabalah: there is a sense in which the four worlds exist in the individual tree of each world; thus, of each world, Kether is its Atziluth, and Chokmah and Binah together form its Briah.

The next six Sephiroth, from Chesed to Iesod, constitute its Ietzirah; while Malkuth is its Assiah. (See Diagram II.)

Not only does the Tree extend itself down the planes, but it also condenses itself, since each Sephirah contains within itself its own tree.

Thus, the Kether of Tiphareth is the highest point or "crown" of the central emanation; conversely, the Tiphareth of Kether is the central point or "harmony" of the highest emanation.

Therefore the complete symbol comprises not forty, but four hundred Sephiroth.

This property of the glyph for extension and condensation shows its aptness for symbolizing the two abysses of the infinitely minute on the one hand, and of the infinitely huge on the other—between which our limited spatial life is passed.

In the *Siphra de-Tzenioutha* or "Book of Concealed Mystery"—one of the texts translated by MacGregor Mathers in *The Kabbalah Unveiled*—they are called the "four hundred desirable worlds".

These "worlds"—here "worlds" means Sephiroth—are produced by "repressing the crest" of the Celestial Dragon Theli, mentioned in the *Sepher Ietzirah.*

This is amplified by a play upon words of a kind which the Qabalah of Numbers often employs; the first letter or "crest" of the Dragon's name, Tau (Th), has the numeration of four hundred. Tau, taken away, presumably constitutes four hundred "worlds" separated from the Dragon whose coils wind round the Netibuth.

Theli, indeed, is said not to touch the Sephiroth with his coils; yet, if he "represses his crest" by sloughing it off as a snake drops its skin, then he is credited with a demiurgic function in respect of the Sephiroth.

He must be assumed to assist in some way in the emanating of the Sephiroth out of Ain Soph Aur, thus giving rise to the "desirable worlds".

The twenty-two Netibuth are likewise extended, becoming eighty-eight in the four planes of being, and eight hundred and eighty if the Tree is both extended and condensed.

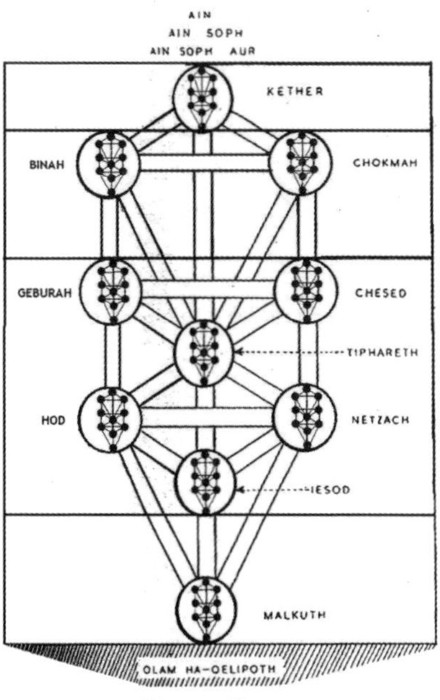

Diagram II

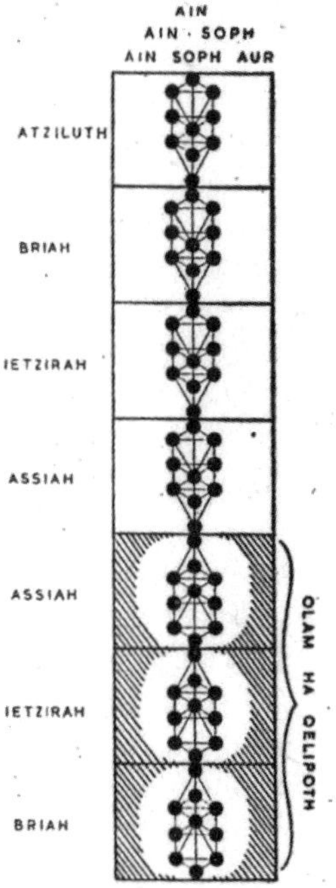

Diagram III

This extension does not take into account the *Oham ha-Qeliphoth* (OULM H-QLIPhUTh) or "World of Shells", a region of unbalanced force depending from the Malkuth of Assiah, and partly interpenetrating it.

This is the habitation of residual forms from which the spark of life has receded so that they are but outward cortices, substance without essence.

We must imagine the Tree as rooted in the Malkuth of Assiah, and reproducing itself upwards through the four worlds. But it stands on the edge of a murky tarn, which returns a distorted reflection of all the Emanations and their interconnecting Paths. (See Diagram III.)

This mirror-image of the "Ineffable Sephiroth" is the Tree in its averse aspect; but it includes only the three worlds of Assiah, Ietzirah and Briah, since Atziluth, the world of archetypes, is beyond the possibility of division.

Thus, for the complete Tree, three hundred "undesirable worlds" and their connecting paths must be added to the original four hundred.

As to the medium upon which this faltering and deceptive image is projected, one can only suppose it to be the "outer darkness"—a state beyond manifestation, but at the opposite pole to Ain.

Though some writers equate the World of Ietzirah with the theosophical "astral plane", this is not generally true. Ietzirah, as the name implies, is the world of formative forces, angels and elemental spirits; but most astral phenomena take origin, not in this upper region, but in the illusory world of shades which subsists below and through the material universe.

In summing up briefly the cosmographic scheme of the Qabalah, one may say that it stands midway between the dualism of Christian philosophy and the monism characteristic of Hinduism and other Oriental systems. Its successive Emanations, paralleled in certain Gnostic cults, make a link between life as we know it and that Absolute Being which is beyond our ken. †

Dimensional Interrelation: A Meditation on the Platonic Solids (c. mid 1960s)

This piece was likely written while Colquhoun was working with the Golden Dawn inspired order Temple of the Pyramid and Sphinx in the mid-1960s. This rather confusing essay was chronicling a series of experiments that Colquhoun was conducting to attempt to achieve some sort of extra dimensional consciousness through manipulating physical models of Platonic solids. She concludes that the solid which was most likely to provide a portal into other dimensions was the cube, which, derived from passages in the Bible, is a foundational solid of several esoteric traditions including Freemasonry and the Golden Dawn. Colquhoun was likely inspired by experiments in Charles Hinton's *The Fourth Dimension* (1931), as well as René Guénon's *The Symbolism of the Cross* (1931) and *The Multiple States of Being* (1932). It should be noted that the swastika, also known as a fylfot cross, is one of the many cruciform shapes that one would meditate on in the curriculum of the Golden Dawn, developed in the late nineteenth century. It is in this context that Colquhoun would have been working.

The five three dimensional figures described by Plato are:

I. The Tetrahedron, 4-sided and ascribed in esoteric tradition to Elemental Fire and the colour red.

II. The Hexahedron, 6-sided and ascribed to Elemental Earth and the colour black.

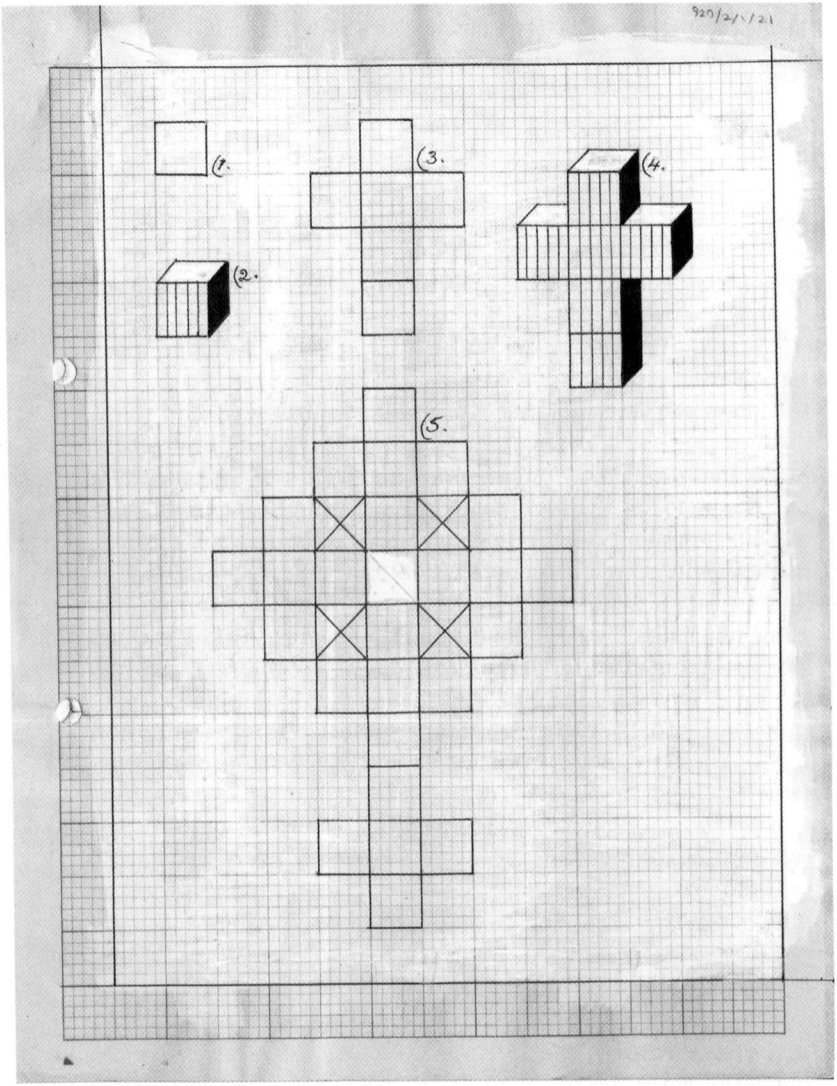

920/2/1/21
(1.
(2.
(3.
(4.
(5.

III. The Octahedron, 8-sided, to Elemental Air and the colour yellow.

IV. The Dodekahedron, 12-sided to Elemental Water and the colour blue.

V. The Ikosahedron, 20-sided, to Aether and the colour white.

Each is defined in space by equal and regular planes, its sides; and a two-dimensional figure may be taken as the basis of each, with a rhythm or pulsation between the second and third dimensions established by experiment.

I. The Tetrahedron

1. The basis is the two-dimensional equilateral Triangle.

2. Take each side of this Triangle as the basal line of a similar figure, raise their three apices to meet above the centre of the original Triangle, and the three-dimensional Tetrahedron (or Triangle-based Pyramid) is produced.

3. Open this Pyramid out as a two-dimensional figure again and it becomes a larger equilateral Triangle composed of 4 smaller such Triangles.

4. Repeat process two with each of these Triangles and each becomes a Tetrahedron joined to the others at basal lines sharing the large triangular base, the complete figure composed of 13 triangular faces (12 small and 1 large) and producing 4 conjoined Tetrahedra.

5. Attempt to open out this figure out into the second dimension and it will be found that many of the triangular faces composing it become impacted. It must therefore be assumed to exfoliate, if at all, in a fourth dimension.

II. The Hexahedron

1. Better known as the Cube, this figure springs from the two-dimensional Square.

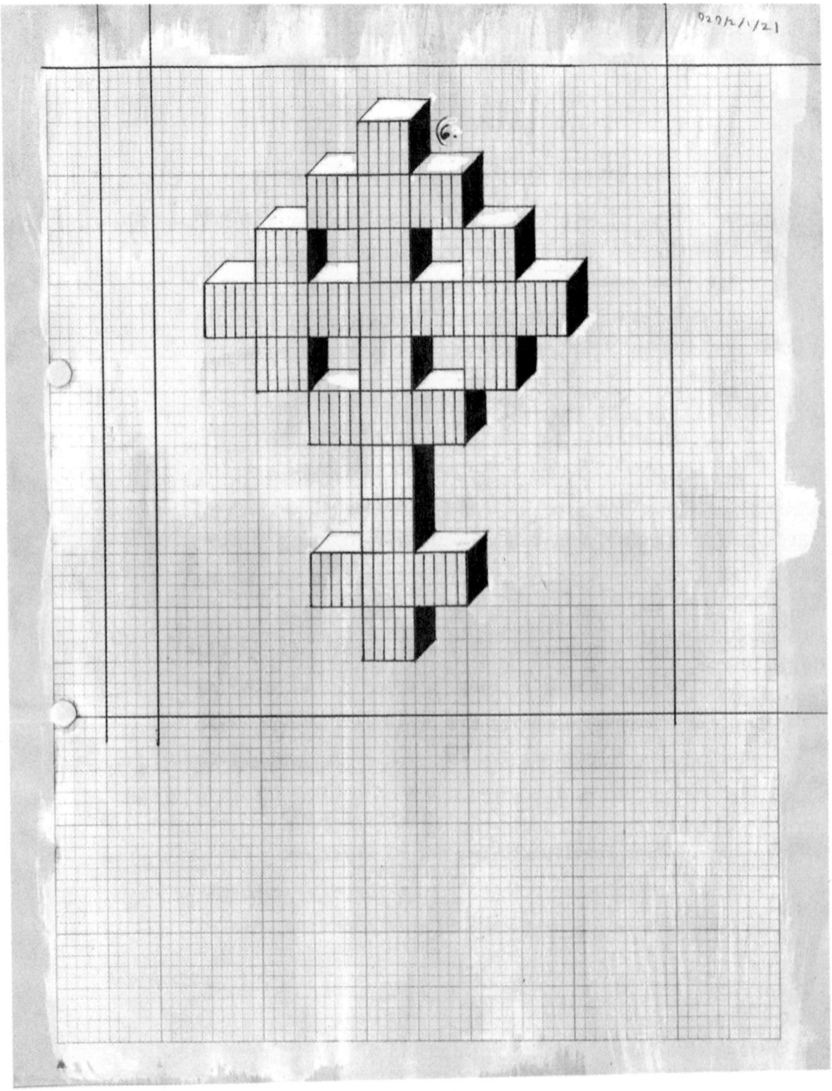
D27/2/1/21
6.

2. Raise each side of this Square to produce another Square, and a solid composed of six square faces will be defined (the Cube).

3. Open this out as a two-dimensional figure and it becomes a Cross, while the number of Squares composing it remains at 6.

4. Construct this Cross as a three-dimensional figure and the number of square faces increases to 26 (6 cubes).

5. Open this out again as a two-dimensional figure and a more elaborate Cross results, the number of square faces remaining at 26.

6. Construct this as a three-dimensional figure and their number increases to 106 (26 cubes).

Though the rhythm of dimensional exchange has been carried out two stages further than in the case of the Tetrahedron, it would seem that this second Cross is the final product of the Square, unless it can be extended into a fourth dimension. But there is the possibility of a "Third Dimension-Plus" in constructing the "Cross of the Six Directions"; at stage four, two more cubical arms are set at right-angles to the first pair to form it (8 cubes instead of 6, 36 square faces instead of 26). At stage six a similar extension gives a Cross consisting of 42 cubes instead of 26, 178 square faces instead of 106. Even at stage two it is possible, instead of opening out the basic Cube into the second dimension, to extend it three-dimensionally by adding a similar Cube to each of its faces, thus producing an equal-armed or Greek Cross (5 Cubes, 22 square faces). Arms added at right-angles to this figure develop it into the "Third Dimension Plus" (7 cubes, 32 square faces).

Figures other than the Platonic solids can be treated in this way: the Double Cube follows a course of stages similar to that of the Cube. Also based on the two-dimensional Square are variations of the Swastika:

1. The Minimal Swastika consists of 17 Squares selected from a larger square of 25 squares.

2. These 17 Squares are developed into 17 Cubes.

3. But they cannot exfoliate without becoming impacted.

4. The Swastika next in degree, that consisting of 25 Squares selected from a larger Square of 49 squares, having passed through the first two stages, exfoliates into an interesting figure of 102 squares (not a Swastika).

5. When in turn its constituent Squares are developed into Cubes, a solid figure (not a Swastika) composed of 378 square faces results.

6. This cannot exfoliate further without becoming impacted.

Interesting figures also result from developing the Double-Square and the Swastika into the "Third Dimension-Plus".

The Square-based Pyramid is not a Platonic solid either but it combines the properties of the first two described (Tetrahedron and Hexahedron) and can be similarly treated.

1. Like the Hexahedron its seminal form is the Square.

2. But when each side of this Square is projected into the third dimension it must be in the form of an equilateral Triangle instead of the repetition of the basic Square, and the four triangular faces must be inclined so that their apices meet above the centre of the basic Square. A four-sided solid results, with 1 face square and 4 triangular.

3. Opened out in the second dimension it appears as species of Tetragram or 4-pointed star.

4. Constructed as a solid, this becomes a central Pyramid bounded along each basal line by a triangular-based Pyramid or Tetrahedron (5 Pyramids in all). Of its 17 faces, 1, the base, is shaped as a Tetragram, 4 are equilateral triangles and 12 Triangles.

5. It cannot exfoliate without becoming impacted.

III. The Octahedron

1. Returning to the Platonic Solids, this one is based, like the Tetrahedron, on the equilateral Triangle as regards its visible faces.

2. But it demands also the concept of the Square since its three-dimensional form is built up of two Square-based Pyramids joined at their two-dimensional bases. This joining results in the occultation of the two squares as they are no longer surface-planes.

3. Opened out, this Octahedron forms 4 Diamonds, or Rhombs, each composed of 2 equilateral Triangles arranged in a horizontal line (8 Triangles). The Squares have disappeared.

4. Constructed as a solid, 4 Octahedra result, arranged in a horizontal line (32 triangular faces in all). In plan-view, each of these Octahedra appears as a Square divided into 4 Triangles (16 triangles viewed from above, 16 from below).

5. Opened out, it produces a double row of 4 Maltese Crosses (8 Maltese Crosses, 32 Triangles). Between each Cross a Tetragram appears.

6. Solidified, this becomes a double row of 4 Maltese Crosses (8 in all), each Cross composed of 4 Square-based Pyramids, joined at their apices (128 Triangles, 16 Squares).

This figure cannot further exfoliate, but it may be projected into the "Third Dimension-Plus" by adding two more Square-based Pyramids to each Cross, setting them at right angles to the other arms as in "the Cross of the Six Directions" (under Hexahedron).

IV. The Dodekahedron

1. The two-dimensional figure is fundamental to the dodecahedron is the regular Pentagon.

2. By projecting each of its 5 sides in a further Pentagon and projecting each of these latter again (in one case double) and by inclining the first 5 outward and the second 5 inward, a 12-sided solid appears.

3. Opened out, a flower-like form results, its pentagon centre surrounded by 5 pentagon-petals, doubled and in one case trebled.

4. This figure cannot be developed in the third dimension, becoming impacted because of the outward inclination of the first 5 pentagonal faces arising from the original Pentagon, which causes an overlap above the shared basal lines. Therefore the figure is not susceptible of development beyond the third stage.

V. The Ikosahedron

1. Like the Tetrahedron and the Octahedron, this solid is based on the equilateral Triangle as regards its faces.

2. Disposed in a particular way, twenty such Triangles form the solid.

3. Opened out, their arrangement is seen to consist of four groups, numbers 1-4, 5-12, 13 and 14, 15-20; and of three horizontal rows, the two last groups forming the third row.

4. Projected three-dimensionally, one face, an irregular polygon, supports 20 triangular-based Pyramids arranged in rows on the Triangles which form their individual bases (1 irregular polygon, 60 triangular faces). Like the Tetrahedron and the Pyramid, it cannot exfoliate beyond this, the fourth stage.

Each of the Platonic solids responds to experiment in a different way, revealing both divergencies and parallels as regards the other figures. Light is also thrown on symbolism: it is surprising to find, for instance, that though the Swastika is traditionally regarded as a fire symbol it has no morphological links with Elemental Fire, being a dependency of the Square, which has affinity with Elemental Earth. On the other hand, the Maltese Cross and the Ikosahedron, reveal links with Elemental Fire, through their triangular morphology. †

An Analysis of the Rose Cross Symbol related to the Spectrum (c. 1960s)

The Hermetic Order of the Golden Dawn pioneered a complex form of colour magic. Light is emblematic of enlightenment, and Golden Dawn initiates are said to be "seeking the light". As the visible spectrum is evidence of the materialisation of spiritual light, the rainbow, and the colours of both light and pigment took on symbolic importance for that order. Colour was also seen as the way in which extradimensional, planetary or Zodiacal forces could be called and experienced. The Rosy Cross Emblem, worn as a lamen or badge by Golden Dawn adepts, contains a colour wheel at the centre, which serves as a key for their colour based magical workings. Here, Colquhoun provides her own derivation of colours through precise colour mixing to ensure that the hues were going to combine in such a way as to have the proper visual and spiritual impact. These principles were seen in Colquhoun's work from the late 1930s onward, but the date for this essay is likely later than that, possibly dating from her work in the Order of the Pyramid and Sphinx in the 1960s when she was actively creating Golden Dawn tools.

To determine the exact hue of each "flashing colour", it is necessary to analyse the spectrum on which the colour attribution of the Rose Cross Symbol is based.

To each of the Primary Colours: Red, Yellow and Blue (Category I) is assigned five units of pure tint. (If less than five divisions are postulated, it is more difficult to determine the proportions accurately, as will be seen from the charts.)

From the Primaries are produced the sub-classes.

I. A. Orange-Red (consisting of 4 parts red + 1 part yellow)
Green-Yellow (consisting of 4 parts yellow + 1 part blue)
Indigo (consisting of 4 parts blue + 1 part red)

I. B. Red-Orange (consisting of 3 parts red + 2 parts yellow)
Yellow-Green (consisting of 3 parts yellow + 2 parts blue)
Violet (consisting of 3 parts blue + 2 parts red)

This brings one to the Secondaries (Category II).

Orange (consisting of 2.5 parts red + 2.5 parts yellow)
Green (consisting of 2.5 parts yellow + 2.5 parts blue)
Purple (consisting of 2.5 parts blue + 2.5 parts red)

These also produce two sub-classes:

II. A. Amber (consisting of 2 parts red + 3 parts yellow)
Blue-Green (consisting of 2 parts yellow + 3 parts blue)
Red-Violet (consisting of 2 parts blue + 3 parts red)

II. B. Yellow-Amber (consisting of 1 part red + 4 parts yellow)
Green-Blue (consisting of 1 part yellow + 4 parts blue)
Crimson (consisting of 1 part blue + 4 parts red)

If a circle is divided into 18 segments and each segment being coloured with tints through the above spectrum series beginning with Red and ending with Crimson, it will be found that the "flashing colours" are exactly opposite each other, e.g. Red opposite to Green, Crimson opposite to Yellow-Green.

If two more concentric circles are drawn within the first and marked in flashing-colours with the appropriate Hebrew letter, the basis of the Rose-Cross diagram will emerge: the Elemental colours may be marked in the smallest circle, the planetary colours in the second, and the Zodiacal colours in the outermost.

It will be noticed that this system leaves the axis Purple and Yellow-Amber empty of letters but helps to differentiate the Red letters since both ה and פ are Red, ו is Orange-Red and ש Red-Orange. ל and נ are also well differentiated as Green-Blue and Blue-Green, while צ is Red-Violet and כ Purple. There is unfortunately no way of {word unreadable} that א is a pale version of which ב is {the full?} Yellow; and ג a pale version of ס's Blue. †

The Tree Alphabet and the Tree of Life (c. 1966)

This short piece is part of Colquhoun's project to synthesise Celtic spiritual systems with the Kabbalah. She was especially inspired by Robert Graves' theorizing about Celtic tree alphabets and Colquhoun created her own versions of the drawings in Graves' popular 1948 book *The White Goddess* to align the Celtic system more closely with Kabbalistic structures. In 1972 Colquhoun had started a project to write 22 poems with accompanying images, reflecting the work she had been trying to achieve synthesizing Graves' tree alphabet with the twenty-two paths of the Kabbalistic Tree of Life. Although only fragments of this project remain, some of them, including the drawings based on Graves' work are found in her small 1973 poetry chapbook *Grimoire of the Entangled Thicket*.

Following up on the essay on *Barddas* (no. 3 *The Druid*), it may be suggested that Einigan, the first man, is equivalent to Adam Qadmon in the Qabalah, his alphabet corresponding to the first ten numbers (i.e. the Sephiroth) on the Tree of Life.

The three rods which Menw saw growing out of the mouth of Einigan after death are the three Vertical Pillars—Mercy, Mildness and Severity—of the diagram. The second alphabet, that of Menw, is the oldest Tree-alphabet, the Boibel-Loth, or Birch Rowan, consisting of sixteen letters, and their augmentations, and corresponds to the paths (Netibuth) which link the Sephiroth. By leaving the first three Netibuth unassigned, the fact that their disposition forms the Awen is revealed at the top of the diagram. This is the Divine Name which Menw did not teach in public.

Both alphabets can be conveniently placed on the Tree of Life by marking the Sephiroth with Einigan's APCETILROS alphabet in Roman capitals, following the order of the descent of the Mezla, and the Netibuth with the Boibel-Loth in Ogham. Thus A=Kether, the World of Archetypes (Aztiluth), while P and C are Chokmah and Binah, which together form the World of Creativity (Briah). The secrets of these two worlds or planes of existence remained secret; the letters from C to S lie below the Abyss, being concerned with manifestation, and comprise the Worlds of Formation (Ietzerah) and Materiality (Assiah).

The Netibuth are twenty-two in number, one for each letter of the Hebrew alphabet; the first three of these compose the Awen, the next sixteen are assigned to the Tree alphabet while the remaining three record some of its augmentations.

When Beli arranged the Boibel Loth, "he left the ten cuttings secret," that is he did not expound the Sephiroth, whose mysteries were known only to the Bards; but he taught the knowledge of the Netibuth, as being nearer to ordinary consciousness, to the people. †

Meditation Begins at Home (1968)

This interesting and rather quietly subversive essay suggests that there is hidden wisdom in many ancient churches that can be revealed by quiet concentration. Of particular interest is Colquhoun's return to the ways in which the Divine Feminine asserts her presence even in Christian contexts.

You don't need to visit the Orient—stimulating as that would be—in order to learn meditation; you don't even need to sit at the feet of an Oriental teacher. (In fact, better not, unless he is a genuine guru—and such are rare—and not someone out to make easy money.) You can find pointers to one-pointedness nearer home, perhaps on your very doorstep.

Don't, if you are a beginner without anyone more experienced to guide your progress, try to "make your mind a blank". This usually results at best in boredom or mind-wandering; at worst in tensions which can precipitate neurosis. Not that the latter is an acute danger: in meditation, as in magic, most people do no harm because they do nothing at all. But wasted effort with consequent disillusionment is to be avoided.

Follow a method suited to your environment and capacity: for instance, choose a glyph or focal point for your attention, a word or picture on which to ponder; it hardly matters what, so long as it is something that interests you. If you choose a picture or diagram, the forms and colours in themselves, as well as what they represent, will become part of your subject. If it is a word not only its meaning but also the shape of its component letters and its sound when spoken will be important. When the actual sound of a word is used as a glyph or starting-point, a branch of Mantra-yoga will have been attempted; but beginners will usually find a visual glyph more useful. It is best to start with a simple geometric diagram rather than a figurative painting: you could do worse than search your parish church for suggestions.

The sixth-century church of St. Sennen[1], "the first and last" church in Britain, shelters its granite walls behind wind-swept bushes with Land's End to the south-west. Inside, four diagrams painted in gold and outlined in dark red on a white ground hang from the pillars of the south aisle; they depict the Alpha and Omega of *The Revelation*, the Sacred Monograms and the Fleur-de-Lys, and invite you to sit and meditate on them one by one.

In a prefatory essay W. B. Yeats tells us: "At Oxford I went constantly to All Souls' chapel, though never at service time, and parts of *A Vision* were thought out there". However, there are hazards to meditating in a church: a friend of mine tried it when the harassments of family life made concentration difficult at home but he was not left in peace. After peering at him on several occasions, the local vicar approached him with an (unwelcome) invitation to attend services. The clergy cannot give effective help in the technique of meditation—and most of them indeed would be nonplussed if asked even to check a meditation-record—but could they not set aside a secluded corner for those who have to practise unaided?

Alpha and Omega are appropriate symbols for meditation at St. Sennen, at the beginning and end of the land, and they bring one face to face with ultimates, spiritually as well as geographically. They may even prove to be the code words opening the safe of apocalyptic vision. The first and final letters of the Greek alphabet, they are often given their Greek form (Fig. 1), sometimes combined (Fig. 2) or interlaced (Fig. 3) as a single glyph; or they may be separate, as the twin panels in a stained-glass window. However presented they can become the "seed-word" of a meditation. Often, as at

1 A church in West Cornwall likely dating from the fifteenth century.

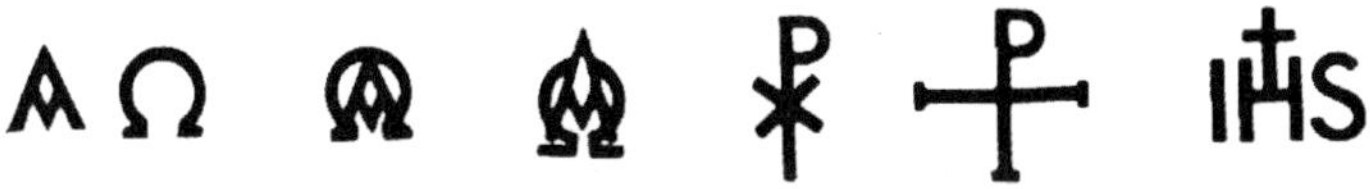

Fig. 1 *Fig. 2* *Fig. 3* *Fig. 4* *Fig. 5* *Fig. 6*

Some of the diagrams and monograms referred to: they can be found in a number of churches

St. Neot's church in East Cornwall, the letter M is associated within them in ecclesiastical decoration and signifies Maria, the feminine creative force. Is it mere chance that a combination of these three letters produces a word, AOM, closely resembling the best-known Sanskrit mantram, AUM?

One of the Sacred Monograms is the famous Chi-Rho, first two letters of the name of Christ, though meditation may reveal in them other meanings. Their Greek form is XP, combined (Fig. 4) as the Emperor Constantine saw them, giant sized in the sky above his army. When a voice told him *"In hoc signo vinces"*, he at once adopted it as his standard. Visualised in gold on a background of purple like the *Labarum* it replaced, this symbol would provide a splendid device for meditation. In the church of St.Just-in-Penwith, a little to the north of Land's End, an interesting variant of it (Fig. 5) is carved on a pillar-slab commemorating the saint's brother, St. Selus. Another example is a small relief in stone above the porch of Phillack church, on the Hayle estuary that almost divides Penwith from the "mainland" of Cornwall.

The letters of the other Monogram, IHS, also figure, both separate and interlaced, in the various media of church decoration whether glass, wood, stone or fabric. They are the initials of the motto *Iesus Hominum Salvator* but again, other meanings may lie hidden in the letters themselves. Sometimes the H is represented with a cross standing on the central bar (Fig. 6); in this form Gustav Meyrink, author of *The Golem* and many other occult novels, was meditating on it one winter's night as he sat beside the river Moldava that flows through Prague. An autobiographical note describes how the symbol activated his clairvoyant faculties which developed thenceforward spontaneously—such can be the power of a traditional glyph.

Last of the Sennen diagrams is the Fleur-de-Lys, Shakespeare's "flower-de-luce" or flower of light, an emblem different from the previous three in that it is not, like them, composed of alphabetical forms. Its symbolic resonance is with the Virgin of the World and it could provide a channel for the forces of cosmic femininity. In heraldry—another abundant source of meditation glyphs—it is usually charged in silver on an azure ground: tincture of the Moon, a particularised aspect of the letter M mentioned earlier. A cognate image is the Egyptian goddess Nuit wearing the blue of interstellar space spangled with stars.

All these four motifs are frequently found in stained-glass windows: the little church at Gwithian on the sand-dunes of the North Cornish coast features the Alpha and Omega and the Monograms alternately, in garnet red and olive green. Such windows need hold no antiquarian interest to provide effective glyphs for meditation: designs in modern glass can prove inspiring and those of the Victorian era when influenced by the Pre-Raphaelite Movement are especially rich in symbolism. Having decided on the symbol you wish to explore, obtain a photograph or other reproduction of it, or better still make a coloured drawing of it yourself, and place this in front of you when you sit down to meditate. Soon you will not need the representation as you will be able to visualise the glyph mentally with your eyes closed, but the diagram will be useful to recall at the beginning of each session.

In Paul church, Penwith, dedicated to the Spanish St. Pol de Leon (a blackened pillar within still recalling a holocaust by Spanish raiders), an unpretentious window hides profound truths in a few simple lines and colours. Bounded by a blue *Vesica*—emblem of "the Mother of God" that precedes all—a white brilliance concentrates its unconditioned splendour into the gold of a background to interlaced triangles, the seal of macrocosmic form. Within this again, a cross of six squares indicates man as microcosm. Meditation on the complete symbol could open to inward sight a whole process of cosmogony, summing up the primal quinary thus:

Ain: the Virgin Mother, the Causeless Cause.
Ain Soph: the Limitless or Unconditioned.
Ain Soph Aur: Light-in-Extension.
Kether: the First Manifestation.
Tiphereth: Consciousness. †

The Thirteen Treasures of the Isle of Britain (1968)

This essay marks a return to Colquhoun's publishing in *Prediction* Magazine, the first of several Celtic themed essays she wrote for them. It demonstrates Colquhoun's deepening engagement with Celtic Spirituality during this time of her life, and also the increasing opportunities to publish on Celtic themes. The Thirteen Treasures in the title are magical objects relating to kingship taken from medieval Welsh literature, although their geographic spread is wider than what is considered Wales today. Here Colquhoun speculates on their nature and relationship to telluric currents, but does not argue a firm conclusion. We also start to see Colquhoun increasingly assert a nativist position, suggesting she is starting to reject the inclusion of Asian esoteric teaching in "Western" systems.

In 1849 Lady Charlotte Guest chose eleven stories from *The Red Book of Hergest*, a fourteenth-century manuscript belonging to Jesus College, Oxford, and translated them into vigorous English prose under the title of the *Mabinogion*. In this she did the same service for Welsh legend as Lady Gregory, with her *Gods and Fighting Men* and *Cuchulain of Muirthemne* did some fifty years later for the Irish mythological cycles.

The word *Mabinogi* denoted a piece of traditional lore, many of which a bardic aspirant had to recite by heart before his status was confirmed. Throughout these tales one finds references to certain precious things of which the translator gives a list. Their full title, "The Thirteen Rarities of Kingly Regalia of the Island of Britain", hint at royalty's link with the numinous. These "rarities" or "kingly jewels" were kept at Caerleon-on-Usk where Arthur held his court: some say that the enchanter Merlin took them with him when he retired to his mysterious abode of glass on Bardsey Island. But others maintain that before his disappearance he concealed them in different localities of the country, where they lie hidden to this day—several in Wales (one on Bardsey, perhaps, and possibly one at Glastonbury, another "glass island"), two in Cornwall, some in the fabric of old cathedrals.

Cathedral builders established their work on sites chosen for their occult significance, whether this was telluric, and therefore natural, or man-made as the result of consecration by earlier priests who knew what they were doing. Most pre-Reformation churches were built on the site of a Pagan sanctuary, often above an underground spring, one of the insignia of a telluric site. This usually forked or "blind spring"—the Classical writer who called occult centres "fountains out of Hecate" was referring to such hidden watercourses. Needless to say, these considerations are ignored today, when churches are built because a suburb or housing estate has sprung up as the accompaniment of industrial development, where the factory nucleus is the real temple and the deity worshipped there is Mammon. Could this be one reason why the churches are empty?

Merlin was perhaps echoing Apollonius of Tyana who, according to theosophical folklore, hid a number of talismans at chosen spots during the course of his travels. A booklet was published in 1966 by Colonel K. Chodkiewicz describing the one supposed to be buried at Krakow. I looked carefully through the volumes of Philostratus' *Life of Apollonius* but was unable to trace a reference to his concealing talismans anywhere, and there is no record of his visiting Krakow. The town, of course, did not then exist, but, as Chodkiewicz says, Apollonius might have wandered to the neighbourhood at a time when no other travels are mentioned. As to his talismans, it seems that the only authority for them is Mme Blavatsky.

However, the Wawel rock, on which the castle and cathedral of Krakow are built, certainly looks as if it might be a centre of occult force: from prehistoric times at least it must have been a striking feature of the landscape, its solitary outcrop rising from fattish lands on a bend of the river. A cleft within it is traditionally the haunt of a devastating dragon which was killed by the local hero, Krakus. (Surely it was the dragon who was named Krakus—this is what the syllable means; and "snake-hole" is a way of indicating chthonic initiations.) The hero must have adopted the dragon's name and having set up the castle on the rock, passed on the name to it and so to the city that grew up around it. One may take a hint from this type of landscape, a high rock or hill above water, crowned with a castle or church or both—when trying to locate the "precious things" of Britain.

First on Lady Charlotte's list is Dyrnwyn, the sword of Rhydderch Hael, this comes into the category of the personal magic weapon, made by (or at least, exclusively for) its owner and so powerfully consecrated as to be dangerous for anyone else to handle. Celtic myth abounds with such weapons, from the well known Caliburn or Excalibur of King Arthur to the spear of the Irish warrior Duftach; when not in use its point had to be kept immersed in a sedative infusion or, like Dyrnwyn, it would burst into flame. The right name for the weapon comes to the operator at the climax of the consecration-ritual.

Numbers two and three, the basket of Gwyddno Garanhir and the born of Brân Galed, can be classified as talismans for abundance of food and drink; so also are number six, a magic knife, and numbers ten and eleven, a pan and a platter. Some of these are plainly related to the Graal in its character of universal provider and it is noticeable that three of the four hallows of the chivalric legend circle, a sword, a Graal and a stone figure among the "wonders of Britain".

Another class includes objects to be used as the instrument of an ordeal. Number seven, the cauldron at Tyrnog, and number eight, the whetstone of Tudwal Tudglyd, were implements for testing masculine courage. (Where was Tyrnog? The name suggests Tír na nÓg, the Gaelic earthly paradise, and makes one wonder whether the treasures are to be found on the material plane of being at all or whether they do not belong to some subtler realm.) Number nine was a garment for the proving of noble birth, and the mantle of Tegau Eurfron, sometimes given as an alternative to the fifth treasure, tested for feminine chastity. Tegau was apparently a good girl as well as one of the triad of beauties who graced Arthur's court. A further category is concerned in the conferring of the magical powers, or siddhis—to use the Hindu term that is more familiar (ironically enough) to Europeans than its Celtic equivalent. We shall continue to employ imported Hindu or Buddhist esoteric phrases instead of those that lie at the roots of our own culture until an occult student who is also a scholar and a linguist gives this subject some attention. Stacks of Cymric manuscripts lie undervalued and therefore untranslated and unpublished in the libraries of Wales; the same is true of Gaelic manuscripts in those of Ireland—to say nothing of continental libraries.

The power-giving treasures are numbers four and five in Lady Charlotte's list, a chariot and a halter that conferred the power of bi-location; they produced instantaneous travel from place to place with the cancelling of space and time. An alternative to number eleven, the ring of Eluned, was set with a stone to make its wearer invisible—as did number thirteen, the mantle of Arthur, while stimulating clairvoyant faculties as well.

Number twelve, Gwenddolen's chessboard, is the most interesting of all: one can be sure that the chess played upon it was something more than a game. In some ancient Oriental forms of chess connected with divination there are four players, one at each corner of the board, linking it with much other fourfold symbolism. Irish legends are full of references to a game called fidchell, a species of chess much favoured by gods and heroes in the Tir na nÓg. These were

> Masterly at making songs,
> Skilled at playing fidchell,

as a poem in the twelfth-century *Book of Leinster* says. The power of Gwenddolen's board was self-acting: once the pieces were set the "playe" followed of its own accord. The board itself was of gold, the chessmen of silver, and it is unlikely that these were the minuscule figures of the present-day game. In *The Romance of Sir Gareth*, the Knight enters the castle of a beautiful fay who invites him to play chess with her. The flagstones of the hall, alternately black and white, serve as a board, while the pieces are great statues of silver and gold which the players activate by means of a "magic rod". Then there is the story of an Eastern potentate who used his dancing girls as "chessmen"; Gwenddolen may also have used human beings, suitably attired in cloth of silver. They may even have been priests and priestesses robed to represent the various pieces, in which case the board would have been a tessellated paving in the precinct of a divination temple. The priestly college attached to this would be headed by Gwenddolen herself, who would thus be a High Priestess as well as a noted beauty of Arthurian legend.

The treasures would be viewed in another way as pertaining to the countryside itself; thus the word "chessboard" may signify a patchwork of fields. If one still follows the *Mabinogion* description, the fact that it is said to be golden must be taken to indicate the colour of its vegetation. The game of chess must be imagined as played with giants for pieces, unless an entire platoon were stationed on each chequer to take the place of individual chess men, and light glinting on their metallic armour would make them look like silver. The game would be at the same time a military exercise and an act of divination, or even the latter in the guise of the former.

Some, perhaps all of the other "precious things" may be of correspondingly huge dimensions, being hidden only in the sense of forming part of the landscape, like the signs of the Glastonbury Zodiac. The basket might be an especially fertile orchard or cultivated valley, the cauldron a hot spring (at Bath?), the Whetstone a rocky ridge, the pan a rock-encircled lake. The chariot could be a mountain-top whose shape suggested a throne: there are many such named after heroes—Arthur's Seat in Edinburgh, Cader Idris in Montgomery, Sei Finn in Co. Kerry.

If, however, one takes the "treasures" as objects fashioned to the use of ordinary humanity, and if one accepts that Merlin or some other sage in the Druid tradition consecrated the treasures as palladia and subsequently hid them, then most of them may indeed survive to the present day. Sword, knife, cauldron, platter, pan, chariot, ring, chessmen large or small, all these could well have been of a substance to withstand the centuries. A band of students combining intuition with a knowledge of local history and geography might succeed in identifying and using at least some of these "precious things". †

Lights In The Air (late 1960s)

This essay is a write-up of a compilation of diary notes related to Colquhoun's experiences of strange light phenomena in West Cornwall in the mid-1960s. Colquhoun kept a detailed record of these experiences and was able to draw them together for this piece. She does not come to any firm conclusion, but her suspicions and observations are clearly tied to wider discourses about UFOs at the time, and also to the many folkloric accounts of strange light phenomena occurring in Cornwall. Although Colquhoun didn't write or paint about UFOs extensively, it is clear that she had an interest in them, given her diary entries and also her collection of press cuttings about these strange phenomena. Her 1955 essay on UFOs for *London Broadsheet* suggests this was a long standing fascination for her.

I live in West Cornwall, and my cottage is surrounded by a garden with a meadow beyond. From this garden and from the lanes and fields in the neighbourhood, I have from time to time noticed the appearance of lights in the air which I can't explain by common sense. Not possessing a car, I have to do a fair amount of walking and can observe my surroundings better than people who always drive. As an artist and writer, I am used to making notes on what I see.

1. The first of these sightings—if that is the right word—happened some years ago, on November 4, 1960, to be exact. I was returning with a companion from a walk to a

hamlet a mile or two away. It was about a quarter to six in the evening and growing dusk but the sky was not dark enough to show any stars. There was some low broken cloud and a north-west wind was blowing.

We had just passed the avenue to a farm when I saw something like a shooting star—though I realised instantly that it was not one since it was only about thirty feet from the ground. It was a ball of light about ten inches in diameter, bright yellow and with a tail like a comet; it darted across the road just ahead of us from left to right, that is, north-west to south-east, and was at once extinguished. I exclaimed in surprise, but it was gone before my companion could look up.

2. A few weeks later I was in my cottage with two friends. It was late afternoon, about sunset, and the weather was fine and rather cold. Happening to glance out of a window which looks over a valley to the east, I saw a bright object, about the size of the previous one, falling through the air. At a height of forty feet or so it vanished but for a second it looked like a burnt-out fire balloon. No ashy fragments were visible, however; it just wasn't there. Neither of my friends had noticed it.

3. I saw nothing of the kind for several years; but one evening about dusk early in July, 1964, I was in my garden with a friend who was staying with me. The weather was dry but not very warm, and the sky was covered by thin cloud. Suddenly my guest called out that she could see "flashes in the air", and I went down the path to where she was standing, but I could see nothing. She was much intrigued, and next evening we both watched for further manifestations, but none occurred.

4. About two months later, however, I was passing through the garden at twilight on a fine evening when my

sleeve caught on a shrub. I turned to release it and in doing so, glanced southwards over the meadow from which I had just come. A bright light flashed in the sky at a height of about twenty feet; it was if an electric bulb had been switched on and immediately off again, but there was no electric installation near it.

I wrote describing this incident to the friend who had been visiting me: she confirmed that it was exactly what she had seen over the garden, only in her sighting there had been several distinct flashes.

5. Further support was provided when, some two years later in the summer of 1966, another friend was seeing me home about eleven on a fine starlight night. As we went through the garden he saw a similar flash of light over the meadow, though I saw nothing.

6. It was back again in the autumn of 1964 (though I did not make a note of the exact date) that I happened to be looking from my garden across to a field on the opposite side of the road. As it is in a valley, I could see the whole expanse of the field, and this was suddenly covered for an instant by a bluish light that flashed across it horizontally at a height of about a foot. The weather was fine but chilly and the time late afternoon, just before dusk.

7. On another day in similar conditions, I saw a light like a lamp among the bushes bordering the adjoining field. It vanished at once and there was nothing to account for it.

8. Again, on a fine afternoon when I was driving to the neighbouring town, I saw a red light falling into the sea near the shore, or perhaps on to the beach itself—I could not be sure as a built-up area intervened and I was some distance away.

9. My next record is about a year later, on October 5, 1965. The weather was mild for the time of year, though there was a light easterly wind. About a quarter to eleven I opened a south-facing window and looked out: it was a fine still night and the moon, about half-full, showed just beyond a clump of trees at the end of my meadow. Suddenly a brilliant disk emerged from the trees some twenty-five feet above ground and passed rather slowly on a level course over the meadow from right to left, that is, north-west to south-east. It seemed about 10 to 12 inches in diameter and when it left the trees it was visible against a clear sky below the moon. But it was much brighter than the moon, and did not look like a metallic object reflecting moonlight; its light had a warmer and more sparkling appearance. In any case the moon was behind it. There was a sudden extinction: I had the impression of quickly-fading incandescence and a change of direction, as though a disk which had been sailing along on its edge with the flat surface towards me had flipped over on its side before vanishing.

10. Some two months later, on December 11, 1965, I was walking home after visiting the next village. It was again about 10.45, a few nights after full-moon; the weather was mild but no moon was visible because of low cloud and drizzle. I happened to glance northwards in the direction of the cemetery and saw two or three pale flashes in quick succession, appearing like an arc from ground to zenith, bluish white in colour. Further on, when I was approaching my cottage, I noticed a sweet scent of flowers though none were growing near enough to account for this.

11. In the same year—though unfortunately I didn't record the exact date—I noticed a similar flash on this road at about the same time of night and in the same weather conditions. But this time it was double and in the opposite direction, that of the southward coast.

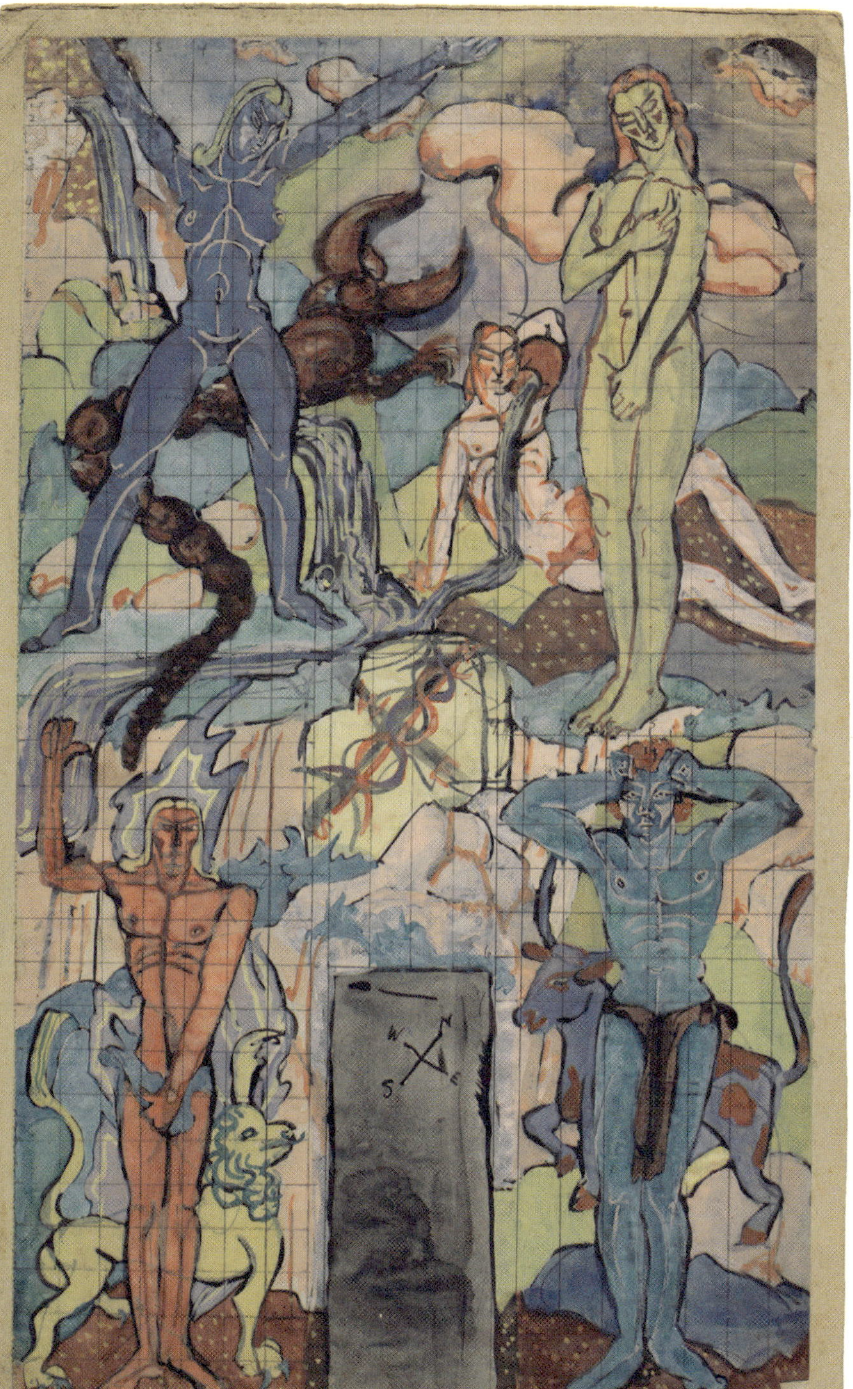

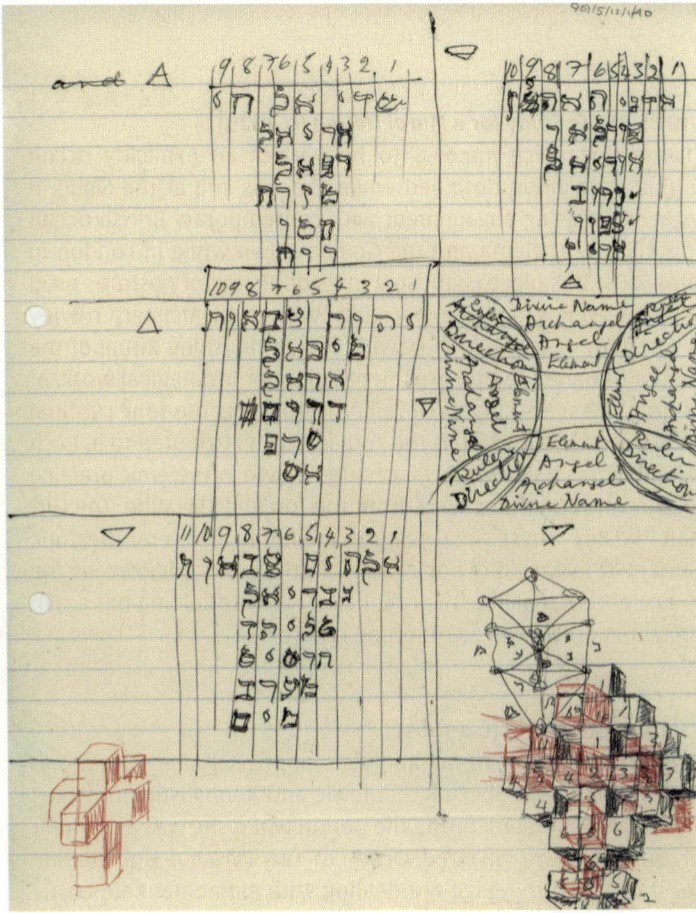
9015/12/1/40
and △
Divine Name
Archangel
Angel
Element
Ruler
Direction

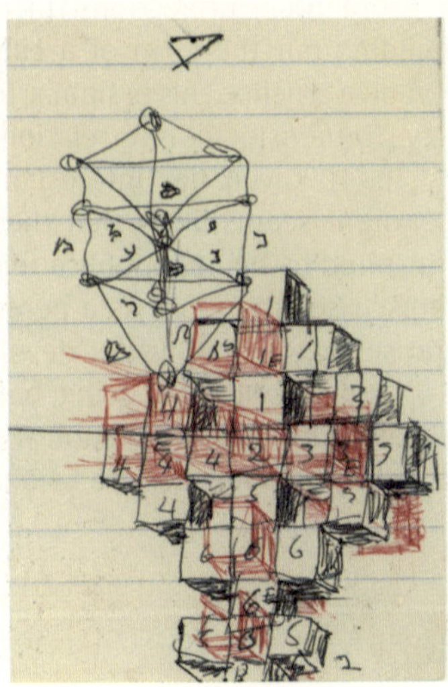

PREVIOUS PAGE: ***Study for a Mural Design*** **(c. 1929)**

This fascinating piece appears to be part of an explicitly occult mural that Colquhoun designed while she was still at the Slade. It shows her increasing engagement with contemporary British occult systems such as Thelema and the Golden Dawn while in London in the late 1920s. This piece is unusual in its depiction of postures used within a Thelemic ritual, The Star Ruby, written by Aleister Crowley. It is a variation of the Golden Dawn's Lesser Banishing Ritual of the Pentagram designed to prepare the practitioner for magical work. At the bottom we see some sort of plinth providing the four cardinal directions. At each direction is the zodiacal sign attributed to it. Each of the four figures is performing a gesture known in Thelemic practice as the signs of N.O.X.: clockwise from the top left, The Wife, The Girl, The Man, The Boy. These ritual gestures are found in several Thelemic rites and in The Star Ruby are enacted in the central known as the Paian, a celebration of Pan, the Greek god who in Thelema has a rich theological significance as a totalising nature deity.

LEFT: ***Kabbalistic Notes*** **(c. 1960s)**

This page likely dating from the 1960s appears to be Colquhoun working through a number of geometric and Kabbalistic principles. This was likely generated during the period when she was a member of the Golden Dawn inspired Order of the Pyramid and Sphinx. Several sections of the page are dealing with elemental Kabbalistic attributions. The detail, however, seems to relate to Colquhoun's experimentation with geometrical projections. In this sketch you can see how she is building out the form of a cube into a three-dimensional elaboration on a crucifix. This is similar to the technique expressed in her essay "Dimensional Interrelation: A Meditation on the Platonic Solids", p.141. Given her interest in the works of traditionalist René Guénon, it seems likely that these experiments were at least partially inspired by his 1931 publication *The Symbolism of the Cross*, where he discusses the cross as a perennial, universal symbol which characterises the metaphysical development of the human condition into a variety of states of being, both material and immaterial. It may be that part of her fascination with the figure of the cross was that at its centre all opposites are reconciled.

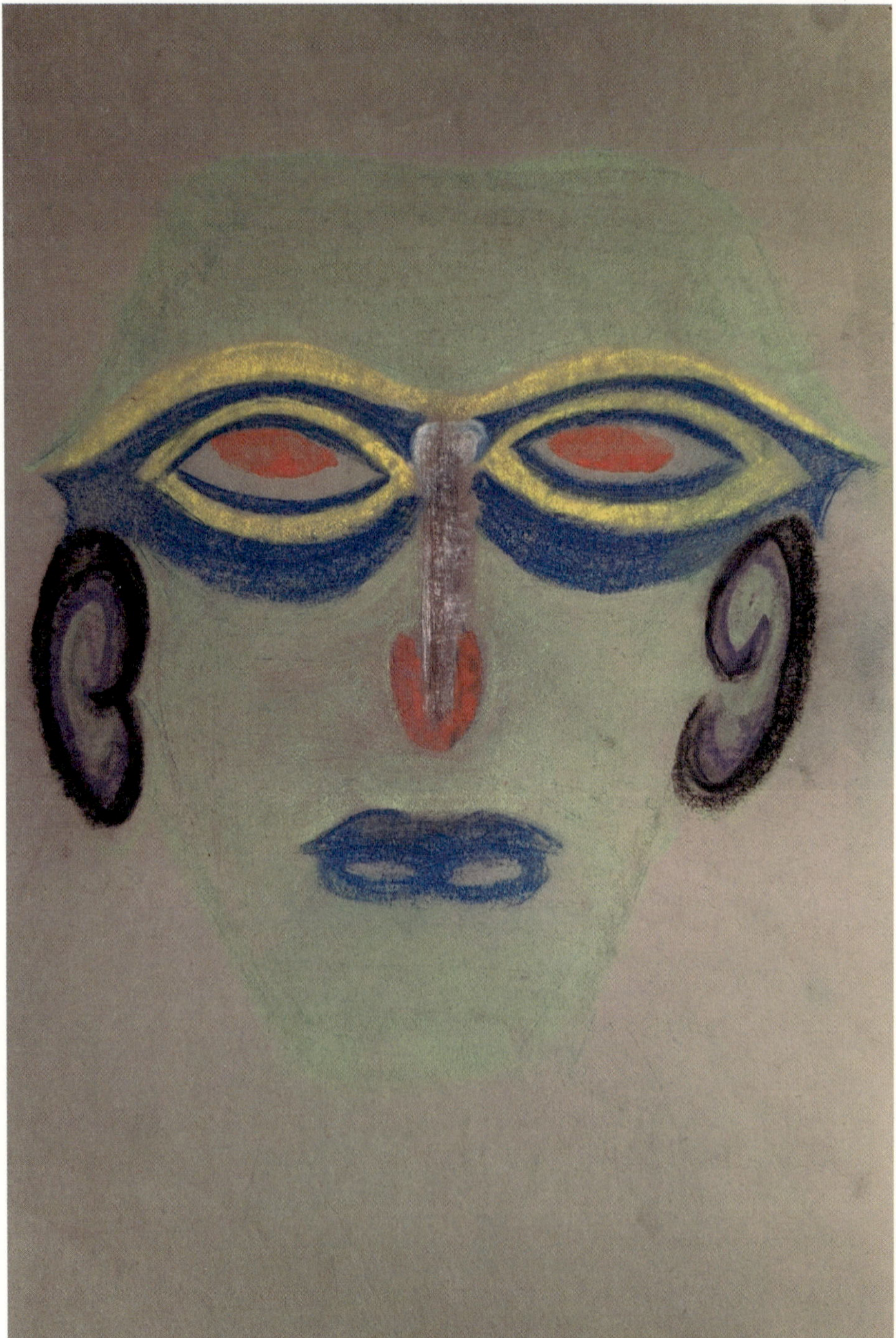

LEFT: *Green Faced Being* (c. early 1950s)

In the early 1950s Colquhoun created a number of rough magical diagrams which were effectively a human in a cruciform shape, coloured according to Kabbalistic, planetary or other esoteric principles. Some of these were studies for block like faces to be used in various mural projects, such as the heads of the Four Evangelists, *Heads of Angels*, created as a study for a mural for the Maze Hill Congregational Church in 1952, a project which never came to fruition. A piece similar to this one from 1951 called "The Green Visage" was created with a colour scheme according to planetary attributes, and eventually became the study for the head of John the Evangelist. This particular piece feels like a softer and more intuitive rendering that emerged from a much blockier original. Perhaps this reveals a true androgynous form of some sort of otherworldly being.

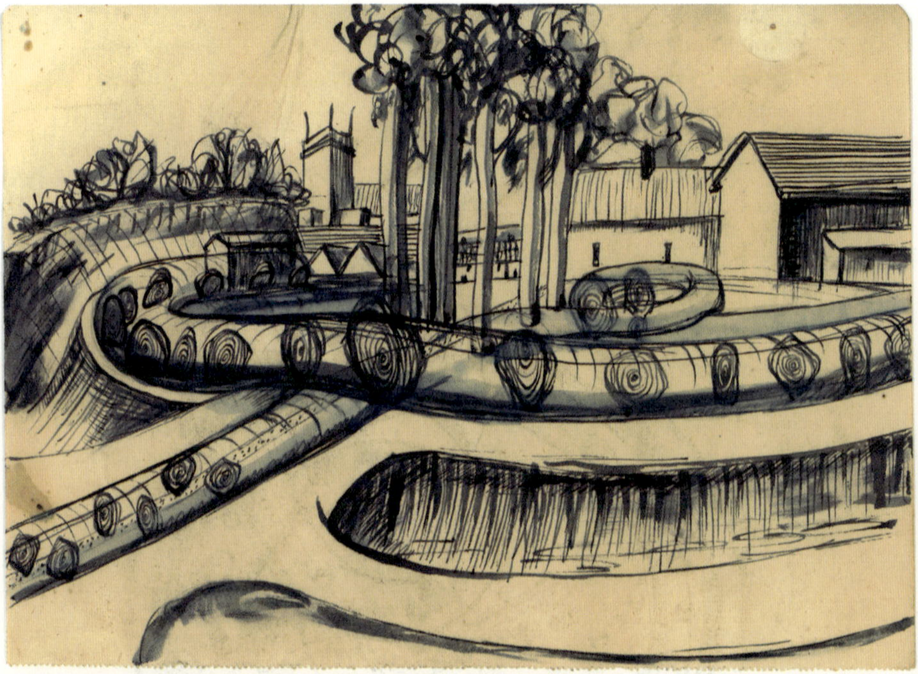

ABOVE & RIGHT: *Snakes Around Avebury* (c. late 1950s early 1960s) These watercolour and ink drawings are part of a series of sketches inspired by the 18th century antiquarian William Stukeley envisioning the stone monuments at Avebury as connected by the body of a giant snake. Stukeley was an influential early theorist writing about the imagined practices of the Druids and their relationship to megalithic monuments, believing them to have been the forerunners of the Christian patriarchs, and thus casting them in a rather pious light. Stukeley's 1743 treatise on Avebury, *Abury* [sic], *A Temple of the British Druids, with Some Others, Described* argued that the stone temples of British prehistory were designed according to the ancients' symbolic understanding of deity, and that in the case of Avebury the temple was designed to represent a serpent. Colquhoun's sketches here demonstrate her continuing engagement not only with contemporary Druidry, but also her continuing interest in antiquarian scholarship.

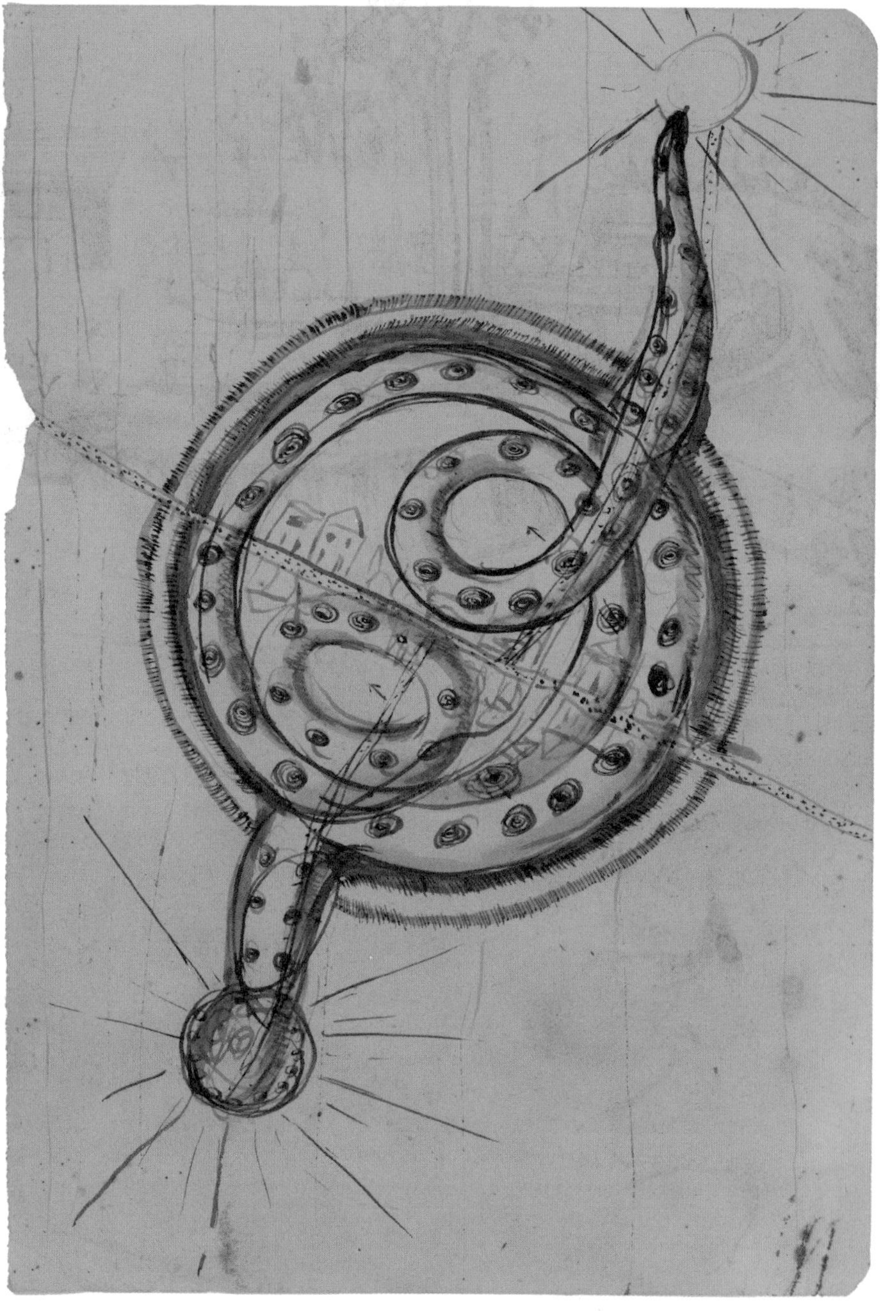

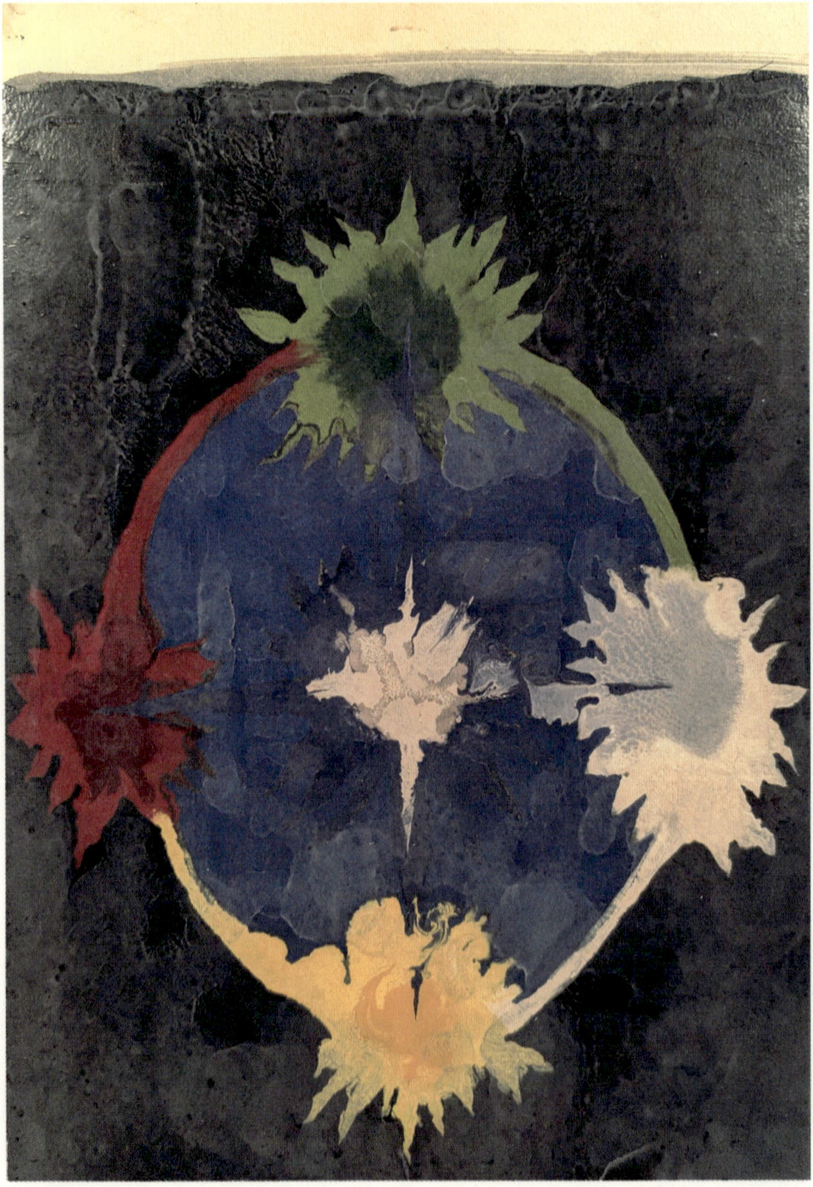

LEFT: ***Mandala of the Five Buddhas* (1979)**

This enamel appears to have been an abstracted version of the Geometric Mandala of the Five Buddhas, which she created at least one version of for a friend in 1979. It contains colours associated with the five Buddhas, with one at each cardinal direction and one in the centre. The positions of these Buddhas are not fixed and can change according to the practice. A draft version of this mandala includes the names of each of the Buddhas in the centre of each of the bursts of colour. From the top clockwise, green for Amoghasiddhi, blue for Akshobhya, yellow for Ratnasambhava, red for Amitabha, and white for Vairocana at the centre. Traditionally Mandalas of the Five Buddhas are used for meditation on wisdom and wholeness, yet in the draft she has also added some characteristics which seem perhaps more aspirational, such as creativity or success, than those characteristics assigned to each of these Buddhas in traditional practice.

OVERLEAF TOP: *Sketch of a Flattened Tesseract* (c. 1940s)

This enigmatic diagram is a detail for a larger study likely from the 1940s. The larger study was of a human form with what appears to be a tesseract in the central part of the torso, surrounding a hexagram in blue and red and purple. A tesseract is a two-dimensional rendering of a theoretical fourth dimensional space. The hexagram at the centre of the figure, situated around the navel, suggests the union of gendered polarities that Colquhoun frequently used as a shorthand for spiritual development and the transcending of gender. The attributes of the twelve coloured sections lining the interior of the square are unclear, but they feature in a number of different sketches in slightly different colour configurations. It is possible that they referenced interior colours of the tesseract, which Colquhoun also attempted to capture in other exercises. Alternately, they may have Kabbalistic attributions. This may have been part of Colquhoun's project to represent the condition of extra dimensionality on the spiritually advanced body.

RIGHT BOTTOM: *Pantacle of the Earthly Paradise* (c. 1950s)
The draft of this magical operation was labelled Pantacle of the Earthly Paradise and may date to the 1950s. Two colour versions of her use of this technique exist and it is difficult to know what the intent of the one pictured here is. The method seems to be an amalgamation of formats and techniques, primarily inspired by Yeats' esoteric readings of Dante's *Inferno* in *A Vision*. There were a number of esoteric readings of Dante's *Inferno* in the early twentieth century, notably René Guénon's *The Esoterism of Dante* from 1925, which may have inspired Yeats' and possibly Colquhoun's approach.

The title and general circular form refer to a Biblical geography of Eden, which is a circle cut into four quarters separated by rivers, although in Colquhoun's working here the quarters are separated by snakes. Colquhoun considered each of the quarters to correspond to Yeats' notion of the Four Faculties, as outlined in *A Vision*, describing functions and tendencies within the human psyche; Will, Mask, Creative Mind, and Body of Fate. Understanding the dynamics of these faculties was key to helping personality integration. In this magical working, Colquhoun attributed one quadrant of the circle to each of these principles, and assigned certain aspirational categories to each one. For instance, in a different draft of this technique, the upper left-hand quadrant was labelled 'Will', and contained the categories of Sex, Health and Esoteric Development. She then created a statement of desire for each category. In the category labelled sex she articulated the desire for "Sex with an appreciative husband, who is also attractive, helpful, loyal, adequately well off, considerate, potent, with an understanding of maithuna (sacred intercourse)." In the section labelled transport, she wrote "Be driven in a comfortable, heated car." Clearly, she understood that good magic requires the most specific intentions. She would then condense her statements of desire into a single sigil, created after the style of Austin Osman Spare. She would likely have eliminated the repeating letters in a sentence of desire, and then combined the remaining letters into a single symbol, concentrating the sentence into a single graphic which she then placed in the centre of a coloured background.

Other drafts of this project have a slightly different arrangement of the quadrants, and colours, which suggest perhaps a separate magical operation. It is notable that this technique has perhaps some of the most detailed documentation of any extant among her papers, providing not only an insight into her magical practice, but also her life and aspirations.

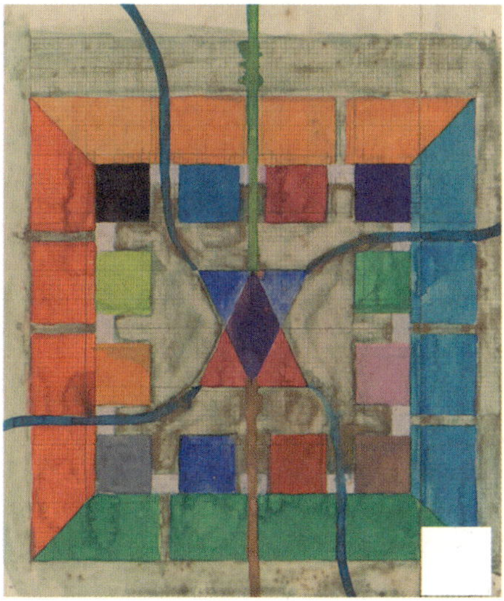

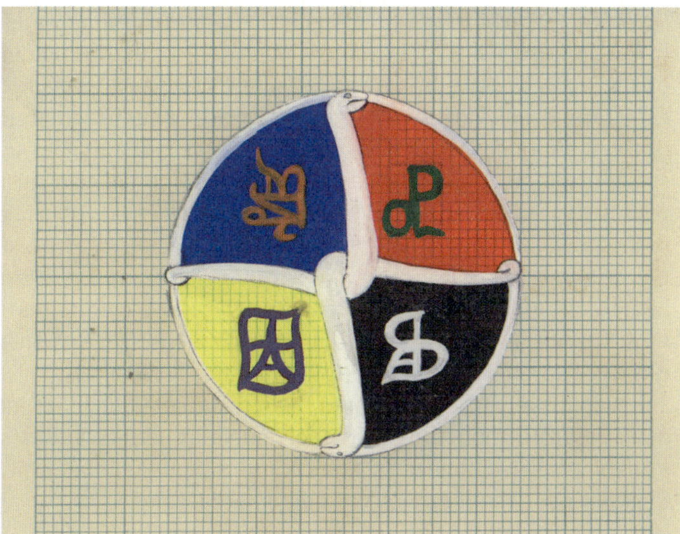

SIGILLVM DEI ÆMETH.

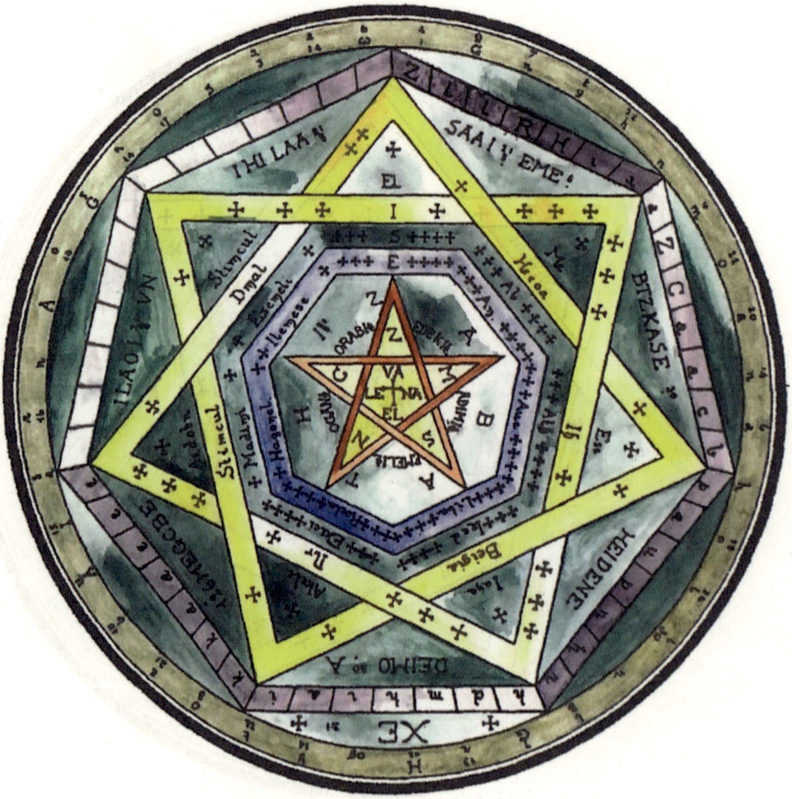

THIS SPREAD: These are two coloured versions of the *Sigillum Del Aemeth*, the sigil developed by John Dee derived from the medieval grimoire *The Sworn Book of Honorius*. These illustrate the essay "Colour and the Two Sigils (1979)", p.290. One version is a more painterly watercolour and the second more a solid version which Colquhoun likely would have favoured for contemplative exercises.

SIGILLVM DEI ÆMETH.

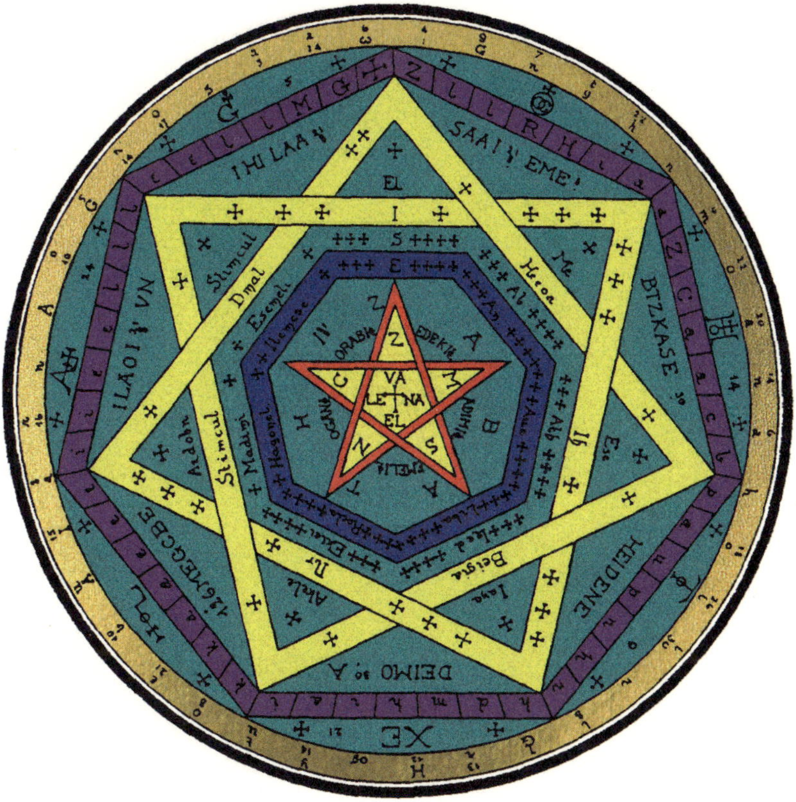

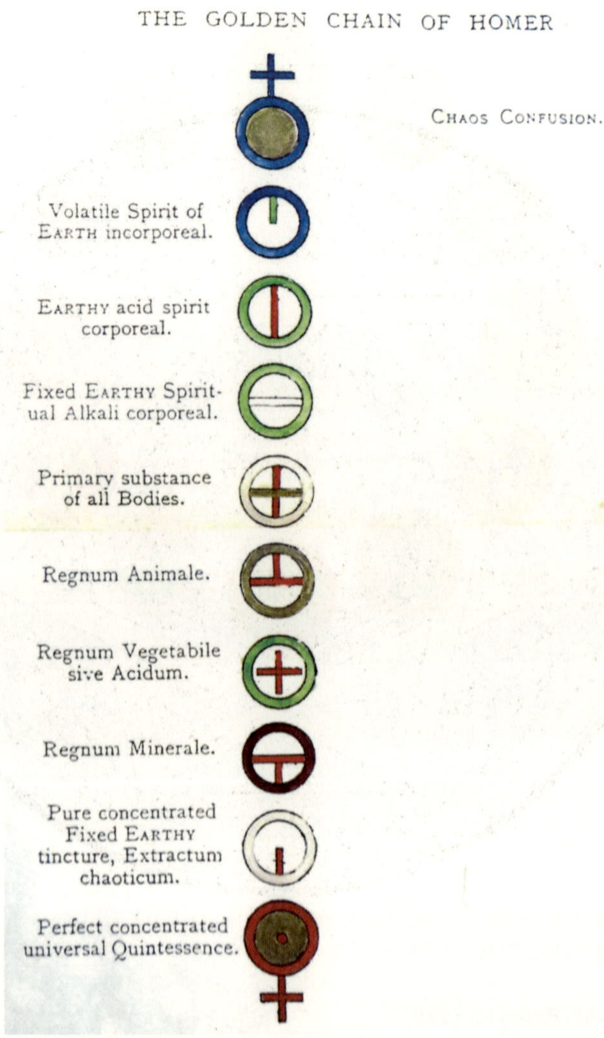

ABOVE: This is Colquhoun's version of the coloured Homer's Golden Chain which illustrates "Note on the Colouring of Homer's Golden Chain Diagram" (1979), p.292. Image courtesy of Marcus Williamson.

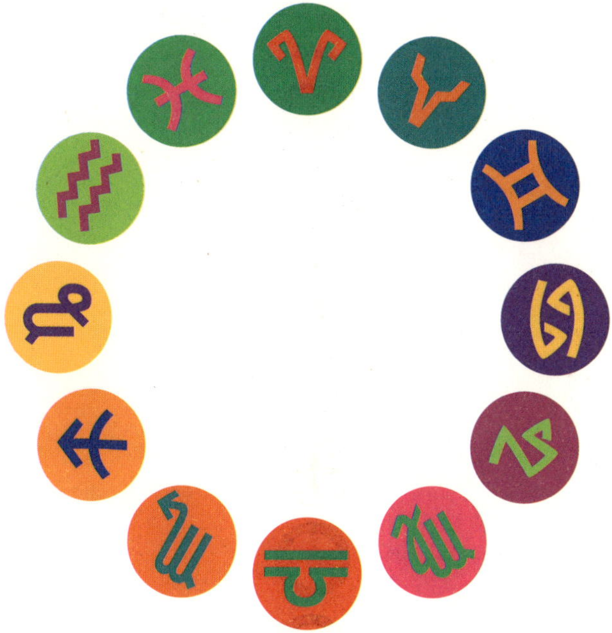

ABOVE: This piece illustrates the technique of placing zodiacal symbols on fields of opposing colours from "The Zodiac and the Flashing Colours (1979)", p.285.

OVERLEAF: ***Angel*** **(c. 1979)**
This lovely luminous angel in flashing colours of gold and purple may possibly be a representation of the Archangel Raphael who in some ceremonial magic systems is associated with the cardinal direction of east and the element of air. Traditionally Raphael would be holding a caduceus, but in this piece he appears to be holding a sword which would be characteristic of the Archangel Michael. The dating is based on other portraits of angels that Colquhoun completed in 1979.

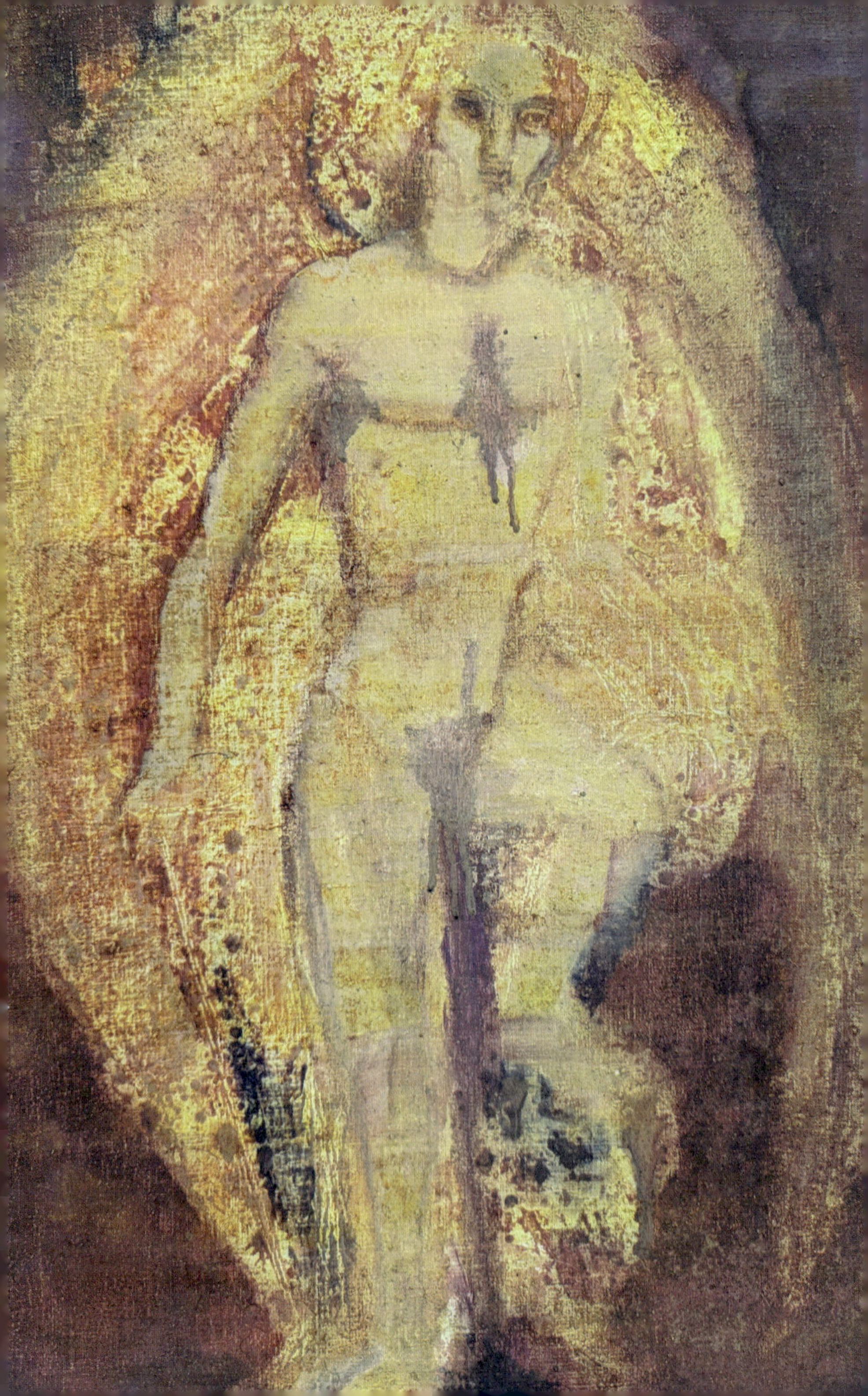

12. A few days later, on December 29, I was walking down the road between the church and my cottage. It was about a quarter to five in the evening and growing dusk, the weather being mild and misty. On my right I saw a point of orange-coloured light in the sky; it was difficult to guess how far away but it seemed between twenty and thirty feet from the ground. It vanished instantly.

13. There is now a gap for almost a year; but on the first of November, 1966, I was crossing the garden about 8.30 in the evening. I saw a vivid white flash that reached the zenith of the northern sky. It was in bright moonlight, the weather being cold and clear except for a few clouds on the eastern horizon.

14. This was followed by a sighting about ten minutes past ten on the night of November 21. The weather was cold and damp with little wind; as I walked up the road leading from the harbour to my cottage, a waxing moon shed a fitful light between the clouds. On nearing the garden gate a light flashed from behind the trunk of a cedar-tree in my garden bordering the lane. Its source seemed to be about ten feet above ground, but its illumination reached the full height of the tree. Compared to the one which I had seen over the meadow and which looked like a domestic light-bulb switched on and off, this was more like a flash-bulb.

15. On New Year's Eve, 1966, I was walking home from the village with my niece soon after seven in the evening. Darkness had fallen, the weather was fairly mild and fine but the sky was covered with a thin mist. As we passed the church-yard on our left I thought I saw a distant whitish flash over the fields to our right—that is, southwards; but I did not mention it as I was not certain. A few minutes later when I was opening the door of the cottage, I saw a double flash in the zenith above us, not brilliant but quite distinct. I remarked on it but my niece had not noticed it.

These lights may be classified into three main types:

(1) **The extended flash** (including the "zenith-flash"), which I have seen five times, whitish or bluish with a subdued but distinct illumination, and often covering half a mile or more of country-side.

(2) **The electric-bulb flash** (four sightings) yellow or orange with brilliant illumination and much usually nearer to the ground.

(3) **The travelling light** (four in number) yellow or orange, bright, moving parallel with the ground or falling through the air.

So far all sightings have occurred from July to December, and most between evening-dusk and midnight. To the suggestion that those on appropriate dates may be explained as fireworks, I would point out that, besides a general impossibility of situation, all the manifestations were soundless. But is it an instance of "synchronicity" that the Celtic fire-festival commemorating the dead, Samhain, occurs in early November and that Guy Fawkes Night perpetuates some of its celebrations?

Though the lights are sometimes seen when more than one person is present, they are noticed by only one at a time. (This may be due to their instantaneous appearance.)

What is the explanation of these phenomena? Some while after experiencing the first instance I have recorded, I was told that near the entrance to the avenue mentioned in my account is a hollowed stone locally called "the Devil's Drinking-Trough". The Devil is supposed to drink from it each evening, and the air about the entrance is said always to strike chill. But this doesn't "explain" anything!

I believe Spiritualists claim to see globes of light at a séance, but what I see is always out of doors and always unexpected: to look out for the lights seems to inhibit their appearance. (Perhaps the reason why I have not seen any lately is that I have grown too alert?) Even if one classes them as "spiritualist" manifestations, what exactly are they?

No special conditions of weather or moon seem to effect the appearing of the lights, and the explanation of "summer lightning" does not meet the case, because of the type of weather prevailing at the times noted. Thunder-storms are rare in this part of the country anyway, since it is a peninsula; and no thunder was reported in local weather-bulletins at the relevant dates. A meteor would burn out well before it reached the short distances from the ground which I describe.

One of my instances, No. 9, agrees with descriptions of the so-called "scouts" sent out from Unidentified Flying Objects; while No. 14 may perhaps be explained as "electric plasma" since there is an electric pole a few yards behind the cedar-tree. The theory of "ball-lightning" might cover some of my examples and that of "static electricity" may account for others. But does anyone know what these "scientific" phrases mean? Some of them seem no more precise than the terms "etheric" and "astral", clear to Theosophists. I'll consider any theory as long as I'm not told that what I have seen is a weather-balloon or the planet Venus! †

The Infernal Worlds of The Qabalah (c. 1968-69)

In this essay Colquhoun explains the need to understand the material impact of the "averse worlds" of the Qabalah, known as the Qliphoth. They are frequently interpreted as shells, distractions or barriers to enlightenment, indicating the dark side of the Kabbalistic sephiroth. This piece, like many of her Kabbalistic essays, is dense, but her purpose is to give the reader the tools through which the powers and rules of the Qliphoth can be known so that they can be effectively managed on a day-to-day basis. She argues that these forces can already be materially identified and are a natural part of the supernatural cosmos, so working with these powers can be worthwhile. It is difficult to know when this essay was originally written, although internal evidence, primarily the reference to *Insight Magazine: A Journal of the Occult*, in which she had published, suggests that she was preparing this version in the late 1960s[1].

In describing these Worlds, the use of spatial imagery, though misleading, is inevitable since the diagram of the Tree of Life is itself a spatial concept. Again, the classification of the Qeliphotic abodes is a near impossibility, entailing as it does the imposition of order upon a realm essentially chaotic. Nor is it easy to find reliable information, as many authorities fight shy of the subject altogether or pass it over with the timidest reference. Exceptions are Francis

---

1 In private correspondence of 22 May, 2024, Richard Shillitoe has also assessed this as a likely date.

Barrett; then later, S. L. MacGregor Mathers, A. E. Waite, Aleister Crowley, Allan Bennett and more recently Idries Shah and E. J. Langford Garstin's unpublished material, apart from the traditional Grimoires and certain treatises dependent from the main texts of the *Zohar*.

Redoubtable as the averse Worlds and their ruling potencies must be, to ignore their existence is merely to give them free play; while to batten them down under hatches, as the Archangel Michael is said to do, is to produce the lamentable results which are plain to be seen. The Anglican Church showed itself indeed when it decided a few years ago that it no longer believed in the Devil! If one accepts the supernatural in any form one cannot, without adopting an attitude of "Pollyanna" complacency, pass over its destructive aspects. Destructive, that is, to contingent humanity; they may fulfil some unknown constructive role in the cosmos. In our world no one can doubt that the Shatterers (averse Chesed) and the Burners (averse Geburah) are as active today as they ever were, especially in the devastations of modern warfare. The Frustrators too (averse Chokmah) must enjoy themselves in the complications of bureaucracy, the Concealers (averse Binah) in the hush-hush activities of industry, commerce and government, the Disputers (averse Tiphereth) in the strife of international relations and the Deceivers (averse Hod) in the double-talk of propaganda. Some would add the influence of the Obscene Ass (averse Iesod) and the Woman of Night (the averse of Malkuth's "Bride") in the pullulation of pornography and the general flaunting of sex, though these are less harmful than the forces of trickery and violence.

In the cosmographic system of the Qabalah, the Tree of Life (Otz Chiim) as generally recognised and employed exists in Assiah (Oshih), lowest of the Four Worlds, that of material form. This is not its only manifestation: it could not exist as Assiah if it did not originate in the higher Worlds. Its first emanation is Atziluth (ATzLUTh), the highest World, that of Archetypes, whose Kether (KThR) is the immediate product of Ain Soph Aur (AIN SUPh AUR, the

Limitless Light), the closest to manifestation of the three Veils of Negative Existence.

The Limitless Light concentrates Itself as the Mezlah (MZLH, the divine Influence) which descends the Tree in the path of the Lightning-Flash, passing through the ten Sephiroth (ShPhRUTh) from Kether, the Crown, to Malkuth (MLKUTh), the Kingdom. This Lightning Flash cuts across the diagram of the Netibuth (NThBUTh, Paths) which connect the Sephiroth one with another, using only eight of them: Aleph, Daleth, Teth, Lamed, Nun, Pé, Resh, Tau (A, D, T, L, N, Ph, R, Th). Having thus reached the Malkuth of Atziluth, the Mezlah overflows as a "current" into the Kether of the World next below, that of Briah (BRIH, Creativity), again following the Lightning Flash down to the Briatic Malkuth, which touches the Kether of the next World—Ietzirah (ITzIRH, Formation). The same process is repeated here and so through Assiah, the Material World, the Kether of one plane always lying immediately above the Malkuth of the one next below.

At the Malkuth of Assiah the descent of the Mezlah ceases, the limit of organised existence as humanly cognised having been reached, though not necessarily the limit of dense matter. The Tree has expanded itself fourfold, becoming "the four hundred desirable worlds"; but beneath it is another Tree, the image of itself reflected as in turbid water giving back a deceitful image; and the Worlds it pictures are undesirable. This is the Tree in the Realm of Shades (Olam-ha-Qeliphoth, OULM HQLIPhUTh). As it is a mirror-image, the reflection of its Malkuth-of-Assiah lies contiguous to the Malkuth-of-Assiah in the "right" Tree; and its Kether, instead of representing a more exalted mode of being, plunges the more deeply into night. The same holds for the intervening averse Worlds: their counterparts, or perhaps better to say counterfeits, replacing "the ineffable Sephiroth." First, the ten Earths subsist in seven "palaces" (Assiah), then similarly the Hells (Ietzirah), next the orders of Qeliphoth (Briah) and finally the ten Arch-devils of the averse Atziluth.

It has been suggested that there can be no Qeliphotic reflection of Atziluth since the Archetype is not susceptible of division—parallel to that of the Red Dragon who writhes around the "right" tree but cannot raise his head above Daath (DOTh) thus leaving the Supernal Triangle untouched. This idea seems too optimistic as regards the averse reflection of the Tree since there is also a tradition of three obscure states, A'athiel (OthIL, Uncertainty) Belia'al (BLIOL, Worthlessness) and Qemetiel (QMThIL, Crowds of Gods) which give back in distorted reflection the Veils of Negative Existence above Atziluth.

A previous study (*Insight*, No. 13) dealt with the seven Earths which comprise the averse Assiah. To amplify this, it is possible that a hierarchy of Cortices or "Shells" should be assigned as rulers of the various Earths. The list is incomplete, as may be expected with Qeliphotic data, but their names seem to be:

> Ogiel, governing Cheled (ChLD) and Thebel (ThBL), "the Wet Earth" of Malkuth and Iesod (ISUD);
>
> Adramalek: Arqa (ARQA), "the Ground" of Hod (HUD);
>
> Baal Chana'an: Tziah (TzIH), "the Sandy Earth" of Netzach (NTzCh);
>
> Zomiel: Nishiah (NshIH), "the Pasture" of Tiphereth (ThPhARTh);
>
> Usiel: Gia (GIA), "the Undulating Earth" of Geburah (GBURH);
>
> Azariel: Adamah (ADMH), "the Red Earth" of Chesed (ChSD);
>
> Aretz: (ARTz), "the Dry Earth" of the Infernal Triangle, is ruled by Ghogiel in the stations of Binah (BINH) and Chokmah (ChKMH) and by Kathariel in that of Kether. These Cortices are beings of a relatively insubstantial nature, able to draw vitality from other life-forms but lacking in active malevolence themselves.

A stage deeper, in the adverse Ietzirah, lie the ten Hells arranged as before in seven "palaces". The Hells of Islamic tradition correspond closely with these, from which they are in fact derived; and the circles of Dante's *Inferno* also provide a suggestive parallel. First of the Hells of the Qabalah, contiguous to the Kether of the Earths, (Aretz) and comprising both the Malkuth and the Iesod of the averse Ietzirah, is Gehinnom (GIHNM). The Biblical Gehenna, translated simply as "Hell", with the dark angel Kushiel as presiding genius.

Next, as counterpart of Hod, and ruled by the angel Labatiel, lie the poetically-named Gates of Death (Sha'ari Moth, Shori Muth) hinting that the Infernal World is as yet scarcely opened.

In the place of Netzach and with Shaphtiel as overlord, is the Shadow of Death (Tzelemoth, TzMLUTh) whose name again implies that the full horror of the nether regions is not yet to be felt.

Averse Tiphareth is found as the Pit of Destruction (Bar Shacheth, BAR ShChTh) under the presidency of Makathiel.

Geburah becomes the Clay of Death (Titahion, TITAHIUN) under Chutriel and Chesed is Perdition (Abaddon, ABDUN) under Pasiel.

The Infernal Triangle is again formed, this time from the averse stations of Binah, Chokmah and Kether, which collectively include the Grave of Death of Earth (Sheol, ShAUL), under the reign of Dalkiel. They are further distinguished: Chokmah and Binah are replaced by Tohu and Bohu, the Formless and the Void—hence the French phrase meaning disorder—and the white brilliance proper to Kether by Darkness (Chaseth, ChShTh).

The Seven Deadly Sins being traditionally attributed to the planets are aptly assigned to the planetary Netibuth of the averse Ietzirah. These are given as tabulated by Christianity, but are closely paralleled in other moralistic systems. Thus *Avaricia* is encountered on the saturnian path of Tau, *Superbia* (Pride) on the solar path of Resh, *Ira* (Wrath), on the martian path of Pé, *Gula* (Greed), on the jovian path of Kaph, *Luxuria* (Lechery) on the venusian path of Daleth, *Accidia* (Sloth) on the lunar path of Gimel, and *Invidia* (Envy) on the mercurial path of Beth.

The last-named Kether (as in the previous world) touches the Malkuth of the plane next below—that of the averse Briah, represented by the ten Orders of Qeliphoth in the arrangement of the demonic hierarchies—as usual into seven "palaces" or abodes—Malkuth and Iesod are grouped together, now as the Younger Lilith, The Woman of the Night and Gamaliel, the Obscene Ass. These entities are to be understood less as individuals than as totems of devilish clans or covens, the direction of whose power is thus signified. One may guess that the same is true of the Qeliphotic Hod—Samael (SMAL), Deceivers of the Netzach, A'arab Zaraq (ORB ZRQ), the Ravens of Dispersion who, averse of Venus' doves, work for the separation of lovers; and the harmony of Tiphereth, marred by the Tagiriron, (TGIRIRUN), Disputers. To the averse Chesed and Geburah, the Ga'agsheklah (GOShKLH), Shatters and the Golachab (GULAChAB) Burners, already mentioned, are attributed; the latter are described as "Giants like volcanoes"—unconsciously suggested in the earth-fire music of Stravinski's *Rite of Spring*. Once again an Infernal Triangle is formulated, now by the Setariel (SThARIAL), Concealers and the Ga'aghiel (OGIAL), Frustrators with the Thaumiel (ThAUMIAL), Dual Contending Forces, usurping the unity of Kether.

While it is probable that in the three Worlds just described equivalents of all the Netibuth (Paths) exist, could their names be traced, it is chiefly in the averse Briatic World that they are documented. Thus the Orders of Qeliphoth are here increased from ten to twenty-two, the Zodiacal paths being ruled by entities comparable to those which replace the Sephiroth (The Clangers, Tzaldimiron (TzALDIMIRUN) replacing Gemini must be having the time of their lives in the din of today's mechanization!) The elemental paths are governed by the Four Demon Kings and the planetary paths by the averse planetary spirits. Thus the path of Shin becomes the territory of Paimon, Demon King of Fire and that of Pé, attributed to Mars, of Bartzabal, the malign spirit of this planet.

The Dual Contending Forces or "Twins of God" mark the limit of this Briatic World and touch the confines of the averse Atziluth wherein the most powerful regents of the Qeliphoth hold sway. In the first "palace" reign Na'amah (NOMH) and the Elder Lilith; in the second, Belial (BLIAL) and in the third, Asmodai (AShMDAI) who according to *The Lesser Key of Solomon* appears with three heads—of a ram, a bull and a man. He rides on a dragon and brandishes a spear—though Barrett's *The Magus* depicts him with only one (cat-like) head. The fourth "palace" belongs to Choia (ChIUA, the Beast); the fifth, to Ashtoroth (AShThRUTh) who looks like an angel mounted on a dragon and carries a serpent—though Barrett gives him (or her?) an ugly face with goat's ears and horns; and the sixth, to Lucifuge, the Fleer-from-Light. Binah in this Infernal Triangle is replaced by Ashith Zenunim (AshTh ZNUNIM), the Woman of Whoredoms; Chokmah by Samael (SMAL), the False Accuser and Kether, by Satan and Moloch, who reinforce the dualism of the same station on the previous plane. It is possible that the elemental paths come under the governance of the four Demon Emperors, superiors of the Demon Kings, according to a variant of *The Lesser Key*; and the two goetic demons of the Decans may be fittingly ascribed, three to each Zodiacal path.

The Elder Lilith is the wife of Samael, so there must be a peculiarly close link between Iesod and Chokmah in the averse Atziluth, stretching (from one direction) across the "Abyss" which, in every World, separates the Triangle from the rest of the Tree. The direction of the Mezlah being reversed in the infernal abodes, one must visualise a flash ascending from Chokmah (Samael) along the fiery and Arien path of Hé, and a dart descending from Iesod (the Elder Lilith) down the fiery and Sagittarian path of Samek, to be conjoined in Tiphereth as Choia, the Beast. Similarly, the Younger Lilith being Asmodai's wife, a link must stretch, not only across an "Abyss" but from one World to another—namely, from the averse Atziluth to the averse Briah. Here the flash ascends from the Netzach of Atziluth (Asmodai) along the lunar path of Qoph, through the domain of Na'amah into that of the Dual Contending Forces of the averse Briah and thence along the lunar path of Gimel, while a dark ray descends from Malkuth (the Younger Lilith) by the Saturnian path of Tau through the region of the

Obscene Ass and along the Path of Samek, to celebrate the nuptials of hell among the Disputers (Tagiriron).

Beyond the depths of averse Atziluth, already almost unimaginable, lie those further profundities mentioned before. The Veils of Negative Existence above the "right" Tree reflect themselves into dark waters where the Limitless Light is given back as A'athiel (Uncertainty), the Limitless as Belia'al (Worthlessness) and the Absolute as Qemetiel (Crowds of Gods)—chaotic multiplicity opposed to the One. As to the medium by which this image is received, it can only be, though a state of potentiality beyond manifestation, the polar opposite of Ain. There is an impression of endless plasticity, of shapes appearing only to merge with other shapes which in their turn melt away in an everlasting flux.

The more one can discover about the lower depths, the better one can deal with them. An attempt has been here made to map them out, recognising that they subsist both microcosmically and macrocosmically. Is anyone invested with the courage and protection needed to explore them in practice? †

Surrealism and Hermetic Poetry (after 1971)

This rather clumsy essay appears to be an attempt to demonstrate the abiding interest in magic and the occult by the surrealists. This may be a response to her parting of the ways with the British surrealists in 1940. While she was not expelled for her occult interest, per se, it was very clear that her desire to participate in occult orders and communities was at odds with Mesens' vision for the wartime British surrealists. Colquhoun noted later that Mesens seems to dislike the occult, which she found strange given the preoccupations of Breton and the early surrealists. It is interesting from a formal perspective in that it is one of the few times that Colquhoun provides translations for her French quotes and uses citations within the text. Although this appears to have stayed unpublished, it was submitted to *Man, Myth and Magic* in 1971, but it was rejected for lack of space. In a personal communication, Richard Shillitoe has stated that he has seen an early version of the manuscript with notes made by Toni del Renzio, Colquhoun's husband from 1943-1947, indicating initial drafts or possibly a collaboration in the early 1940s[1].

Reminiscences in the earlier essays of W. B. Yeats hint at a subterranean current reappearing in the culture of his time; he recalls, for instance, Strindberg's search for the Philosophers' Stone in the Montparnasse of the nineties; and "a young Arabic scholar who displayed a large, roughly-made gold ring which had grown to the shape of his finger.

1 Shillitoe, personal communication, 22 May, 2024.

Its gold had no hardening alloy, he said, because it was made by his master, a Jewish Rabbi, of alchemical gold"[2].

Who could resist the excitement of such glimpses as these? Yeats was fond of quoting the words of Stéphane Mallarmé, "All our age is full of the trembling of the veil"—and he often mentioned Stanislas de Gaeta; at the epoch with which the essays, *Ideas of Good and Evil*, are chiefly concerned, none was more assiduous in the hermetic quest. De Gaeta's chief work, published before his death at the age of thirty-seven, was the three-volume *Essais de Sciences Maudites*. Little known in Britain, being of blood drawn from Italy, Germany and Lorraine, he is nonetheless the revered ancestor of a double line—modern alchemy, and that "alchemy of the word" which is poetry after Rimbaud.

Whatever its prime intention, most alchemy is recorded, and these records are a branch of imaginative literature. They may take the form of verse, like *The Book of Lambspring* by Nicholas Bernaud Delphinas, favourably comparable to Quarles' *Emblems*:

> In India is a most pleasant wood,
> In which two birds are bound together.
> One is snowy white; the other is red.
>
> *The Book of Lambspring*. Figure VIII.
> (Tr. A. E. Waite, 1893)

or the form of poetic prose, such as the tracts of Thomas Vaughan, to name only one of the many who could be cited:

> There is in every star and in this elemental world a certain principle which is the "Bride of the Sun"... Know then for certain that the magician's sun and moon are two universal peers, male and female, a king and queen regents, always young and never old. (*Anima Magica Abscondita*, 1650).

2 From the Epilogue in Yeats' *Per Amica Silentia Lunae*, (1918).

The twin brothers, Henry and Thomas Vaughan, are an instance from English literary history of magic poet and poetic mage.

Alchemy may be many things—it may be medicine, psychology, chemistry or metaphysics. Today alchemy often takes the form of psychology or of metaphysics—though there are some practitioners with a laboratory in the back garden—since medicine and chemistry have, in the historical process, developed in a different direction. As psychology, alchemy has been profoundly explored by Jung, and Silberer made some earlier reconnaissance. The patients of these men have often been unwitting alchemists, in so far as their dreams and hypnogogic phantasies have provided material for the *opus*; but Jung himself, through deliberate effort and sympathetic perception in such works as *The Secret of the Golden Flower* brought to light the significance of this material. In an essay "The Idea of Redemption in Alchemy", he notes:

> ...there are good and bad authors in alchemistic literature as in all others... inferior writings are easily detected by their abundant recipes, their careless and unrefined composition, their obtrusive mystification, their terrible dullness and their shameless insistence upon the manufacture of gold. Good books are recognised by the industry, the care and the obvious mental integrity of the author. (*The Integration of the Personality*. Tr. Stanley Dell. 1939).

Jung goes on to suggest that the practical work of the alchemist was sometimes little more than a pretext to set going the process of projection—that is, the throwing out upon external nature, wherever attractive analogies are found therein, of unconscious psychic contents, which are then perceived as visions or "hallucinations". This is what the alchemists called *imaginatio*; and though there are some points of contrast, there are also many analogies with the various kinds of automatism discovered and practised by surrealists. The alchemistic philosophers were also familiar with the inner dialogue well-known alike to poet and analytical psychologist, which Jung defines as "a living dialectic relation to certain dominants of the unconscious"; and they knew of the "dialectical opposites" in the psyche upon which the researches of analytical psychology have thrown light. These are some of the present-day concepts with which alchemy deals; and Jung suggests that we are nearing a moment in history when that intermediary realm—between matter and the psyche—with which alchemy is occupied "may come to life again, the physical and psychic be once more blended". In the words of Hermes:

> It is necessary that at the end of the world heaven and earth be bound together, this being the philosophical word.

One is reminded of the confession of faith of André Breton (1896-1968), founder of surrealism:

> Je crois à la résolution future de ces deux états en apparence si contradictoires, que sont le rêve et la réalité, en une sorte de réalité absolue, de surréalité, si l'on peut ainsi dire[3]. (*Manifeste de Surréalisme*. 1924).

The alchemistic search for the Elixir of Immortality that should, as Jung has shown, "produce a *corpus subtile*" or Body of Light, may be compared with the aspiration of a writer sympathetic to surrealism, Nicolas Calas, towards the conquest of death:

> If death is not a biological necessity and already tends to be outworn, then old age is no longer a fatal biological necessity, and we must overcome that too. (*Foyers d'Incendie*. Tr. *Partisan Review*. 1940).

Much inspired poetry of our time stems from the Symbolist movement—taking this word in its widest sense—which flourished, together with its many magical and occult connections, at the end of last century. This descent is clearly traced by André Breton in *Arcane 17*. (1944):

---

3 "I believe that in the future these two states, dream and reality, which seem so contradictory, will be resolved into a kind of absolute reality, a *surreality* if such it may be called."

> grands poètes de ce dernier siècle l'ont admirablement compris, depuis Hugo dont viennent d'être révelées les attaches très étroites avec l'école de Fabre d'Olivet, en passant par Nerval, dont les sonnets fameux se referènt à Pythagore, à Swedenborg, par Baudelaire qui emprunte notoirement aux occultistes leur théorie des "correspondences", par Rimbaud, dont a l'apogée de son pouvoir créateur, on ne saurait trop souligner le caractere des lectures—it suffit de se reporter a la bibliothèque de Charleville—jusqu'à Apollinaire chez qui alternant l'influence de la Cabale juive et celle des romans du cycle d'Arthur.

> ("The great poets of last century understood this perfectly from Hugo whose close links with the school of Fabre d'Olivet have just been revealed, passing through Nerval whose famous sonnets make reference to Pythagoras and Swedenborg, through Baudelaire who notoriously borrowed the doctrine of "correspondences" from the occultists, through Rimbaud, the character of whose reading when at the peak of his creative power cannot be underlined too strongly—it is enough to refer to the already-published list of the works he borrowed from the library at Charleville—up to Apollinaire in whom the influence of the Jewish Qabalah alternated with that of the stories in the Arthurian Cycle.")

That the nucleus of surrealism, in the figures of such men as André Breton, Pierre Mabille, Kurt Seligmann, André Masson and Max Ernst, were excited by occultism and maintained close links with magic is not surprising. Even a superficial observer, glancing through the pages of the review *Minotaure*, would be impressed by this pre-occupation. Throughout his writings, Breton stressed the fact that poetry and magic are two aspects of the same thing; as early as 1924, in the *Manifeste du Surréalisme*, he says:

> Héraclite est surréaliste dans la dialectique. Lulle est surréaliste dans la definition. Flamel est surréalist dans la nuit de l'or.
>
> ('Heraclitus is surrealist in dialectic. Lully is surrealist in definition. Flamel is surrealist in the night of gold'.)

And later, in the *Second Manifeste* (1930) he draws attention to the words of Nicholas Flamel:

> Il aimait a montrer ainsi "un Roy avec un grand coutelas, qui faisoit tuer en sa présence par des soldats, grande multitude de petits enfans, estoit puis après receuilly par d'autres soldats, et mis dans un grand vaisseau dans, lequel la Soleil et la Lune du ciel venoient se baigner" et tout près il y avait "un jeune homme avec des ailes aux talons, ayant une verge caducée en main, de laquelle il frappoit une salade que lui couvrait la tête. Contre iceluy venoit courant et volant à aisles ouverts un grand vieillard lequel, sur sa teste avoit une horloge attachée". Ne dirait-on pas le tableau surréaliste?
>
> ("He liked to show thus "a king with a big cutlass, who caused a huge crowd of small children to be killed in his presence by soldiers, and then afterwards gathered up by other soldiers and put into a great vessel in which the Sun and Moon of the sky came to bathe" and nearby there was "a young man with wings on his heels, having a Caduceus wand in his hand with which he was striking an antique helmet covering his head. Towards him came running and flying with wings out-stretched a tall old man who had a clock fastened on his head". Wouldn't you call this <u>the</u> surrealist picture?")

In fact, Breton quoted Raimond Lully as early as 1928 in *Le Surréalisme et la Peinture*, nor did he depart from the position which he then occupied in regard to the occult. The long poem *Fata Morgana* (1942) and then

Arcane 17 are, as their titles suggest, saturated with hermetic ideas and imagery; from the former here are some lines of the celebrated "ibis-mummy" passage:

> Ibis-mummy of combustion leaving a red spot
> in every cinder
> Ibis-mummy of perfection calling for the
> ceaseless fusion of imperfect creatures...
>
> ("Momie d'ibis de la combustion qui laisse en toute
> cendre un point rouge
> Momie d'ibis de la perfection qui appelle la
> fusion incessante des créatures imparfaites"...)

Four illustrations to the latter by Matta were based on designs for the Major Arcana of the Taro—the Lovers, the Chariot, the Blazing Star and the Moon. (According to Eliphas Lévi's system, the Blazing Star is numbered seventeen in the Atonts or Major Arcana.)

The contributions of Breton to *Le Surréalisme en 1947* show the same pre-occupations; these had been shared by a group of surrealists and sympathisers gathered temporarily at Marseilles in 1940-41 where, while awaiting a chance to escape to the Americas, they evolved their own card-pack. Here Génie, Sirène and Mage replaced the usual King, Queen and Knave, and each court-card of the four suits was given a name from surrealist hagiology, twelve personages in all being thus commemorated.

The essay *La Parole est à Péret* (1943) situates this writer[4] among those fascinated by esotericism; while Kurt Seligmann's *History of Magic* and the studies of Dr. Mabille supplied a more scientific angle on such themes.

Much more could be quoted to show the common ground between hermetic language and the imagery of surreal poetry, but one example must suffice. Compare Breton's line from *Le Revolver aux Chevaux Blancs*, (1932):

4 "La parole est à Péret" was a short 1943 essay by leading surrealist automatist poet Benjamin Péret addressing the idea of mythic thought.

> Ouvre sur le faux univers deux yeux de couleurs differentes
>
> ("To open two eyes of different colours upon the deceitful universe")

with a passage from the *Greater Holy Assembly*:

> In the eyes which are inferior are a right eye and a left eye, and they are of two diverse colours.
> *Kabbala Denudata* (Tr. S. L. MacGregor Mathers ed. 1938)

Was Breton's text obtained through that species of automatism evolved by him some years previously, or was he directly influenced by the Qabalah which he might well have known from de Pauly's translation of the *Zohar*, (1906-11)? †

Wisdom Tradition Of The Gael (1970)

This was a two-part series on Irish mythologically-inspired spirituality that Colquhoun wrote for *Prediction* Magazine, likely informed by her Druidry, and her work with Yeats' Irish esoteric material in which he was working to fuse Irish mythology and Kabbalistic structures to form an ideal Celtic esoteric system. Much of the legendary material here was taken from the *Lebor Gabála Érenn* (*The Book of Invasions*) a pseudo history of Ireland dating from the eleventh century, drawing heavily on legend and mythology. While these esoteric readings of Irish mythology are common among some Celtic enthusiasts, it's useful to keep in mind that they do not reflect current scholarly interpretations of this legendary material, although this was believed to represent historical fact for centuries.

In the first essay Colquhoun is proposing actual locations for the mythological cities of the Druids from *The Book of Invasions*. In a shared theme with a previous essay, she is exploring the idea of magical objects that have been placed in the landscape. There is an emphasis on the number four, a key organising principle in Hermeticism and Kabbalah, which helped Yeats and Colquhoun transpose one system onto another. The second essay in the series makes for rather uncomfortable reading. It is one of the few times that Colquhoun adopts a racialised perspective of esoteric systems. Earlier in her life she seemed to embrace an East West synthesis, but it may be that trends in the communities she was

working with during this period were unfortunately advocating some type of "racial purity" with regard to spiritual practice.

Wisdom Tradition Of The Gael; Part One: The Green Diamond (1970)

The bardic literature of the ancient Irish hints, notably in *The Book of Invasions*, that a wisdom-centre existed whence the gods brought their occult knowledge and magical treasures, and which chosen mortals could visit for instruction. It is mentioned as "the four cities of the world that was" and is situated "in the Northern Isles of the World". Here dwelt the Tuatha-de-Danaan, race of the mother-goddess Dana, before they came to settle in Eire and name the land after another of their goddesses.

So when they looked back to their place of origin, "northern" must have meant somewhere north of Ireland: the "isles" cannot be identified with the Hesperides, the Islands of the Blest, Hy-Brasil or any others lying westward in the Atlantic—survivors, perhaps on some subtle plane, of the Atlantean cataclysm some 11,000 years before. Rather do these "Northern Isles" belong to a still earlier age, that of the Hyperborean continent, and their remains must be sought among the Hebrides, the Faeroes, the Flannan Isles, Rona, St. Kilda and possibly parts of the Scottish mainland. Iceland may lie too far westward, and the Orkney and Shetlands too far to the east for inclusion.

Located somewhere in this area were the Four Cities[1] where the people of Dana practised their skills, whether magical, artistic or military. They were not (happily) cities in the modern sense, but sacred Colleges, each ruled by a "Druid" or spiritual teacher. The names of these Druids have come down to us—or perhaps their titles, since they may represent office or line of succession rather than individual: they are Uiscias, Esras, Semias and Morfesta.

1 In *Lebor Gabála* the Four Cities are Falias, Gorias, Finias and Murias.

The literary journalist William Sharp (1855-1905) when inspired by his poetic anima "Fiona Macleod", laments "the world that was" in his "Dirge of the Four Cities":

> Finias and Fallas
> Where are they gone?
> Does the wave hide Murias
> Does Gorias know the dawn?
> Does not the wind wail
> In the city of gems?...

Later in the poem he relates each city to one of the Four Elements and the cardinal points. He also describes in *The Divine Adventure* a vision of "the four ends of the green diamond which is the earth", giving a valuable hint as to the location of the Cities.

By cutting out a diamond-shape in paper and sliding it over a map of the Western Isles of Scotland one discovers possibilities for field-investigation.

Remembering that the Irish hero Cuchulain went for his training to "the land of shadows" or Skye, the island which maybe was named after the goddess Skatha, his instructor, one may guess that among the Cuillin Hills, whose name echoes the hero's own, the city or "college" of Findias was to be found.

Cuchulain's military training included esoteric exercises, some of which could be put to military use. He attained many "excellencies" (*Buada*): his ardour could heat three vats of water, a feat reminiscent of certain Tibetan adepts whose "psychic heat" could dry a succession of soaking sheets at midwinter. Then he possessed "the excellence in fine language", the *beurla na filed*, the language of poets (who were also prophets)—a metaphorical riddling code for use between initiates.

Apart from "the excellence in beauty", he achieved many athletic excellences useful in warfare. His training also included the nineteen "accomplishments" (*Clessa*), among them levitation and the ability to stand on the point of a spear, comparable with the fakir's invulnerability to sharp instruments or the yogi's to his bed of spikes. *Buada* and *Clessa* are terms comprising what a student influenced by Sanskrit texts would call *siddhis* (occult powers); and it is a measure of the ignorance of our own heritage that we have gone so far away in order to find phrases expressive of such matters.

As the city of Findias is properly attributed to the eastern quarter (though Fiona Macleod calls it "Finias" and assigns it to the south), the right-hand point of our diamond-shape can be placed on the Cuillin Hills in Skye, bringing the left-hand point (Murias, the west) to the Outer Hebridean island of South Uist. Here the site of the wisdom-centre may well have been the mountain called Hecla, where later "St. Michael" in his seaboard-aspect took over from a Celtic marine god.

The top point (Falias, the northern city) rests on an island, Eilean Shithford, between Harris and Lewis, though a mountain on the mainland of Lewis nearby is named Sithean an Airgid, Sithean meaning "bespelled" or "enchanted".

The bottom point (Gorias of the south) indicates the island of Tiree. This is one suggested allocation, based on the hint given by the site of Cuchulain's "college" but there are other possibilities which may be discovered by moving the diamond-shape about the map. More certain intuitions would no doubt result from a visit to the actual sites, combined with the exercise of clairvoyant faculties.

From each of the Four Cities the Danaans brought a "treasure"—talismans, palladia or magical instruments for the use of a whole people; and each treasure was associated with a particular Danaan divinity.

From Findias, city of Elemental Air, came the Sword which belonged to Nuada of the Silver Hand, a sky- or possibly moon-god. The Golden Spear of Lugh, god of the Sun, was fashioned in Gorias, the Fire City. The Cauldron of the Dagda Mor, father-figure of the pantheon and "lord of thunder and silence", came from Murias, the city of Water.

The Liath Fail (the Stone of Destiny) was brought from Falias, city of Elemental Earth, and is linked with the goddess Teltia since it was at one time guarded in Telltown, Co. Meath, her stronghold, and the centre-point or omphalos of Ireland. The four divinities may be seen as a variant of the masculine trinity—in this case, the three volatile Elements, plus the Earth-mother as basis of all.

If I understand a passage in *The Unicorn* by Virginia Moore, W. B. Yeats and his associates, who at one time devoted much research to this subject, assigned two of the Cities to other deities, namely Findias to Brigid and Falias to Dana. "Moon-crowned Brigid, of undying flame", may have a relationship with Nuada, and Teltia could be looked upon as an aspect of Dana, the earth goddess.

It is now a truism to equate the Danaan treasures with prototypes of the Hallows figuring in the Grail-cycle of legend. All were once material objects, though endowed with a subtle counterpart; the first three were probably works of art, beautiful in design and skillful in workmanship. All were consecrated or "charged" to their special purpose by powerful magicians. The only one to be identified with any certainty today is the Liath Fail, traditionally surviving as the Stone whose wanderings run: Falias—Tara—Telltown—Iona—Dunstaffnage—Scone—Westminster.

Though the Cauldron (as Grail) has inspired a voluminous literature down the centuries, it is impossible to judge between the various cups, bowls and dishes which have been claimed to represent it. One is said to lie in a cave below the church at Priddy on the Mendip Hills; another was found near Glastonbury earlier this century and, when I last heard of it, was preserved at Letchworth (of all unlikely places). This one is distinct from that supposed to have been concealed by Joseph of Arimathaea in the Chalice Well; but the entwinings of Christian legend, absent from the Liath Fail, here complicate the issue.

Then there is the Healing Cup of Nanteos (Cardiganshire) and the story of a chalice rescued before the sacking of the Castle of Montsegur and hidden—where? The Abbey of Montserrat in the mountains near Barcelona is another fabled repository of the venerated vessel: it seems that one is indeed in the watery realms of uncertainty and illusion. But beyond an equation with the perforating lance of Longinus and the name of the Golden Spear Mountain outside Dublin, even legend is silent as to the identity and whereabouts of the invincible Spear and Sword, which seem to have been vaporised into the subtle regions of Fire and Air whence they came.

What subjects did the Four Druids, those mysterious poet-sages, impart in their magical fastnesses? Bearing in mind the respective Elemental rulership of these, one may surmise that the privileged mortals who were accepted at Findias would follow the arts of war, government, justice and healing; they might learn the power of levitation, and would practise divination by astrology.

At Gorias they would study transmutation, evocation, magnetism and the training of wild beasts: they would master not only ordeals by fire but the projection of that Druid fire, deadly in combat, of which the myths are full, and would employ pyromancy for purposes of divination.

In Murias they would absorb the mysteries of shape-changing and bi-location—now called astral projection—necromancy and the casting of enchantments and illusions, especially by the production of mists and other weather-changes; and would divine through the use of the magic mirror.

In Falias they would work at all kinds of craftsmanship, particularly those connected with gems and metals and the construction of pentacles and talismans; they would practise the inner side of agriculture and acquire the secret of physical strength and of parthenogenesis, using geomancy as their mode of divination.

All four centres would give a grounding in magic, warfare and art, since every Danaan divinity was adept in these; but it seems that at Findias the student would go on to train for what would be called today the more intellectual professions, while at Falias he would perfect himself in crafts and manual skills.

Gorias and Murias would provide advanced occult training each with its own specialities. But it must not be forgotten that in "the world that was" work of any kind had an esoteric significance both as to method and aim, differentiating it from the soulless toil of modern industry and commerce.

Later in date than *The Book of Invasions*, the romance called *The Voyage of Maeldûn* describes an "Isle of Four Precious Walls" made respectively of gold, silver, copper and crystal, which is inhabited by Kings, Youths and Maidens—an obvious parallel with the court cards of the (initiated) Tarot pack.

These categories link up with the four Elements, inferring a place difficult of access, and dedicated to mystery-teaching, where the skills of each Element could be taught and learned in the appropriate College. One is reminded also of the Four Watchtowers in the Enochian system of magic. †

Wisdom Tradition Of The Gael; Part Two: The Danaan Tree Of Life (1970)

What were the Danaans like and how should they be visualised in meditation—those "people of the goddess Dana" who form the major part of the Gaelic pantheon? In the absence of a monumental sculpture comparable to that of Egypt and Greece to show them to us in the round, we have to rely on descriptions in the epics and in other poetry, both ancient and modern, to know how they looked.

Gods or demi-gods, they were never completely humanised though they were of human stature and possessed some human characteristics. They were the Lordly Ones, the Bright Ones, in appearance tall and fair-skinned with red or golden hair:

How beautiful they are,
The lordly ones,
Who dwell in the hills,
In the hollow hills...
Their limbs are more white
Than shafts of moonshine:
They are more fleet
Than the March wind...

as "Fiona MacLeod" (William Sharp) sang of them in *The Immortal Hour*. Older readers may remember that this verse drama was set to music by Rutland Boughton and ran successfully as an opera in the West End some 40 years ago.

Most favoured by poets of all the Danaan deities is Angus Og, Angus the Young, "Flame-haired Angus, lord of love and death": his physical type reinforces the theory of their Hyperborean provenance—so far as they can be equated at all with earthly races—and distinguishes them from possible remains of the Atlantean peoples, who seem to have been dark-haired with reddish or brownish skins.

In a similar way, the myths contrast the Danaans with their predecessors in Ireland—on the one hand the Fomorians, whose aura of the dark, gigantic and terrifying identifies them as Titans to the Olympian Danaans; and on the other hand, with the Firbolgs who are dark and small and, though sometimes tricksy or comical, have an air of dwarfishness and subjection. From the Firbolgs derive later stories of Leprechaun, Clurichaun and similar goblin-like beings who in folklore haunt the remoter Irish countryside even today.

The theme of *The Immortal Hour* is the love affair between a Danaan, "Midir of the Dew and the Evening Star" and Etain, wife of a mortal king, Eochay Airemh. Seemingly a mortal herself but actually a Danaan princess exiled from her own place in the form of a butterfly through the jealousy of Midir's wife, she had dropped exhausted into the drinking-cup of a queen and was thence conceived and born as a mortal child. The following passage, translated from a fifteenth-century manuscript but drawing on much older sources, is taken from A. H. Leahy's *Heroic Romances of Ireland*, and describes her beauty in great detail:

> On her head were two tresses of golden hair and each had been plaited into four strands... Each of her two arms were as white as the snow of a single night, and each of her cheeks was as rosy as the foxglove... Her eyes were as blue as the hyacinth, her lips delicate and crimson... Her feet were slim and white as the ocean's foam; evenly set were her eyes; her eyebrows were of a bluish-black, such as you see upon the shell of a beetle.

Equally splendid is the description of her lover, Midir, as he emerges from the mysterious Tír na nÓg and appears to the High King Eochay on the ramparts of Tara:

> ...his hair was of a golden
> yellow and of such a length that it
> Cached to the edge of his shoulders.
> The eyes of the young warrior were
> lustrous and grey...

Small wonder that the elderly Eochay stands no chance against this handsome couple: when he tries to detain them, they are levitated into the air and, passing out through the palace-roof, are wafted back to the Country of the Young. In the stage directions, "Fiona MacLeod" takes the liberty of making both Etain and Midir dark-haired, which is not in accord with Danaan tradition.

Some verses from the twelfth-century *Book of Leinster* translated by Kuno Meyer describe the inhabitants of Magh Mell, the Plain of Honey—another name for the Gaelic Otherworld:

> On their heads are
> Beautiful golden-yellow manes.
> With smooth comely bodies,

> With bright blue-starred eyes,
> With pure crystal teeth,
> With thin red lips.

Admiration for the Danaan-type dies hard: in the traditional ballad-literature of the British Isles, the blonde is always celebrated:

> He has ta'en three locks o' her yellow hair
> And with them strung his harp sae rare.

If a racial type is associated with a certain kind of inherited wisdom which it is considered desirable to keep unmixed, such pride is understandable; and thus it goes a little way towards explaining the exaggerated theories about Nordic superiority put forward by such writers as Gobineau, Houston Stewart Chamberlain and later, Dr. Alfred Rosenberg[1].

In view of recent research on the ductless glands, it would be a bold theoretician who maintained that there is no relationship between the type of the physical envelope and that of the Subtle Body (or bodies) associated with it. In most cultures there have been instances of the sacred gens or clan which communicates initiated wisdom through descent: hereditary priesthoods like the Roman Flamens are an example. An abraded form of the same thing occurs today, though usually undeveloped and unacknowledged, in those families where some psychic gift such as precognition is passed on from one generation to another.

The balanced view is that, while many lines of traditional knowledge exist, all equally valid, the Hyperborean may be the one best suited to the nations of northern Europe because it is their own. (Within this

---

1 This is a most unfortunate list of ugly pseudo-scientific and explicitly Nazi race theorists. Colquhoun does not seem to be endorsing these writers. Her argument appears to be that if one were to take these descriptions of beautiful people as cultural standards for deities that it would explain why these theorists concluded that these "races" were superior. Colquhoun backs off to call this view unbalanced, and instead calls for the development of racialised and separate "wisdom traditions". She likely felt she was being much more even handed and equitable, but that is not how it comes across today.

context, the Norse is a sister-tradition to the Celtic, matching as it does a greater metaphysical force with the latter's realm of sensuous glamour.) One need not be a racist to suggest that better results might ensue if fewer occult students in Britain imitated Tibetans or Japanese and fewer West Africans tried to become Hellenised gnostics, but each worked instead to develop their own native traditions.

"Who dwell in the hills, in the hollow hills"—but the Danaans are certainly not mere *dei terreni* (earth-gods) as the eighth-century *Book of Armagh* calls them: they are primarily Sky-gods and deities of Light, "sky-set Lugh who leads the hosts of the stars", "Dagda, Lord of Thunder and of Silence", "moon-crowned Brigid of the undying flame". When in their turn they were invaded and conquered by the Milesians—the first fully-human race to inhabit Ireland, from whom the oldest Irish families still claim descent—the Danaans retired to the duns and raths of the countryside which henceforth concealed a subtle counterpart of the physical world, an Earthly Paradise. Herein they pursue a life free from sickness, old age and death; their dwelling-place impalpable palaces, their nourishment a delicious food and drink conferring immortality. They make war, but their dead and wounded are miraculously restored next day; they range over sea and land, but though they inhabit a timeless element—the Tír na nÓg or Country of the Young—they are precisely localised in regard to "surface" geography: Aillel Olum, for instance, is King of the Danaans of Munster. They make love, and their more-than-permissive society though usually hidden by invisible veils is not far removed from ordinary human consciousness; the myths tell of frequent links between them and humanity, notably when there is a question of a love-affair between a Danaan and a mortal. The story of Midir, Etain and King Eochay shows this interchange as clearly as any. Thus Midir sings to Etain a chant of enticement when persuading her to return with him:

> O fair-haired woman, will you come with me to the marvellous land, full of music, where the hair is primrose yellow and the body white as snow?

> There none speaks of "mine" and "thine"—white are the teeth and black are the brows; eyes flash with many-coloured lights, and the hue of the foxglove is on every cheek.

How is the transition made from the Country of the Young to our earth, and vice versa? Before this can be answered, one must take notice that though the Tír na nÓg can mean the whole of the Otherworld, it should strictly be applied to the first part of this only, i.e., the part lying nearest to the physical world.

The Celtic Otherworld is divided into four "stages" or "layers": it is said that one crosses Earth (no doubt Earth as esoteric Element is intended) in order to reach the first of these, the Country of the Young.

Beyond it lies the Tir-Fo-Thuinn, the Land-under-Wave, sometimes called the Many-coloured Land, and to get there Elemental Water must be crossed.

Beyond again is the Land of Wonder, and Air must be explored to gain it; lastly one comes to the Land of Promise (which could mean Potentiality) and to enter it one must pass through Fire.

Here is a system of four interpenetrating states, each composed of more subtle matter than the last, which is not very different from that of the Qabalah. Thus Assiah is equivalent to the Earth, interpenetrated by the Country of the Young; Ietzirah—the World of Formation—is interpenetrated by the Many-coloured Land; Briah—the Creative World—by the Land of Wonder and Atziluth—the World of Archetypes—by the Land of Promise.

From another point of view, the figures of Gaelic mythology could be placed on the diagram of the Tree of Life as projected successively into these Four Worlds. The Tree here is the Hazel of Wisdom—complement of the Ash tree Yggdrasil in Norse legend—and bears ten Nuts in each of the Worlds. In Atziluth the Nuts are manifested as the chief deities; in Briah, as the Heroes; in Ietzirah, they are represented by the voyage-myths (of Bran and of Maeldûn, the Quest of the Sons of Turenn, and the Swan-children of Lir); in Assiah, by our own earth as influenced and interpenetrated by the beings of the Tír na nÓg.

In the late nineties and the early years of the present century, the poet W. B. Yeats, sometimes in company with his Sligo uncle and cousin, George Pollexfen and Lucy Middleton, sometimes with Maud Gonne, "Fiona MacLeod" or other associates from the Order of the Golden Dawn, successfully practiced evocations of the Gaelic Divinities. Records exist of these collective visions in which such beings appear, speak and conduct the mediators on journeys through the subtler realms.

This work was undertaken by Yeats as a preliminary to establishing his Castle of Heroes, which was to be a centre for the revived Hibernian Mysteries. A site was found—a castle on Loch Key—and rituals were composed, but the Irish literary theatre claimed Yeats and politics Maud Gonne and without these leading figures the project came to nothing.

A touching glimpse of the poet on his last visit to Madame Gonne MacBride records him as saying: "Maud, we should have gone with our Castle of Heroes." †

The Order of the Sun and The Moon, Nicaragua (1971)

This essay references the dream origins of a wonderfully eerie, richly layered painting, *The Grotto of the Sun and Moon, Nicaragua*, from 1952. It is notable that she was compelled enough by these themes to be writing about them nearly 20 years after the production of the painting, although she captured the original dream in a prose poem shortly after it happened. This piece may have been inspired by the marriage of Nicaraguan activist Bianca Jagger to Mick Jagger in 1971, as she seems to have interpreted her press exposure at the time as some sort of trigger for the meaning of the dream. She concludes that this particular instance of Nicaragua may be an extra dimensional space where an alchemical order exists and has the ability to communicate with her. Although this in many ways is a whimsical notion, it also shows the richness of Colquhoun's imaginal life and the influence it had on her.

Why Nicaragua?

It began with a dream in the late 1940s, and I can't do better than quote a prose-poem in which I recounted this dream soon after it had happened.

> *The Grotto of the Sun and Moon, Nicaragua*
>
> The approach to the grotto is a wide unroofed corridor or narrow courtyard, something like the entrance to one of the circular

tombs of Mycenae. (One remembers the very pale Mycenaean gold, thinly beaten out.) Above the high wall at the opposite end the sky burns intensely blue. In the middle of this wall a triple archway is hollowed out, the surfaces at right angles painted in true fresco with deep yellow, flower pink and slate blue. This design is mainly abstract, but sun's rays are suggested at the top of the central arch on the wall surface facing the spectator.

Inside the arch rises a mass of dark porous substance like pumice stone, but each of its holes is large enough to admit the passage of a ray of light. These rays seem to shine through the holes from the hidden core of the grotto, some are paler than others, and I understand that they proceeded from the sun and moon. Each hole represents some crisis in the annual cycle of these luminaries, and, as at Stonehenge, a gap in the circle allows the sun, rising on Midsummer's day, to strike a certain stone, so here the light streams through each hole in its own season; yet all appears to be happening at the same time, bringing the greatest satisfaction.

I also painted this dream as a picture. The title of both poem and painting was heard as a disembodied voice in the dream. I didn't know anything about Nicaragua then, but since—and fairly recently—it has been in the news for volcanic eruption, political revolution and Bianca Jagger. There is water in the name Nicaragua, and Bianca means white; this suggests aspects of the lunar element. A friend whom I consulted at the time of the dream was of the opinion that I should have a series of such dreams with obvious interconnections, but this did not occur. However, I tried to find out if there was such a place as the grotto by studying books about the country and found that very little had been published on its topography or archaeology. There was no mention of such a frescoed temple.

Perhaps "Nicaragua" is not to be taken geographically but to be understood in the same sense as the place names in alchemical literature, like the "India" of *Lambspring* or the "Andalusia" of *The Book of Ostanes*. The central archetype is prefigured in the first illustration to the *Splendor Solis* of Salomon Trismosin, though the commentary on this seems to be at fault since it calls the luminary on the ground "a second sun", whereas it is plainly intended for the moon.

The grotto may be the sanctuary where the chemical nuptials of the sun and moon are celebrated; and I had the impression that there was, now or at some former time, an initiatic group called something like the Order of the Sun and Moon, perhaps localised in Nicaragua. Having discovered nothing of any relevance I assumed that the grotto was an occult centre used by an eponymous order which existed in the past or still exists, either in that state of being commonly recognised as reality today or else in regions variously called the Higher Worlds or the Inner Planes. For some reason I obtained a glimpse of this mysterious centre, and now if I receive an idea or perception which does not seem to be a direct result of anything I have read, heard or thought, I take it to be a message from the order.

At least the volcanic character of Nicaraguan geology is aptly indicated by the tufa-like formation of the rock in the grotto, and the weather also seems to be typical, as perhaps other matters will be verified in the future. One may speculate that the teaching of the order takes up an equally balanced position between the forces of Yang and Yin, to use a Far-Eastern term now modish in the West where the words sun and moon were once understood in a similar sense. †

Aspects of Graal Symbolism (early 1970s)

This essay helps to unpack the importance of castration symbolism and sexual wounding in Colquhoun's work of the late 1930s and early 1940s, most notably seen in *The Pine Family* (1940). In her poems she frequently refers to a wounded or bruised thigh, and the iconography of wounding and impotence is a recurring visual theme in her early representational surrealism and in her erotic *corpus*. Key to the emerging esoteric readings of Arthuriana in the late nineteenth and especially the early twentieth century is the idea that Arthurian legend concealed a fertility cult, popularised by Jessie Weston's 1920 bestseller *From Ritual to Romance*. For Colquhoun overcoming this wound is a precursor to wholeness. Although there is no firm date for this essay it may have gone through multiple drafts over decades. This essay may have started in the 1950s as she refers to the 1948 play *Le Roi Pécheur* by surrealist ally Julien Gracq as "recent".

Before trying to establish what the grail—the quested substance, state or object—in fact is, one may note the characteristics of the quester. In all versions of the legend, he is described as simple, rustic, or unsophisticated. He is the "holy fool" who "could know all wisdom could he know anything". He may be likened to the pictured Fool on the Taro who does not look where he is going. This implies that intellect is bypassed by the quester in his search, since something other than intellect is the necessary instrument.

This search may be correlated with creative work on any plane, but refers especially to a quest for the essences of life, some universal germ. Though the written word had and still has a certain magical (practical) potency, it cannot convey this essence nor of itself produce a change of consciousness. The essence is to be sought in some field other than that of verbalization, the discursive intellect, the logical formula—other than that of the conscious mind at all. Some other intuition animated the movement called Acéphale, "The headless", a later branching from surrealism, though this movement manifested an orgiastic element absent from the grail legend as known today[1].

The syllable "Per" meaning a bowl or a vessel, occurs in all forms of the quester's name. The grail, when described at all, is specified as a vessel, also sometimes as a stone, possibly a hollowed stone. Thus, it would seem that the quester is in some sense the object of his own quest: he himself, or some aspect of himself <u>is</u> the grail. "The Fool is his own body of fate" as W. B. Yeats says in *A Vision.*

If Perceval is the grail, what is Amfortas? He is another aspect of the quester, or another (and earlier) stage in the quest. He is indeed the wound, a figuration encountered before that of the grail itself. Amfortas is said to be a blood-relation of Perceval, in most versions his great uncle or, taken at dream level, he is his father by displacement. The wound of Amfortas is a sexual wound, presumably he has been the loser in a struggle with his son for sexual supremacy. The location of the wound differs slightly in various versions, some saying vaguely that Amfortas is "lame", which perhaps might be better translated as "maimed." Others are more specific, one version placing the wound in his side, another in his thigh, a third in the groin and a fourth, more frankly, in the pubic bone. All accounts make the meaning clear: Amfortas is symbolically castrated; wounded almost mortally, by Perceval's death-wishes toward him; and only Perceval can heal him. Amfortas is both alive and dead, but more dead than alive, as shown by the barren and ravaged state of his domains. In order to restore

1 *Acéphale* (Eng. "Headless") was the name of the publication and secret society formed by Georges Bataille from 1936-1939, intending to counter fascism and populism through engaging with myth and ritual, marked by violence and transgression.

these to prosperous fertility, Perceval must cure the wound, and this before he can "win the grail" or himself attain to unity of being.

Amfortas' asceticism is the enforced self-denial of the invalid who cannot take his full share in life. In one version at least the wound is attributed to a forbidden union with the seductress Kundry; but this does not explain why in Perceval should reside the only possible healing agent, unless Kundry is in fact some aspect of Kondwiramur, Perceval's bride. The wound would then be the guilt feeling at a broken incest-taboo.

In the story as told by Wolfram von Eschenbach, Perceval (Parzifal), does not enter the grail-castle until after his marriage with Kondwiramur; therefore his purity cannot be interpreted as virginity, asceticism, sexual abstinence or any kindred notion, as in later and sentimentalised versions. This purity may, however, be connected with his character as simpleton, or it may indicate the single-minded concentration necessary to the achievement of an arduous undertaking. If the grail represents the hidden depths of his own psyche for which he is seeking, then the finding of the grail is that complete differentiation of the self from father-and-mother figures which ideally accompanies conjunction with the anima, personified as the bride Kondwiramur.

Amfortas, sometimes identified with the Fisher King, is lying sick in the graal castle; and as a preliminary to his healing, he shows Percival the castle treasures, chief among which is the graal itself. The cure of Amfortas' wounds depends on whether Perceval asks their meaning. In some versions he must do so, and is rebuked for sloth and stupidity if he does not; in others he must not ask, and is equally rebuked for curiosity and disobedience if he does. In one version, that of Chrétien de Troyes, he is first warned against his curiosity and subsequently reproached when he fails to show it. Whatever the graal-castle represents, with its inhabitants and its treasures, the quester's attitude to it is seemingly ambivalent. R. W. Cruttwell has suggested that the castle is a multiple symbol—that to Perceval it is not only his father's tomb and his mother's womb, but the vagina of his bride. If this is so, then it carries an almost intolerable load of different (and contradictory) affects.

The pivot of the legend turns on the asking of a fatal question. T. W. Rolleston suggests in *Myths and Legends of the Celtic Race* that the versions in which the question is forbidden are authentic—adducing, rather feebly, the fact that curiosity is often punished in fairy tales[2]. As the prime function of the quester is discovery, it would seem more in keeping with his character that he should inquire. Also, being the holy fool, he could rush in where angels fear to tread. How could the mere fact of remining silent when the mysterious treasures are produced, cure the ailing Amfortas? But if the graal-castle is taken as a hall of initiation, Perceval as the candidate, the old man (the "wise ancient" of dream symbol) as the hierophant, the treasures as initiatory objects (comparable to those used in mystery cults such as the Eleusinia, or to the salt and phallos in Aphrodite's sanctuary at Paphos) and their ritual display in procession as part of a mystery-drama, then some kind of dialogue or catechism would naturally ensue. The candidate would be expected to ask, and probably later to answer: he could scarcely remain a mere passive spectator.

Whichever alternative Perceval takes, he is "had". If he poses the question the castle and all that it contains will dissolve, and he will subsequently be scolded for his temerity. If he remains silent, he will be reproached for his lack of enterprise, and again sent forth on his travels. In neither case is an answer vouchsafed. Even when, after long wanderings, he finds the castle again and passes through the ordeal successfully—either asking or not asking the meaning of the hallows, according to version—there is still no recorded reply. The legend remains silent on the crucial point, merely stating the fact of his achievement. To the investigator of today the form of the hallows themselves point to an answer. What could Percival be told, except that their meaning is, in the widest sense, sexual? They are symbolic sexual pairs; and the healing of the castrated Amfortas will result from

2 The Irish writer T. W. Rolleston was known for his anthologizing and popularizing of Irish and Welsh legend. *Myths and Legends of the Celtic Race* was published in 1911 and in 1912 he produced his own poetic reading of *Parsifal.*

their restoration to a place of honour and knowledgeable veneration. The aim is a consecrated well-being on every plane, including the physical, depicted as the healing of Amfortas and the restoring of his lands to fertility.

The treasures consist in the graal itself, pictured as a hollow vessel of some sort, cup or bowl, and later equated in Christian tradition with the eucharistic chalice; a blood dripping spear, later identified with the blood dripping spear of Longinus; a sword and dish. These treasures, or "hallows" of the castle are almost exactly repeated in the four suits of the Taro pack, the Fool being the first of its Major Arcana. Designated as Cups, Wands, Swords and Pantacles or Deniers, the suits provide two phallic and two vulval symbols, as in the case of the hallows. The element of reduplication is somewhat mystifying; the pantacle echoes the cup and the sword echoes the wand, as with the hallows, the dish echoes the graal and the sword the lance. The repetition is not exact, and suggests that a slightly differing object indicates a slight difference of function in the symbol. This reduplication is no late addition to the myth, but is integral to it from the beginning. To recognise this, one has only to examine the very similar treasures brought, according to Celtic myth, by the Danaans from the Land of the Dead. Their treasures—cup or bowl, spear, sword and stone—may well be the antecedents of the castle hallows, since the graal myth first appears in Celtic culture. The vessel is sometimes called "the cauldron of abundance' and the stone 'the stone of abundance", both foreshadowing the graal's attribute of cornucopia. In the nineties of the last century, Yeats spent some time working out, with one or two colleagues, a Celtic initiatory rite embodying these four objects, that was to be enacted at the Castle of Heroes on Loch Key.

As to the ultimate provenance of the myth, what can one say but that it is probably Indo-European, vague as that may sound? It might be useful to compare the objects held by Shiva and other deities in traditional Hindu iconography. Though Christian and ascetic ideas are found in the myth, these are late additions and did not form part of the original teaching which it enshrined. Of the "hallows", the cup and the dish appear in Christian ritual as the eucharistic chalice and the paten, but sword and lance (even the lance of Longinus) are missing. In other words, the two vulval symbols are retained, but the two phallic symbols are excluded. Iconography redresses the balance to some degree, as for instance in delineations of the Instruments of the Passion.

Of this myth's recent avatars, *Le Roi Pécheur* of Julien Gracq signalises clearly the Christian and Pagan elements. The hermit Trévizrent and Klingsor are made to stand for the Christian good and evil, while Perceval and Amfortas represent the profounder Pagan dichotomy of light and shadow. This is, however, too sharp a definition, since there are Christian elements in the character of Amfortas. He is the "sick saint" of which hagiography teems with examples: his wound is also a stigmatisation. But Gracq ignores this, confronting in his two "pairs of opposites" the Christian sin and resistance to temptation with the Pagan sterility and fertility, death and life. For him, Amfortas is the dead king lying in his tomb (the castle) and Perceval the youth destined to succeed him—winter and spring the setting and the rising sun, in seasonal pulsation. †

Banners from the Sky (1973)

Published in *Prediction* in 1973, here Colquhoun returns to the topic of strange lights in the sky, but with a perhaps unexpected twist, an intersection with heraldry and esoteric visions. Colquhoun had a longstanding interest in the esoteric associations with heraldry, something that may have been a feature of her associations with Traditionalist occultist W. B. Crow, who ran an order Colquhoun belonged to that took an interest in heraldry. While this might seem odd, heraldry was of interest from an esoteric perspective in that it was a source for several features of interest to Colquhoun: the notion of lineage and inheritance, a powerful and symbolic use of colour, the use of emblems, and also the adoption of mottos. Colquhoun's archives show her research into various family crests. In this quirky essay we see Colquhoun attributing, once again, an extradimensional origin to earthy symbols of order and authority. In Colquhoun's world, the colours and shapes of flags and shields provide a key to the essential qualities of nations and people.

Unexplained phenomena observed in the sky are not new, although in recent times they have attained prominence through the numerous "flying saucer" reports that have appeared in the mass media. Strange shapes and lights have long amazed watchers of the skies and their reports were recorded in early times just as they are now. Sometimes huge star shapes or crosses were seen in the heavens, like the well attested star form which in 1967 sped through the night air above Devon, to cite just one modern instance. What are now called "sightings" would formerly have been termed "visions".

Throughout history such luminous portents—for as such they were usually taken to be—have inspired the design of banners. Carried into battle, these were believed to bring victory. Whether they boosted the troops' morale through suggestion alone is anybody's guess.

Most famous of these "banners from the sky" was Constantine's modification of the *Labarum*, standard of the Roman emperors, a purple flag supported on a golden spear topped by an eagle. To Constantine, the *Chi-Rho* monogram—the Greek letters looking like an X combined with a P—appeared shining against a dark sky on the eve of the Battle of Saxa Rubra (Red Rock) in 312 AD. A dream-voice told him to inscribe the monogram, representing the first two letters (ch) of Christ's name, on the shields of his soldiers, together with the motto *In hoc signo vinces* (In this sign shalt thou conquer). Constantine obeyed and, seemingly in consequence, won the battle. He promptly adopted the design as his banner, superimposing motto and monogram on the imperial purple flag and replacing the eagle with a crown.

The so-called St. Andrew's cross (basic form of the crossed swords, batons or keys of heraldry) is also of celestial origin. When allied against Athelstane of England, Achaius, King of Scots, and Hungus, King of the Picts, saw such a diagonal cross gleaming pale against the midnight blue prior to their encounter with the enemy. The brothers-in-arms were victorious, and making a barefoot pilgrimage to St. Andrew's church, vowed to take the symbol as their national emblem.

A white decussate (diagonal) cross on a blue background remains the flag of Scotland even today and as such contributes to the design of the Union Jack. That St. Andrew was martyred on a cross of this type is a popular fallacy which degrades the symbolic significance.

The oriflamme (flame of gold) was first used as France's national flag in 1119. Described as *vermeille* (crimson), which would today probably be rendered as *sanguine* (blood red) in heraldry, it was cut into three "tongues" at one end to represent flames and mounted on a golden shaft like a sword. Its provenance is uncertain: but may not a glimpse of the flame-like tongues of the aurora borealis have suggested it to some night-wandering traveller?

First held at the abbey of St. Denis outside Paris, it passed to the Count of Vexin when he took possession of the abbey. When Philip I of France assumed the Vexin territory he also took the oriflamme. This banner was reputed to blind France's enemies or even strike them dead; it was also said to possess the Druidic power of calling up fog or dispersing it, whichever was most advantageous. In spite of these remarkable qualities it was finally abandoned in favour of a blue flag scattered with golden fleurs de lis. The oriflamme was returned to the abbey of St. Denis whence it disappeared, being last mentioned in 1534.

Next in date comes the *Dannebrog*. It was in 1219 that Waldemar II of Denmark saw a fiery cross in the sky betokening his victory over the Estonians. On the flag he afterwards designed, his vision was commemorated as a white cross on a red background.

When a banner is assumed by a monarch it becomes the symbol of his nation as well as his personal standard. However, families and even individuals have claimed supernatural origins and magical properties for their chosen emblems.

A legend of the Macleods of Dunvegan tells how an ancestor of the clan was given a flag by a "fairy-bride"—no doubt a member of the Danaan race of demi-gods who in Celtic countries are said to have maintained close human contacts both in love and war. A hereditary standard-bearer was appointed to take care of the Macleod flag, together with 12 guardians who carried it into battle, enclosed in a casket, to ensure victory.

In extremity, it is said, the flag can be waved (but only on three occasions) and the "Host of the Air" will come to the bearer's rescue.

It has been waved twice, apparently with good effect, and during the Second World War many a serviceman named Macleod carried a photograph of it as a talisman.

Today the flag hangs, framed, in Dunvegan Castle on the Isle of Skye. Discoloured and much darned, it is of an Oriental silk which museum authorities have identified as a piece of a Crusader's surcoat. Otta Swire, however, suggests in *Skye: The Island and its Legends* that, since the Macleods had Norse connections, the flag may in fact be Harald Haardrada's treasured banner *Landoda* (The Land Ravisher), brought back from his Near Eastern travels.

Before the Battle of Ourique which ousted the Moors from Spain in 1139, Don Alonzo sighted a bright cross in the eastern sky. Like other leaders before him, he adopted it as his insignium, arranging on a silver shield five *azure* escutcheons (smaller shields) each bearing five golden bezants or circles so as to form an equal-armed cross.

Two different flags compete as the banner of the prophet Mohammed, one being the Bajura Standard and the other the *Sinjak-Sherief* (Lofty Banner), a strip of green fabric some 12 ft long embroidered with gold. It is (or was) preserved at a mosque on the outskirts of Istanbul named in honour of the prophet's devoted standard-bearer Eyub, who fell in defence of the city while carrying it and who was interred there. This banner ran according to type as a luck-bringer, and though it does not seem to have originated in an aerial sighting, it was probably presented, like other of the prophet's possessions, by some heavenly visitant.

A glance at the connection between astrology and the heraldic colours from which those of flags derive is quite illuminating. Thus each heraldic "tincture" evokes the powers of the planet to which it is attributed:

gules (red): Mars
vest (green): Venus
azure (blue): Jupiter

sable (black): Saturn
purpure (purple): Mercury
or (gold yellow): the Sun
argent (silver White): the Moon
tenne (tawny): Uranus
murrey (mulberry/red-purple): Neptune
sanguine (blood red): Pluto.

Following this lead, the national standards evoke, through their colouring, various planetary powers as do the insignia of individuals:

Imperial Rome: Mercury and the Sun
Scotland: Jupiter and the Moon
Don Alonzo: the Moon, Jupiter and the Sun. †

Paganism (after 1973)

In this essay Colquhoun works to reconcile her animist spirituality with her Indian birthplace. Her own sense of ethnicity and family identity was always a challenge for her. In the end she comes to define Paganism as being characterised by a strong relationship with the currents of place and the land.

Religion is largely determined by locality; a pagan means one who lives in a country place, a heathen one who lives on heathland.

I used to claim that I was a Hindu because I was born in India. A strict Hindu must not only be born there, but must remain there, never leaving the sub-continent. (Should acceptance of such a doctrine prove awkward, a financial transaction may satisfy theological niceties in India as elsewhere.)

On investigating the area where I was born in Shillong, Assam, I discovered that the native inhabitants were not of Aryan stock but were ethnic Mongols. Even as lately as 1681-1826 a dynasty of Shan kings ruled the region, whose northern border backs onto the foot hills of Bhoutan and Thibet. Vedic Hinduism was an intrusive system which gradually imposed itself on the age-long animism of the population. This explains and underlies my support of the animist viewpoint.

Animism, of which pantheism is a philosophical version, postulates a life-energy informing all natural manifestation. Characteristically it tends to equalise expressions of this energy, and so to lessen humanity's claim to supreme importance.

The central area of the Assam valley surrounding the capital Gauhati, from ancient times was called Kamrup. It was and perhaps still is one of the chief power zones of the Tantrik cult, having been recognised no doubt from the earliest times as a centre of wide-spreading chthonic force. Tantrism being less a system than an attitude easily absorbs the cult of the many faceted Kali, the Hindu Isis of Nature, and it is as earth goddess that she chiefly figures in this area.

On an island in the Bramapoutra opposite Gauhati, the shrine of Umananda may be found and about two miles down-river on the Nilachal Hill stands the temple of Kamakhya. I surmise that both these are devoted to Kali in some form, Kamakhya certainly is. I have heard that in or near one of them is a carving (or possibly a natural rock formation?) representing the external sex organs of the goddess which are said to menstruate at regular seasons. Perhaps a chalybeatic spring and the oxidization of iron in the soil provides the material cause.

Kenneth Grant mentions a certain secret temple in Assam; this may be Umanda but can scarcely be Kamakhya, a pilgrimage centre already much frequented, unless some part of it is inaccessible to the public. He refers to an image with "breasts of electrum magicum, an alloy of the seven planetary 'metals', and a body of vitrified Ojas" (electro-magnetic energy). It seems from his further description that here the goddess shows herself in a lunar aspect.

Any temple established in the Kamrup district would draw upon a "fountain out of Hecate", an uprush of force from the macrocosmic underworld which, focused by ceremony, may coincide at precise times with the microcosmic unconscious. Paganism, therefore, depends in a special way on qualities of a locality in the earth itself, which some other cults have tried to ignore or suppress. It would seem that importance attached to the influence of birthplace is more than subjective phantasy. †

Excerpts from *The Sword of Wisdom* (1975)

The Sword of Wisdom was Colquhoun's love letter to Samuel Liddell "MacGregor" Mathers and the Hermetic Order of the Golden Dawn. Although it is most frequently characterised or described as a biography of Mathers, *Sword of Wisdom* is truly an interesting patchwork of a text. It often reads as a memoir, starting with Colquhoun's own magical autobiography and frequently including her own views, but it also includes interesting history about Mathers, and chronicles the impact and offshoots of the Hermetic Order of the Golden Dawn. The text itself has often come under criticism for a lack of historical accuracy, but Colquhoun had many interesting sources and connections, and most certainly some of the anecdotes she shares in the text have some truth behind them. As is common with most of Colquhoun's writings, she inserts herself and her opinions into the text frequently, which sometimes makes for a jarring reading experience. Interestingly, despite the comprehensive history of Golden Dawn spin-offs and splinter groups covered in this text, Colquhoun does not mention her former order, Order of the Pyramid and Sphinx, suggesting that the separation was an unpleasant one.

In the appendices to the text, Colquhoun adds several magical essays of her own which combine history and pedagogy. Although they demonstrate Colquhoun's deep understanding of the topics at hand and certainly her familiarity with both primary and secondary magical texts, it would seem as though the main reason

for the inclusion of these essays was to highlight the Golden Dawn history and curriculum with respect to these esoteric practices, namely Enochiana, Tantra and Alchemy. It is hard to evaluate how successful any of these essays are, as they are not particularly well structured, but they do contain interesting historical nuggets. One feels as though Colquhoun may have also been working to establish the legacy of her cousin Edward Garstin, Cancellarius of the Alpha Omega lodge, as a forgotten Golden Dawn writer and magician, as she works in these essays to highlight his writings. †

Enochiana (1975)

Enochian magic refers to the angelic language that was derived from the scrying practices of Elizabethan magicians John Dee and Edward Kelley. Enochian magic is a central practice in the magical system of the Hermetic Order of the Golden Dawn. Additionally, Enochian Magic was a particularly important facet of the Golden Dawn-style magic that Colquhoun practiced with Tamara Bourkoun's Order of the Pyramid and Sphinx that she was involved with until just prior to the publication of the *Sword of Wisdom*. Here she seems to wander into quite a bit of speculative philology, again demonstrating Colquhoun's interest in empiricism.

The Enochian system of magic and its vehicle, the Angelical language, are usually attributed to Dr. John Dee (1527-1608) and his Skyrer or clairvoyant, Edward Kelley. However, in a Latin treatise published at Venice in 1531, *Vaorchadumia*—itself an Angelical word—the script of the Angelical alphabet is already to be found[1]. From 1475 onward, a secret Lodge of the same name, with which Marcello Ficino is said to have been connected, was operating in Venice. Chwolsohn[2], in his misleadingly-

1 This is a reference to the *Voarchadumia Contra Alchimiam* published in 1530 by alchemical writer Giovanni Agostino Panteo also known as Pantheus. Barry William Hale noted in personal correspondence that this is an earlier version of an Angelic language to Dee's, also said to be derived from Enoch. Dee had this manuscript in his collection but their alphabets are distinct.

2 Russian Arabic scholar Daniel Chwolson. *The Nabataean Agriculture* was of interest to students of esotericism in the nineteenth and early twentieth century as it seemingly portrayed an account of the beliefs of and practices of pre-Islamic Arab culture.

named *Nabataean Agriculture* published in German at St. Petersburg about 1860, also gives the Angelical letters though it is not likely that he knew of Dee's investigations. Mme. Blavatsky mentions Chwolsohn's work but not Dr. Dee's: by her references to Enochian literature in *The Secret Doctrine* she means the apocryphal *Book of Enoch*. Even considering the links that obtained between the early Theosophical Society in England and the early GD, it is not likely, though it is possible, that she gave MacGregor Mathers and Wynn Westcott a hint to investigate the system. However this may be, they did so, using not only the resources of scholarship but those of clairvoyance through the skrying of Moïna. Kenneth R. H. Mackenzie, who died just before the founding of the GD, left manuscripts wherein the Angelical language was used; and if these were accessible to the founders they would have provided further incentive. Mackenzie's documents are not to be discovered in the British Museum Library nor, I am told, in that of the *S.R.I.A.*, of which he was at one time a member; they may be hiding in some private Masonic collection.

A letter to me dated March 5, 1954, from the late C. R. Cammell[3] states that a MS in the Angelical language, of a much earlier date than the time of Dr. Dee, exists in the library of a Syrian monastery. The learned Doctor could scarcely have known of this; and it has since been classified as "in an unknown tongue and indecipherable". I regret that Mr. Cammell was not more specific; he did not say which monastery nor even which of the Eastern Orthodox Churches owns this relic: I repeat what he wrote in case someone can fit in the missing pieces of the puzzle.

Dee was, among much else, the founder of modern "Spiritualism" and Kelley was his most powerful medium though by no means the only one he used. His chief spirit-guides—or better to say, communicators—were not discarnate human residues but were the same Archangels—Michael, Gabriel, Raphael and Uriel—as those who instructed the Hebrew patriarch Enoch: hence Dee's adoption of the latter's name for the system they dispensed. The difference between this and most of what has since passed for spirit-communication is that Dee's contacts did actually *say* something, and something of profound interest: they did not merely maunder on

3 Author and poet Charles Cammell who wrote a biography of Aleister Crowley.

with unverifiable speculations and moralistic platitudes[4]. Whether they were or were not identical with Enoch's Archangels, whether they were or were not angels at all in a theological sense, they were certainly a notch above the spirit-controls who have manifested themselves since, most of whom come into Mme. Blavatsky's category of "flapdoodles".

Among the unpublished work left at his death in 1955 by Edward Garstin was a Glossary of the *Enochian Language*. J. W. Brodie-Innes had previously compiled one and Elias Ashmole had long before attempted something of the kind, but whether Edward consulted these I do not know. Dr. Israel Regardie has also been working on such a Glossary for some time in consultation with a philologist, and this should soon appear. Edward completed his investigations without consulting Regardie, of whose revelation of GD material he disapproved, so they reached the same conclusions (where they did so) independently.

In a brief introduction, Edward makes the point in the 48 *Angelical Calls* the communicating Angel sometimes needed to insert words, implicit in the language of the text itself, into the English translation so as to make the latter intelligible. He compares the telegraphic style of the original with that of the *Sepher D-Tzenioutha* (= The Book of Concealed Mystery), one of the three Zoharic texts comprising *The Kabbalah Unveiled* as translated by Mathers. He further tries to sift these added words from their original text, at the same time analysing their roots. He notes that the splitting into syllables found in Dee's MSS—the object of this being to aid pronunciation—has resulted in some syllables being wrongly re-allocated.

Edward suggests a possible Angelical derivation for certain words in the Hebrew and other languages, comparing the Hebrew *Zion* with *Siaion* (= temple), the Latin *Lux* with *Luc* (= bright) and the Egyptian *Ra* with *Roa* (= east).

Some students have speculated that Angelical is the *Ur-Semitisch* language, source of all later Semitic tongues. Part of its uncouth impression, on the latinised eye when written is admittedly due to the omission of some

4 Colquhoun did not approve of mediumistic Spiritualism, finding it to be a degenerate practice.

vowels, which must be supplied by the reader from previous knowledge, as in all Semitic languages. I prefer the opinion of Regardie (*The Golden Dawn*, Vol. 4) that it may rather be the language that "lies behind Sanskrit" in the words of Charles Johnson, namely, the language of Atlantis. It is not adapted to ordinary conversation, being primarily a "tongue of lore", a hieratic tongue to be used in ritual, its vocabulary referring to transcendental matters. Like all sacred alphabets this one consists of numbers as well as letters—the individual signs composing such *are* numbers as much as letters; but in a more recondite sense each letter is also a sigil or glyph. Each has an entity of its own, of which the form of the letter is an emblem or signature.

A method of pronunciation was taught in the GD and a disc survives of Crowley reciting the first of the *48 Calls*, beginning *"Oel Sonuf Vaoresagi"*. The timbre of his voice is insufficiently sonorous to do such a Mantram justice, but it does suggest how impressive this language could sound if adequately vibrated. The last word on its pronunciation, or rather vibration, has not yet been uttered.

Enochian magic is, among other things, a Western equivalent to Hinduism's *Mantra-Yoga*—I use the Sanskrit term for want of a Western synonym. The prime purpose of Dee's elaborate diagrams is to produce the Names of divine, angelic or demonic beings so that these may be evoked by sound to aid the operating magician: "Move, therefore, show yourselves!" adjures the first Call. By certain manipulation of sound, the system can, if my intuition serves, give access to an early world of Atlantean pellucidity: based on an employment of occult mathematics, it raises a superstructure unimaginably attenuated and jewel-clear, what the *Egyptian Book of the Dead* symbolises as "the lily of green felspar". An echo of its nature can still be heard in Egyptian Tradition, perhaps a gleam of it may be caught in Celtic wonder-tales like *The Voyage of Maeldûn*:

> Thereafter they voyaged till they found a great silvern column. It had four sides, and the width of each of these sides was two oar-stroked of the boat... And not a single clod of earth was about it, but only the boundless ocean. And they saw not how its base was below or—because of its

> height—how its summit was above. Out of its summit came a silvern net far away from it; and the boat went under sail through a mesh of that net... And they heard a voice of the summit of yonder pillar, mighty, and clear, and distinct. But they knew not the tongue it spoke, nor the words it uttered.

Is the image of sailing through one of these meshes equivalent to entering "in the Spirit-Vision" an Enochian square? Another passage describes "a lofty island" divided into quarters by fences of gold, silver, brass and crystal, and containing respectively Kings, Queens, Warriors and Maidens. Do these Tarot-like figures body forth the entities whom Dee called Little Daughters of the Light, and Sons, Daughters-of-Daughters and Sons-of-Sons of Light, and whose names he drew from the Great Seal forming the top of his skrying-table? Or alternatively, are the quarters of this mysterious island another way of picturing Dee's Watch-Towers? Are they hinted at again by the "woman in strange raiment" who invited another voyager, Bran son of Feval, to embark for

> ...a distant isle,
> Around which sea-horses glisten
> A fair course against the white-swelling surge—
> Four pedestals uphold it.

To my mind, the Enochian is further removed from everyday consciousness than any of the classic systems of medieval magic. A mathematical friend draws an analogy between these latter and Euclidian geometry—which he relates to the Briatic World of the Qabalah—on the one hand, and Enochian magic and the non-Euclidian systems of Riemann[5] measuring the space-time continuum by the geometry of *positive* curvature (ellipsoidal forms)—which he relates to the Ietziratic World—on the other. The former magic evokes entities from the realm of mind; Enochian magic, entities external to the human mind. I put this idea forward in case other mathematical magicians or magus-mathematicians can follow it up. I feel myself, though I cannot yet prove, that the Enochian Tables conceal a musical system; Dee's terms "Call" and "Aire" themselves suggest an auditory reference;

---

5 German mathematician Bernard Riemann (1826-1866).

Crowley's substitution of "Key" and "Aethyr" may thus obscure a facet of meaning. It is possible that the Tables provide a method of notation, or record frequencies on which the Calls should be sent out; they may even suggest the construction of an instrument. This is a field which awaits further experiment.

Of several novelists who have fallen under the spell of Dee, the most distinguished is Gustav Meyrink (1868-1932). His long and fascinating novel, *The Angel at the Western Window*, of which a French translation appeared in 1962, deals extensively with Dee's family-origins, his relationship with Kelley, intrigues with Elizabeth I and her secret service, travels and contacts with Central European monarchs, spiritistic experiments, alchemical investigations, and astrological predictions. But Meyrink leaves aside the basis of Enochian magic as revealed in the séances of Dee and Kelley, perhaps as material indigestible in a romance, though he describes some of the séances themselves.

In this country Gerard Heym was, before his recent sad death, one of the few people with any understanding of Enochian magic, and I recommend his all-too-brief essay, "Le Systeme Magique de John Dee" in No. 11-12, *La Tour Saint Jacques* (Paris), to those seeking a technical exposition. Heym believed that the Angelical alphabet was known to the erudite of Islam from the early years of their epoch. I am also acquainted with a fraternity appointed from an undisclosed source to carry further Dee's magical system and it is now operating to this end.

J. W. Hamilton Jones, a member of the TS [Theosophical Society] and also a Freemason, in 1946 published his annotated translation from the Latin of Dee's *The Hieroglyphic Monad*. This is a mathematico-astrological work with alchemical overtones, written in a style both cryptic and elliptical; it does not touch directly upon this magical technique. The fact is that hardly anyone knows anything about this technique from a practical angle, nor understands its theoretical basis.

Ivor Jones, in an appealing booklet called *The Green Rainbow* (c. 1967), brings out the relationship between the—chiefly alchemical—work of Dee and that of a later transcendental Welshman, Thomas Vaughan, brother of the Silurist poet. But he gives little account of the content of Dee's experiments with spirits, merely recounting anecdotes about his theories and their sometimes-awkward domestic consequences. He states that Dee left written works to the number of seventy-nine but does not say how he arrives at this figure. Only a few have been published, the most important from the viewpoint of his magical system being *A True and Faithful Relation of what passed for many years between Dr. John Dee and some Spirits* (1659)—though even from this the first five parts were omitted. About half-a-dozen other magical works remain in manuscript in the British Museum Library, others at the Bodleian, Oxford. A. E. Waite collected the *Alchemical Writings of Edward Kelley* in 1893.

Even Dee's manuscripts provide little more than the skeleton of a system, rudimentary when compared to the consistent and elaborate magical corpus taught in the GD. In his introductory paragraphs to the Enochian section of *The Golden Dawn*, vol. IV, Regardie remarks with wonder that someone has welded disparate texts, scattered in different libraries, into a coherent whole. Who was this consummate welder but MacGregor Mathers, who signed with one or other of his magical mottoes nearly all the Order's instruction-papers relative to the Enochian system? These formed an important part of the study-course undertaken after the grade of Adeptus Minor and in preparation for the grades of the Second Order. It was mainly if not solely through Mathers that Dee's magical working was injected into the GD syllabus and hence through him that it differs from that of most other esoteric Schools. Though Elias Ashmole before him had attempted a rescension of Dee's system, he did not fuse it with other Hermetic material.

It was Mathers—or was it his Secret Chiefs?—who composed *The Book of the Concourse of the Forces*. This stupendous amalgam combines Egyptian Tradition, initiated Astrology, Taro, Geomancy and the Qabalistic Tree of Life with Dee's intense Elemental constructions, to make a single monumentally-impressive whole. No one without the profoundest knowledge of all these symbolic "paths" could thus have built up from them a workable synthesis. Henceforth I will call this system, devised by Mathers on the basis of Dee's pioneer investigations, by the name of Enochiana, to distinguish it from the undeveloped texts of Dee himself.

Taking the Hebrew Qabalah, particularly those of its treatises which expound the Tree of Life, as basis of the Near Eastern magic which, absorbed by Europe, became the classic form of the art for the West, Enochiana is recognisable as different though in no way contradictory. It has developed the Kameas or Magical Squares of the former system into another dimension—at right angles, if one may so phrase it, to Qabalistic magic. (A study in depth, *Le Cara Magique SATOR AREPO*, by the late Alex Bloch is one of the few authoritative texts on the subject of Kameas). Similarly, it has expanded the Qabalistic equivalent of *Mantra-Yoga* in its elaboration of Words-of-Power. So much we owe to Dee or to his communicators: Mathers devised beyond this an Enochian parallel to the Hindu *Tattvas*—more properly *Tanmatras*—as taught in the GD when he elaborated the Elemental Universe as revealed to Dee. This Tattva-teaching was taken more or less directly from *Nature's Finer Forces* by Ram Prasad, but whereas the Tattvas represent, for example, Air of Fire as a red triangle charged with a (smaller) blue circle, Fire being the Element and Air the Sub-element, its Enochian equivalent is to be found in one of the squares of the Lesser Angle of Air in the Watch-Tower of Fire. Enochiana is much more detailed, its Elemental potencies being more finely sub-divided as to classification; therefore, the visions produced by skrying in its squares should be at once more elevated and more precise than those resulting from Tattva-skrying. While this is usually the case, judging from members' records which show that they contacted—in appearance at least—the "Sphynx", the "Angel" and the "God" of each pyramid as they were taught, they seldom experienced the full power and knowledge of such entities, and their records sometimes read like an account of mere pageantry. The following is from *A Vision of the "X" Square in the Watery Lesser Angle of the Fire Tablet* by Annie Horniman, reproduced in Francis King's *Astral Projection, Magic and Alchemy* (1971):

> I made the Signs and called on the Names and begged to be allowed to see the Angel. She appeared with a blue lunar

> crescent on her head and brown hair which was very long. Her robe was pale blue with a black border, and a pentagram in red on her breast; her wings were blue also, and so was the Cup in her left hand, in her right hand she bore a red torch. Around her was a diamond of red yods. She told me her office was "Change and purification through suffering such as spiritualises the material nature".

Such visions seem at once too decorative and too anthropomorphic; there is no reason why the appearance of the Angel of a pyramid, or of its lesser elemental inhabitants, should even recall a human shape. In the words of Yeats' superb poem:

> Once out of nature I shall never take
> My bodily form from any natural thing,
> But such a form as Grecian goldsmiths make[6].

I should rather expect such entities to manifest themselves in some abstract geometric shape suggesting jewellery, simple or complex according to their nature; or perhaps in forms resembling crystals or the basic cellular structures of organic life. This is only to say that further exploration is needed.

The primary concern of Enochiana is with the World of the Five Elements, whose doctrine is common to both Western and Eastern occultism; it sets forth a geometric method of mapping this "World", and a means of exploring it, in the Four Watch-Towers (of Air, Water, Earth and Fire) which are held together by the Tablet of Union (Aether). These Watch-Towers are represented by diagrams divided into squares in twelve columns and thirteen ranks, the Tablet of Union consisting of five columns and four ranks. One can imagine—or construct—a cube with one Watch-Tower diagram on each of its sides and the Tablet of Union at the top; or perhaps a cylinder would be more appropriate. This solid figure, whichever it is, should be surrounded by a series of concentric spheres, each symbolising one of the Thirty Aires. The diameters of these spheres increase in geometrical progression with their distance

6 From Yeats' poem "Sailing to Byzantium" (1927).

from the Watch-Towers—than which they are modes of being, "worlds", or "dimensions" still more attenuated. Thus the diagram reproduced in *The Monolith*, Vol. 1, No. 4 which represents the Aires as a mass of circles (bubbles?) all the same size above a terrestrial globe would seem to be misconceived. Since 1964 the Order of the Cubic Stone[7] has experimented with Dee's Calls, publishing results in its journal as just cited. It goes back for inspiration to Dee, ignoring as far as possible the developments of Mathers.

The system is both macrocosmic and microcosmic, related as much to the human psycho-physical organism as to the depths of space. Though Dee presented it in austerely diagrammatic form, he also recorded a vision seen by Kelley of four actual castellated Watch-Towers, with appropriate colours, banners and guardians. He gives their colours as white, green, black and red; Mathers assigns yellow to Air, blue to Water, black to Earth and red to Fire, reserving white for Aether. It is perhaps significant that his attribution employs the five colours regarded as sacred in the Far East, though his motive for the variation may have been a practical one: when these diagrams are painted as talismans or "flashing-tablets", Mathers' colouring proves more effective.

In the same way as Mathers projected the two-dimensional diagram of the Tree of Life into a sphere and actualised the *Fama*'s description of Christian Rosenkreutz's tomb, he raised the Enochian tablets into the next dimension. Each square of the Watch-Towers thus becomes the base of a solid, a truncated pyramid with six surfaces, four sides, a base and a top. He recognised that a three-dimensional *Mandala* has a wider application than a line-drawing. He further assigned to each face of a pyramid an Elemental attribution, a Taro Arcanum, a Zodiacal or Planetary sign, a Geomantic symbol, a Sephirah, a letter or an Egyptian deity. Sometimes he allotted two of these to one face. Each pyramid thus became a "concourse" of several different yet congruent forces which, manipulated by an effectual operator, could dispose of immense power.

---

7 The Order of the Cubic Stone was a magical order active from the late 1960s with a curriculum based in Hermetic and Enochian magic. Their publication was *The Monolith*.

GD members were warned about the dangers of mere dabbling in this system, as in the Sacred Magic of Abra-Melin which also makes use of Magical Squares. To experiment in the latter method without undertaking the preliminary praxis enjoined by its author would be asking for trouble. Initiated by ceremonial skrying and the vibration of words-of-power, Enochiana also should be approached gradually, with serious intent, and by members of a dedicated group. Should anything go wrong, the load will then be spread, and the impact neutralised or at least mitigated.

Crowley of course paid no attention to such warnings: whatever he lacked, it was not energy nor courage, even to the point of foolhardiness. In 1909 he undertook the peripatetic exercise in Enochian magick which he records in *The Vision and the Voice*; accompanied by his disciple Victor Neuburg, he tramped across the deserts of the Algerian hinterland, pausing only for ritual and skrying with Dee's *Calls*. Perhaps he felt himself a second Edward Kelley as he gazed into his own particular "shewstone", a huge topaz set at the centre of a scarlet cross, while Victor scribbled down what he reported seeing therein. His purpose was to explore those recondite regions symbolised by the Thirty Aires, or Aethyrs as he called them; but I do not feel that he penetrated far into their essence, remarkable though his results are. The account of his visions set down by Victor reads too much like that of his other visions. These are obsessively concerned with interpreting the magical world of the Golden Dawn by his own magickal extension of it—whereas Enochiana goes beyond either, and in a different direction. Crowley's atmosphere is often loaded and lowering if sometimes technicoloured, and the frequency of nightmarish episodes, like the following from a vision based upon *The Cry of the 18th Aethyr which is called Zen*, suggests that he failed to pierce through the turbid clouds of his own aura to any clearer sphere:

> And now there dawns the scene of the Crucifixion; but the Crucified One is an enormous bat, and for the two thieves are two little children. It is night, and the night is full of hideous things and howlings.

Later, he set out the basis of Enochiana with admirable lucidity in *The Equinox*, Nos. VII and VIII, though without acknowledging that the work had already been done by Mathers: such omissions can be as damaging as lies.

Yeats also must have delved some distance into Enochiana since he took part in the game of Enochian Chess—another development of Dee's investigations for which Mathers was responsible. Enochian Chess is more than a game: as Regardie says (*The Golden Dawn*, Vol. IV), its chess boards can, when prepared according to the Mathers formula, become "flashing-tablets" and "The Playe or Raying of the Chequers" a method of divination. I know of a group of occultists in the USA who in the 1940s did just this and came up with some remarkable results. One of the prophecies thus obtained declared that before the end of this century Russia would lose Mongolia to China. Time will show.

In Celtic mythology references to *fidchell*, a kind of chess played by its heroes and divinities, are frequent; skill in this more-than-game is a mark of magical power. Yeats worked out what may be called a Celtic extension of Enochiana and describes some Tables which he calls "chessboards" in an unpublished manuscript, National Library of Ireland, 13568 (2). Here a Cromlech[8]—a capstone supported by four uprights—replaces the concept of a pyramid with four walls sloping to a flat top; and changes in colour-attribution as well as in the allotment of the direction of space to the four Elements are introduced. There is no indication of date, so this material may have been given out as Second Order teaching, which is known to have varied that of the First Order in some respects; or Yeats may have arrived at it after the Schism through his own researches.

8 A cromlech is a type of megalithic monument with a capstone and side walls.

THE EVOCATIONS OF THE CROMLECS[9]

The chess board was undoubtedly of great mystical importance and in ancient times is attributed to certain Cromlecs. There are twenty different attributions corresponding to the reflection of the powers of the four gates of each of the four cities and to the reflection of the four gates of the city that is above the gods and above form. As these cities correspond to the four elements and the spirit, so do the reflection of their gates correspond to the sub-divisions of the elements and of the spirit.

Each square of the chess board represents a cromlec seen as from above; and all the uppermost stones of the cromlecs of the chess board, when it is attributed to the city of Fire are red or red yellow, and when to the city of Air a blue green, and when to Water violet or silver, and when to the Earth yellow. Each uppermost stone is supported by four supports corresponding to the four angles of each square, and these supports are allotted to the elements and the colours in a certain order.

I will take the allotment of the chess board to the forces of the Western gate of the city of Gorias for an example. Gorias corresponds to the element of Fire and as the West is the place of Water, the Western gate is the Water of Fire.

The upper left-hand quarter corresponds to the East and the Air, the upper right-hand quarter to the South and Fire and the lower left quarter to the North and the Earth and the lower right quarter to the West and Water respectively. Each of these quarters is again divided into four quarters this again divided into four quarters containing a single square each.

The place of Earth is considered the place of greatest elementary power and the place of Water the next and the place of Air the next and the place of Fire the least, for the elements decline in weight in

9 This refers to Yeats' own version of "Enochian Chess", where he merged Golden Dawn material with Irish mythology.

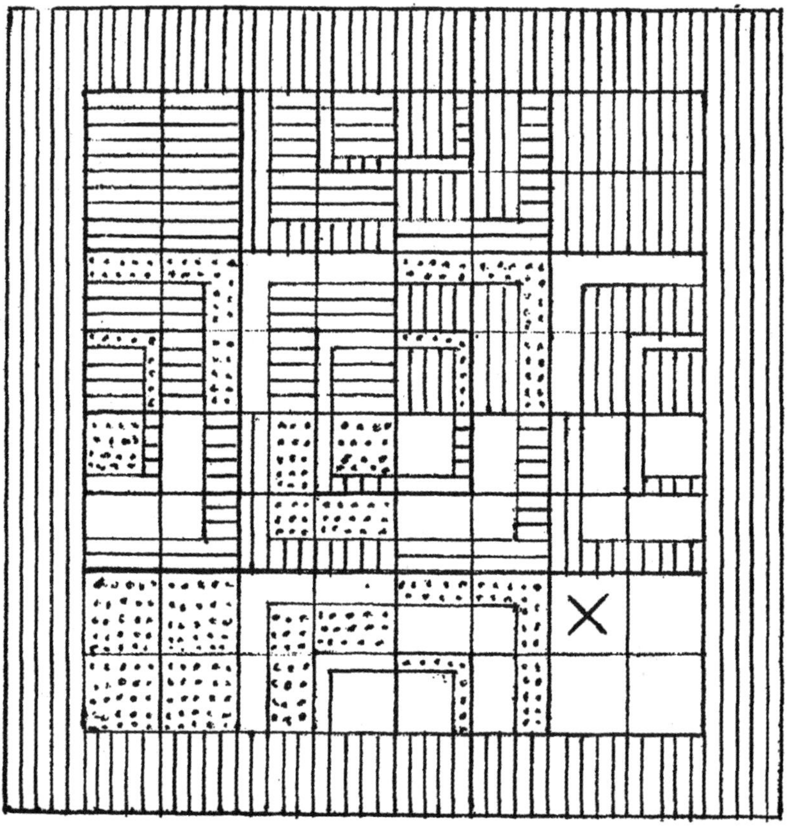

this order. The strongest sub-element, in the allotment, which will be Earth in the chess board when allotted to a Northern or Earthy gate of a city and Fire if the allotment be to a Southern gate, etc., will always belong to the Northern support which will therefore be coloured yellow; and the next strongest sub-element, which will be Fire in the case of the Southern quarter of the board, will be allotted to the West, and so on. I will take the square marked X as an example.

It is the Eastern square of the Western quarter of the chessboard allotted to the Western gate of the city of Gorias. Its cromlec will therefore be the cromlec of Air of Water of Water of Water of Fire. The main element Fire is represented by the uppermost stone; the most powerful sub-element, Water, by a violet or silver Northern support, and the next most powerful sub-element, which is still Water, by a violet or silver Western support, and the next sub-element, Water, by a violet or silver Eastern support and the least powerful sub-element, Air, by a blue green Southern support. (Yeats' diagrams are *oblong*, very roughly drawn; I have made them *square* as they cannot otherwise be related to the chessboard. I have coloured them according to his directions, and have also retained his spelling of the word cromlech as he is using it in a special sense.)

I do not entirely share Regardie's scorn for later Enochian students since I have studied some papers by members of the Hermes Lodge of the *Stella Matutina* describing in great detail the attribution of Egyptian deities to the squares of the Watch-Towers—though whether these were ever used in a practical way is open to question.

Dee's Watch-Towers were communicated by a spirit called Ave; another, called Nalvage, revealed a further Table which, though modest in size, seems to me of considerable importance. Again it consists of letters geometrically arranged, this time naming four classes of entities, forces—angels if you will—which rule jointly and perhaps also severally over the Watch-Towers. Dee particularised them as *Laudantes* (= Those who praise), *Ministrantes* (= Those who minister), *Confirmantes* (= Those who establish), and *Con-fundantes* (= Those who throw into disorder). In so far as humanity partakes of the Elemental realms, these four classes of beings bear sway over it: therefore, though the first three would seem to be beneficent, the

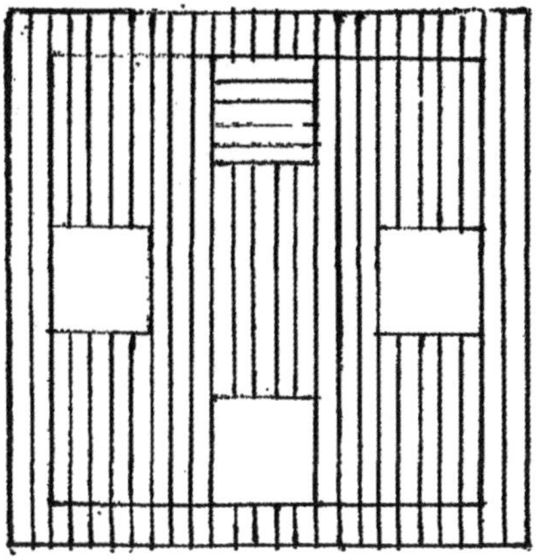

Key:

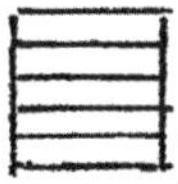 = East, 🜁, Blue-green

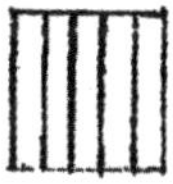 = South, 🜂, Red

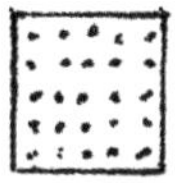 = North, 🜃, Yellow

 West, 🜄, Purple (or Silver)

Confundantes in the course of their destined function can cause chaos in human affairs, from the most trivial to the most momentous. I suggest that the entities whom Yeats experienced as "the Frustrators" when he was receiving the communications on which he based *A Vision* came from that class. Their existence alone is enough to advise caution.

This is not to maintain that the *Confundantes*, or any other Enochian entities, are essentially evil, even in the restricted sense of hostile to humanity, but disturbed inexpertly, they may prove as destructive as electricity or any other natural force mishandled. They are the vehicles of particularised Elemental energies; in some cases personalised, but in a different mode from that of human beings.

Good is, for ordinary consciousness, whatever contributes to the well-being of humanity; but the provision or maintenance of such well-being may as a goal be utterly unimportant in a larger cosmic scheme. Whatever undermines it or sweeps it away may not in a wider context be evil at all. "Between mutability's teeth let us make our dwelling"[10]—one would be wise to take Rilke's suggestion to heart. †

Tantra (1975)

This is an odd essay in that it is not at all concerned with the practice of Indian Tantra. It is mostly a consideration of whether or not the Golden Dawn or any of their offshoots in the early twentieth century were engaging in sex magic or esoteric sexuality. The section on A. E. Waite may be the most revealing in this regard. Although Colquhoun appears to have been working on a system of sex magic in the years between 1939-1943, she does not address any of the theoretical material she was previously working with in this essay.

The magical system taught in the GD is to be classed as Theurgy, the Magic of Light, as distinct from all types of sex-magic and even exclusive of them. In the Preface to his monograph of the same name, Edward Garstin defines Theurgia as:

10 This quote from Rainer Maria Rilke is also found in *Goose of Hermogenes.*

> the practical part of spiritual alchemy

and later continues:

> ...the Egyptian Theurgists, who said that the Gods were Spiritual Essences, and were partaken of as light, leaving the light unaffected, while the partaker was filled...

He adds:

> ...nowhere in the truly sacred mysteries—at any rate in the West—was any teaching given involving any sex-practices, such as the introversion of sexual forces, endeavouring to draw these up the spine and into the brain.

It follows from this that he disapproved of Aleister Crowley—indeed, when I first met my cousin he was very bitter against him, though less on account of his supposedly-harmful influence than because of his treatment of Mathers, which was shabby by any standards. Edward was always intensely loyal to Mathers and Moïna; but it is fair to say that towards the end of his life he modified his attitude towards Crowley and grew less blind to the latter's merits—though he still deplored his oath-breaking, libelling and pilfering of others' material. Perhaps Edward was becoming more tolerant of the strangely-juxtaposed tendencies which constitute a human being.

While I believe Edward's view of sex-magic to have been generally held in the GD of his time—Regardie (in *My Rosicrucian Adventure*) expresses the same opinion concerning the absence of sex-magic in GD teaching—I also believe that certain of its earlier students of Second Order rank were given more than a hint of processes which might today be classed as "Tantrik". This speculation is difficult to substantiate since the teaching, if such there were, would not be committed to writing in any explicit way. In all occult sodalities the student receives—in addition to graded rites—instruction by stages:

1. From books in libraries, and by means of public or semi-public lectures, to which correspondence-courses are a possible adjunct or alternative.

2. Through "Knowledge-lectures", as the GD called them: usually duplicated or privately printed papers available to members only; and in private lectures or seminars.

3. Through secret MSS lent only to the more advanced students; and individual teaching "from mouth to ear"—the Unwritten Qabalah or its equivalent in other systems.

In these days of scientific enlightenment and universal education, should not information of any kind be available to all? Esoteric fraternities may be thought a little out of style in demanding secrecy or even discretion from their adherents. Yet how far do unqualified investigators penetrate into a nuclear research-laboratory, or non-initiates into an office where the policy of a financial consortium is decided, or the profane into a Government Department concerned with Defence? (The result of the last type of intrusion may well be imprisonment.) Even the International Committee of the Red Cross at Geneva—*La Maison* to its members, who never exceed twenty-five in number—meets for its major decisions in strict secrecy. These examples demonstrate the fact that when matters are considered important enough, secrecy is the rule; those who demand admittance must be in possession of the equivalent of a password.

Returning to the field more usually designated occult, the problem is to determine if there is in the West any *corpus* of tradition comparable to the Tantras of the Orient whether Taoist, Buddhist or Hindu. While sex-magic of various kinds is common to all cultures especially at the level of folk-practice, I doubt if one can find Tantra properly so called in Europe unless as an importation from the East. Those writers who profess to discover it tend to stress one of Tantra's "Five M's"—*Maithuna*, sex-intercourse—at the expense of its other four. Nonetheless Tantra is, according to Philip S. Rawson, organiser and cataloguer of the Arts Council's exhibition of Tantrik Art in 1971,

> ...a cult of ecstacy focussed on a division of cosmic sexuality. Life-styles, ritual, magic, myth, philosophy and a complex of signs and emotive symbols converge upon that vision. The basic texts in which these are conveyed are also called Tantras.

This exhibition, one of the most inspiring, aesthetically and metaphysically, I have ever seen, gave a clear insight into a specialised and sophisticated world-view. (I did not hear of any complaints about "obscenity" and I hope there were none.) I suggest that Tantra in art, philosophy, feeling, represents the Magian strain in Oriental culture: I take the term from Spengler's *Der Untergang des Abendlandes* (a title too-briskly translated as *The Decline of the West*) where this style, distinct equally from the Classical and the Romantic modes, was first isolated.

Had one the opportunity to study them in depth, certain of these Tantrik exhibits would, I feel sure, cast light on Dr. Dee's Enochian system: I think of geometrical arrangements of the letters of the Sanskrit alphabet, and other diagrams consisting of squares for astrological computation and again, Tantras representing the origin of the lingam. If Dr. Dee is the most profound example of Magian thought in the West he may be also a Western exponent of Tantrik thought. Another theme (just one more!) which lies awaiting exploration.

As any equivalent of Tantra would belong to the third and most secret category of esoteric instruction in a magical fraternity, one can only collect scattered references, gossip even, as indication of its presence in the GD—much as, in the sphere of national politics, one can sometimes gain insight from the Questions asked in Parliament rather than their replies, often phrased in an "officialese" designed to bewilder rather than enlighten. Following such faint trails one can pick up traces of a Tantrik or anti-Tantrik attitude in several GD members; in Mathers and Moïna themselves; then in Dr. Edward Berridge and Annie Horniman (remember her expressed disapproval of him in this regard); in W. B. Yeats, Dr. Brodie-Innes, Aleister Crowley (of course) and A. E. Waite with Arthur Machen as his disciple.

Why did the Mathers' select Isis from the Egyptian pantheon for a cult-revival? (Or were they rather selected by her?) Who or what was she, besides the power of the Invisible Station which should inspire the Praemonstrator of a GD temple? She was the Moon as Queen of Heaven but also the earth and its corn, nourisher of mankind—both Iesod and Malkuth on the Tree of Life. Archetype of mother, sister and wife she was, beyond that, the Great Goddess of all the pantheons, Mother Nature herself—Binah but also Ain Soph Aur, the all-pervading and all-producing. When Moïna assumed the god-form of Isis she became the universal Shakti to her husband. Did they feel some "lunar" influence as needed to balance the GD's Magic of Light and was this the motive for their revival of Isis-worship?

Waite's interest (with the exception of Crowley's) is, surprisingly to say, the best-documented. In the Gerald Yorke collection of MSS at the Warburg Institute, London, is a work by Waite entitled *The House of the Hidden Light* (1903) which was never published though bound into a volume through the assiduous care of Mr. Yorke. It mentions *The Veritable, Ancient and Rectified Rite of Lilith, called* ל *in the Great Book of Avalon*. Whether this *Great Book* was ever written does not appear but as to the portion of it called *The Rite*, one can guess at its intention by analysing the names in its title. In Qabalistic tradition, Lilith is ruler of the Qliphoth (= "Shells" or Evil Demons) pervading the averse aspect of Iesod, microcosmically the sphere of sex. Rabbinic lore characterises her as Adam's first consort, a succuba and mother of succubi—which suggests that this *Rite* concerned sexual congress with praeternatural beings. Legends elaborate further, assigning the Younger Lilith as wife of Asmodai, who rules the sphere of *Venus Aversa*, the Qliphotic Netzach; and Lilith the Elder as spouse of Samael, prince of the Qliphoth of Chokmah, sphere of the Dark Father. It seems as though Waite were dealing, not only with sexual magic, but with its "blacker" side. He had investigated Andrew Jackson Davis during an earlier Spiritist phase and was to publish in 1922 an account of Davis' Harmonial Philosophy. But this *Rite* would seem to go much further than Davis' fairly tentative sexual theories. The Hebrew letter ל (=L, Lamed), however is allotted to the sign Libra, mansion of Venus and to the Major Arcanum known as Justice, both without goëtic undertones. (Crowley re-named the card Adjustment and ascribed to it a phallic-vulval significance as "The Woman justified by Iod".)

Waite goes on to say that the *Rite* is symbolically related to the third letter of the Sanskrit *mantram* AUM : as A and O (U) were already in use as emblematic of the Magic of Light and typified sunrise (Greek *Eos*, Ἔως), M must have indicated another path—"lunar" as distinct from "solar", perhaps, one which utilised the feminine current as such. The Magic of Light expresses the unisex idea in an occult sodality either by admitting men and women on an equal footing, irrespective of their sex, or by restricting membership to men only. Tantra, however, needs women because in its view their psycho-physical constitution contains elements absent from that of the male. This is the basic inspiration of all cults devoted to the Great Goddess and the reason for the suspicion with which they are commonly viewed in a male-oriented society. Thus, while a Tantrik group admits women, it cannot do so on a unisex footing since the reason for their presence consists in their very difference from men. This view may be aptly suggested by the letter M; any fraternity making use of the powers which the Goddess subsumes could come under the same designation, also those women-only groups deriving from myths of the Amazons. These are not necessarily of a Lesbian tendency, though I understand that such exist: in Elliott O'Donnell's *Secret Societies of Modern London* one of them is mentioned as The Gorgons, but there is no evidence of such sororities in connection with the GD.

Waite's *Rite* is not given in full so it is impossible to say how far it openly made a cult of the Goddess. Evidently his initiates formed a secret group within his HOGD (like certain of its predecessors in *Isis-Urania*) but were not drawn exclusively from it. All his members had left the original *Isis-Urania* by this time and were consequently in schism, Waite lists them under their GD mottoes and I append their names in the profane world:

Soror Shemeber	=	Pamela Carden—Mrs. P. Bullock
Soror Hilaria	=	?
Soror Vigilate	=	Mrs. (Helen) Rand

Soros Fidelis	= Elaine Simpson
Frater Resurgam	= Dr. Edward W. Berridge
Frater Levavi Occulos	= Percy Bullock
Frater Finem Respisce	= Dr. Robert W. Felkin
Frater De Profundis Ad Lucem	= Frederick L. Gardner
Frater Anima Pura Sit	= Dr. Henry Pullen Burry

One should add Waite himself and his great friend Arthur Machen; also perhaps Crowley, since he was already associated with Elaine Simpson and Dr. Berridge in the loyal *Isis*-Temple. The connection of these Hermetic students with the *Rite* sheds an unexpected light on the personality of some of them, not least on that of Waite himself; and one may also speculate on how Mrs. Rand reconciled herself to Dr. Berridge, to whom shortly before she had been almost as much opposed as was Annie Horniman.

Waite gives another list of names, seemingly in respect of Offices rather than individuals, which includes:

Frater Aquarius
Frater Elias Artista
Frater Christophoron
Soros Benedicta in Aqua
Soror Gloriosa in Igne

The two last obviously represent a version of the GD Stolistes and Dadouchos—Stolistria and Dadouché if the Offices are taken by women-initiates—niched on the Tree of Life in Hod and Netzach respectively. Christophoron (= Christ-bearer) could be an Office attributed to the sphere of Tiphereth, while *Elias Artista*, which has alchemical overtones, and *Aquarius* would be referred respectively to Geburah and Chesed. Waite himself probably took the Office of *Elias Artista* since he used this title in other places almost as if it were an extra magical motto, and Machen was sometimes called *Aquarius* instead of *Filius Aquarii.*

Waite belonged to a generation which tended to veil in Latin the franker parts of any discourse, and this one is wrapped up as well in his usual obfuscated prose. He casts oblique glances, however, at a mysterious *Locus Faunorum* (= Place of the Fauns) and a *Locus Inferioris Zion* (= Place of the Lower Zion) which can scarcely imply anything if not sexual polarity. The latter name is in fact a Zoharic locution for the female genitalia (*Idra Zuta Qadisha*, ch. XXII, 744); the passage is a clear example of the sexual basis to much Qabalistic thought. Even if all is to be taken symbolically, what is said must concern a rite oriented to sex-magic and therefore distinct, not only from the Magic of Light but also from the Christianity to which Waite continually animadverted—to use a word of which he surely would approve! I call to mind the fringe-Masonic ritual recorded by Crowley in *Energised Enthusiasm* (*The Equinox*, No. II) which I once assumed to be fantasy.

If it is surprising to find Brodie-Innes as a collaborator of Waite in this sense—the two were personally as oil and water—it is no surprise at all to find him an advocate of Tantra, in which he had already shown an interest. If Kenneth Grant is right in thinking that *Shakti-tantra* or its Western equivalent formed the basis of Dion Fortune's occult work, then she received an initial impetus towards it from Brodie-Innes. Nor is the co-operation of Dr. Berridge astonishing since one of the first serious squabbles to strain the fabric of *Isis-Urania* arose from his adherence to the Brotherhood of the New Life. This was founded by the naturalised American Thomas Lake Harris who with his followers, one of whom was the fascinating Scotsman Laurence Oliphant (1829-88), author of *Sympneumata*, established several communities to put his ideas into practice. Here belief in a double-sexed deity replaced extreme monotheism, group-marriage and the search for the soul-mate were advocated and trance-states induced by means of Karezza (what the O∴T∴O∴ was later to call Dianism) were encouraged. Mild enough by present-day standards, Berridge's propaganda for these notions would have been found generally shocking in the Britain of last century, and Annie Horniman was not the only occult student to be scandalised. Complaints soon reached Mathers, by that time domiciled in France, that Berridge was leading the younger members astray. Mathers, however, refused to discipline him as Annie demanded and told her (more or less) to mind her own business. He made it clear that in his opinion everyone should reach a conclusion on sex-questions without interference from their fellow-students, though they could apply to their superiors in grade (i.e., himself and Wynn Westcott) if they felt the need of guidance. His attitude is remarkably broad-minded in a man who, as far as one can judge, himself led a life of considerable abstinence. Berridge repaid the tolerance of his Chief by rallying support for him in the hour of need, which struck some years later on the defection of most of *Isis-Urania*'s initiates.

Whether Lake Harris evolved his ideas out of his own *ingenium* or otherwise, they certainly bear some resemblance to Tantrik Yoga. The Tantrika avoids "wasting" semen in orgasm; the substance is valued for its occult properties and is ideally absorbed into his psycho-physical being where, especially, its subtle counterpart reinforces his subtle body or bodies. Oliphant advocated a system of "internal respiration", related to yogic breath-control, to be used especially during the sex-act. A booklet by Alice B. Stockham entitled *Karezza* (1895) describes this sex-praxis in some detail; it would seem to be indistinguishable from what Catholic theologians, when listing permissible methods of contraception, call *coitus reservatus* and which they classify as a type of continence.

This instance of Casuistry makes one wonder whether the relationship of Mathers with Moïna was strictly and permanently "platonic", that is, based upon continence as ordinarily understood and as her letter of December 31, 1895 to Annie Horniman would imply. Could it be that Karezza was not excluded, being assumed to be a "spiritualised" praxis far removed from ordinary sexual stimuli and their satisfaction? If Mathers exercised as much mesmeric ascendancy over his wife as Westcott opined, he may have persuaded her that *coitus reservatus* was not a sex-act and to overcome to this degree her repugnance from intimate physical contacts. Seated face to face, ritually robed in nemyss and mantle, the scarlet and blue reversing the traditional colouring of Boddhisattva and Dakini, they may have remained entranced for hours in a mutual enthronement.

Whatever their relationship consisted in, continence (in either the accepted or the casuistic sense) did not injure Moïna in any way: one never hears of her as physically ailing, nor does she seem to have been emotionally victimised. I am not sure that the same can be said of Mathers: though he was of tough physique and always took steps to maintain his health and strength, accounts dating from before the turn of the century and stretching forward to the outbreak of the 1914 War note in him symptoms of nerve-strain. May not these have been due in some measure to the taxing control which Karezza demands? Several sexologists have warned against the practice on these grounds.

There may be further reason for misgiving: while one knows that Crowley is not a trustworthy reporter, especially when his subject is an ex-friend, an assertion which may be pertinent occurs in *Liber Agape*. This is an O∴T∴O∴ instruction-paper dealing with sex-magic quoted by Kenneth Grant in *The Magical Revival*. Having indicated the use of the mouth in a vampiric manner at the culmination of intercourse, Crowley continues:

> It was used by the late Oscar Wilde, and by Mr. and Mrs. "Horos" also, in a modified form by S. L. Mathers and his wife, and by E. W. Berridge. The ineptitude of the three latter saved them from the fate of the three former.

As the said fate involved prosecution and a long prison sentence, the implication would seem to be that the practice Crowley hints at, if completely performed, would so pervert the judgment of its practitioners as to urge them into crime while obstructing their escape when the Law prepared to catch up on them. But Crowley was irresponsible in such accusations and he may, knowing Berridge's predilections, have thrown in a snide remark about the Mathers's for good measure.

Whether or not they used or attempted to use this species of vampirism, wherein the partners become Sage and Victim, it is plain that Karezza in itself could have brought them some advantages. Not only could it provide an occult launching-pad for exploring the realms of mystery but a contraceptive whose near-safety would obviate concern in respect of family ties—rather than which both undoubtedly desired occult advancement. In view of the continually-precarious state of their finances the care of dependents would have frustrated the mission to which both had been called.

Mathers' teaching dealt with sex in another, more recondite manifestation—that of the Elemental spouse. Both he and Wynn Westcott not only believed in the possibility of such a union but must have taught methods by which a partner from praeternatural regions could be attracted. They recommended an Elemental marriage to Mrs. Carden, despite the fact that she was married already in a less rarified fashion to A. J. Carden and had produced a daughter. Without more detailed documentation than is at present available, it is impossible to say more than that here again the two GD Chiefs were in accord with Tantrik tradition, for the advanced Tantrika has methods of obtaining a Daimon-lover. Such beliefs are not confined to specialised cults in the Orient, however: the folk-lore of the world teems with stories of the fairy-bride or fairy-bridegroom, whether beneficent or averse, from the seal-man and seal-woman of the Hebrides through the Lady of the Lake or the Lamia to the mermaid ancestress of the Lusignan line. If such unions result in offspring—and they are often said to do so—it is difficult to dismiss them as mere fantasy without also classifying all our forebears as mentally deranged. While Moïna disliked the idea of Elemental mates as much as human ones, she did not doubt the possibility of such, and one wonders how long she continued to resist it in face of what she sincerely believed to be Rosicrucian teaching. She must in the A∴O∴ have given instruction on such subjects as *The Esoteric Philosophy of Love and Marriage* if she banned, as too revealing, Dion Fortune's book of this title.

Mathers need not have gone as far afield as the secret systems of China, India or Tibet: Islam hides a similar tradition with the Beni Udhra sect and for several reasons it is more likely that, if Tantra (so called for the sake of convenience) formed a part, albeit hidden, of Rosicrucian doctrine, it came from the Near rather than the Far East. Mathers himself was temperamentally opposed to Oriental borrowings and there is no evidence to suggest that he ever joined the O∴T∴O∴. Though I cannot find anything in Europe comparable with the extensive Oriental systems properly designated as Tantrik, some residues of the Pre-Christian Gnosis which taught similar doctrines may have survived the centuries. In general, however, Europe owes its Tantra to Eastern lore brought back in more recent times by enterprising travellers like Carl Kellner who have penetrated exotic cults in the course of their wanderings.

The seal was set on these graftings when Crowley was initiated into the O∴T∴O∴ in 1912. Mathers may well have given him an inkling in his early studies and, like others, he no doubt gleaned something from his travels, though too much has been made of his Tantrik Gourous. Crowley stayed in the neighbourhood of Madoura, South India, for only a few days and could not have taken any advanced initiations there in so brief a time. Later in Benares he had a talk with Shri Swami Swayam Prakashananda Maithila, and with Munshi Elihu Bux at Agra; but neither was a Tantrika and there is no reason to think that Tantra was discussed. As to Shri Mahatma Agamya Paramahamsa Gourou and Bhima Pratap Sen, who are claimed by some as his mentors in Tantra, he did not ever meet them but only received their teaching, at third hand and much later, from Theodor Reuss: they had been the initiators of Karl Kellner. Towards Agamya, Crowley did not feel the respect due to a revered master, judging by the scornful account by Col. Fuller which he published in *The Equinox*, No. IV. While Crowley was one of nature's Tantrikas, his proclivities were not channelled in a workable system until his reception into the O∴T∴O∴.

I do not belong to that school of thought—whose chief exponent is, perhaps, Serge Hutin[1]—which sees in love-stories by several poets of the *Belle Epoque* the work of Tantra-initiates. Dr. Hutin thus claims Rimbaud on the strength of the sonnet "Voyelles", and de L'Isle Adam[2] of *L'Eve Future*; earlier, there was de Nerval and Aurelie. In no case is there hard evidence for membership of a closed group—nor for anything more than erotic sensibility. I append my own translation

1 Serge Hutin (1929-1997) was a French writer about the occult and Freemasonry. He and Colquhoun were close for some time in the 1960s and may have had a romantic involvement.

2 French Symbolist writer Auguste Villiers de l'Isle-Adam (1838-1889). *The Future Eve,* published in 1886, was an early science fiction novel in which the term android was said to have been coined.

of "Voyelles" so that all can judge whether it mirrors "An Ascent unto Daath" or any similar occult praxis:

VOWELS
A black, E white, I red, U green, O blue—
Vowels, I'll tell your hidden origin!
A, swarthy coat of glistening flies that whine
Round disenchanting stenches there below

E, white of curtain-mist, the glacier's proud
Spear-shaft, pale kings, rustle of umbel-bloom
I, lovely in ire or sad delirium
The crimson laughing lips that have spat blood

U, tides, celestial murmur of green seas
Peace of herd-scattered pasture, wrinkled peace—
Alchemy's imprint on a studious brow

O, the last trumpet of strange stridencies
Omega, violet radiance of Her Eyes—
Aeons and Worlds rise through their silence now!

It seems to me that Dr. Hutin confuses fantastic love-affairs with an obscure but exacting discipline. With W. B. Yeats, however, one is on firmer ground; one knows at least that he spent the greater part of his adult life as a member of a secret fraternity. Though never closely associated with either Waite or Crowley (and this is one reason for divining a Tantra-like strain in the illuminations of Mathers himself), Yeats set a high metaphysical value on sex, both in his personal life and in his work. The latter falls into Spengler's category of the Magian; many of his poems celebrate what he calls "the solved antinomy", of which he sees marriage, and indeed all sexual love, as a glyph. He extends this idea in the prose of *A Vision* (1926 and 1937) where it recurs as one of the basic themes. In "the union of man and woman" he sees "a symbol of that eternal instant where the antinomy is resolved". The book is full of abstruse statements like:

> ...passionate love is from the Daimon which seeks by union with some other Daimon to reconstruct above the antinomies its own true nature.

and:

> ...in the most acetic schools of India the novice tortured by his passion will pray to God to come to him as a woman and have with him sexual intercourse, nor is the symbol subjective...

While I have no wish to overestimate the "Tantrik" tradition in the GD there are some hints suggesting its existence. Whatever leakages there may have been previously, it was Ellic Howe's publication in *The Magicians of the Golden Dawn*, of Moïna's revealing letter to Annie which brought the matter to the surface. While Mathers and Moïna communicated this and any other sexual teaching only to pupils who in their view were ready for such instruction, Waite must have come at it by another, probably transatlantic route.

It is plain from such intimations on the lore of Elementals and their relationship with humanity that much Order-teaching has not yet reached the general public. Material already given out lies hidden in mundane recesses; more remains undisclosed, in the keeping of Guardians who await those qualified to receive it undistorted and transmit it with discretion. Will the year 1975 see them emerge?

The Order has spread—not as its Chiefs would ideally have willed, but it has spread; and its name is more powerfully evocative than ever before. If a complete revival is to take place in the future, its master-spirit must be, as Mathers aimed to make himself, both a scholar and an adept. He must have a good knowledge of Hebrew, Greek and Latin, preferably of Arabic also; and he must possess at least several of the occult *buada* (= excellencies) and *clessa* (= accomplishments)—to substitute Gaelic terms for the Sanskrit *siddhis*. How far Mathers succeeded may be gauged by comparing his attainment with that of most present-day occultists.

I *may* fail but I *will* be renowned, like the race of the echoing Morven[3]! †

---

3 This is a line from a famous eighteenth century literary forgery, by James MacPherson, *Fingal: an ancient epic poem, in six books: together with several other poems, composed by Ossian the son of Fingal*. It's a strange choice to conclude this essay.

Alchemia (1975)

While much of Colquhoun's earlier interest in alchemy tended to centre around individual and spiritual transformation, this mammoth essay is notable for Colquhoun's focus on operative alchemy and the work of practicing alchemists in the twentieth century. Her assertion that alchemy is a branch of nuclear physics is an interesting indication of her framing of magic as a science that is still not fully understood. She seems to have a particular interest in the medicinal applications of alchemy and refers to the ingesting of metallic tinctures of silver and gold, both of which are still used as treatments and cures.

I use the word Alchemia for the science or art of alchemy as seen through the GD temperament, in the same way as I employ Enochiana for the Enochian system of magic similarly seen. Today, if anyone thinks alchemy dead or exploded they had better think again. Though in the West the Establishment has always tended it to the dustbin of "rejected knowledge", arising as it does from the underground stream of Magian thought, it is as much alive in the present as in any previous century. Without racking my memory I can think of several Operators on the Continent—the late Armand Barbault, author of *L'or du millième matin* (1969), just published in an English translation; Eugène Canseliet, pupil of the mysterious Fulcanelli whose identity is in debate although he was active in the very recent past; Roger Caro, Bernard Husson and the painter Louis Cattiaux who wrote *Le Message retrouvé* (1955). All maintain (or until lately maintained) an alchemical laboratory in back room or back garden. M. Canseliet has even been shown on television at his labours there.

Roger Caro, author of *Pléiade Alchimique* (1967) and *Concordances Alchimiques* (1968) has also published a coloured photographic record of the Great Work in its different stages and is associated with a fraternity known as *Les Frères Ainés de la Rose Croix* which operates two Temples, the *Ajunta* and its offshoot the *Vrehappada*. Their members are European adepts, some of whom have taken magical names in Sanskrit; the following lists are probably not complete:

Ajunta Temple
Kamala Jnana (Superior; author of a *Dictionnaire de Alchimique*, 1961, published at Argentière, Charlet)
Theophoreonai (Hierophant Major)
Mustagogos (Hierophant)
Erebus
Ermeion
Jethro
N' Palinga-Dhara
Teletourgos

Vrehappada Temple
Pasiphae (Hierophant)
Nitiçastra
Tejasrasa

It would be rash to assume that these Temples function in India—it may well be in France, with a theosophical inspiration. They engage in practical as well as theoretical alchemy: during the course of a visit to M. Caro, Dr. Serge Hutin was shown a specimen of the Quintessence: "*liquide rouge en masse compacte, mais prenant la couleur d'or une fois qu'il se trouve étalé*" as his Preface to *Concordances Alchimiques* recounts. The popularity of Dr. Hutin's own books on alchemy is a proof of a Continent-wide interest in the subject. He writes from a theoretical viewpoint without attempting (as far as I know) either the physical or the spiritual praxis[1].

Perhaps I should at once say what I think alchemy is *not*—difficult though it is to define it positively. It is not a moralistic allegory, but neither is it mere furnace-work, the "torturing" of metals by extreme heat: authorities unite in decrying the *Soffleurs* (= Puffers) whose one idea was to transmute metals into gold in order to get rich quick. It is not chemistry of any kind, not even so-called Hyperchemistry; it is rather an aspect of nuclear physics, and its well-attested

1 This appears to be another shot at Serge Hutin, with whom she was once quite intimate.

transmutations result from nuclear reaction brought about by a still-unknown process.

No doubt there are alchemists practising in Britain; there are certainly several theoreticians with magnificent personal libraries like Michael Innes (not the novelist!) and Robert Lankiewicz [sic][2], to say nothing of the late Gerard Heym, whose unique collection was dispersed some years before his death. He was a founder-member of the Society for the Study of Alchemy and Early Chemistry, and of its journal, *Ambix*. His Introduction to the French translation of Gustav Meyrink's novel, *Le Dominicain Blanc* (1963) shows his insight into the theory of Taoist alchemy, traceable to China in the sixth century B.C., with especial reference to the tradition that a Sword is found materialised in the coffin of an adept whose corpse has been transmuted by the Elixir into a Body of Light. In the 1930s, London possessed a genuine adept in Archibald Cockren, a physiotherapist and masseur then living in Boundary Road, N. W. 8, who wrote *Alchemy Rediscovered and Restored* (1940). Edward Garstin visited his laboratory, where he was shown the Philosophers' Egg, a glass vessel of ovoid shape containing layer upon layer of basic matter in the traditional colours of black, grey, white and yellow. At the top these had blossomed into a flower-like form, a pattern arranged like petals around a centre, all of a glowing orange-scarlet. One remembers Sir Epicure Mammon's anxious query in *The Alchemist* by Ben Jonson:

> Thou hast descried the flower, the sanguis agni?

By keeping his basic matter for a long time at a constant gentle heat, Cockren had caused it to grow; it had branches like a tree, as Edward told me. Cockren would not divulge what substance he had used as basis, but remarked that he always kept "an open pentagram" in the laboratory while he was at work. I took this to be something like the GD Pantacle, the magical implement related to elemental Earth, and I suppose he kept it wrapped in silk when not in use, as instructed.

2 Robert Lenkiewicz (1941-2002) was a Plymouth based painter who had a great interest in witchcraft and the occult, with a staggering and significant personal library dedicated to the topic that was sold at auction after his death.

Other adepts have maintained that the laboratory also be an oratory. Though I feel sure he was not a member of Edward's Lodge, he may well have had some other GD connection.

Cockren followed directions he found in the writings of Sir George Ripley, a disciple of Raymond Lully—probably in *The Bosom Book* which gives a method for preparing the Philosopher's Stone. Ripley was also the author of *The Compound of Alchemy ... containing Twelve Gates* (1471). Cockren prepared oils from all the metals and prescribed them in minute doses to his patients: to take more than would tinge a litre of water would poison one. Oil-of-gold was the most effective healing agent, but Mrs. Maiya Tranchell-Hayes was cured of a nervous breakdown by taking three drops of oil-of-silver, presumably in as many doses.

By the 1940s Cockren had moved his place of work to the Holborn area where Gerard Heym, who was a friend of Edward's from Quest Society days, used to see him frequently. Gerard was by this time in the Fire Service, and when he was injured on duty Cockren gave him a balsam which, as he believed, saved his life. The laboratory was wonderfully equipped—the finest since the eighteenth century so he said—by the generosity of Mrs. Meyer Sassoon, who had great faith in Cockren after he gave her potable gold as a medicine and to whom his book is dedicated. He was killed when a direct hit destroyed the laboratory; and there was no successor to carry on his work. It would be impossible to set up his experiments from the sketchy and elliptical descriptions in his book. As lately as 1965 Gerard told me of a friend, then aged ninety-five, who still took potable gold with great benefit; its effect was to prolong life and youth. He could not, or would not, reveal this patient's identity, but there may be others even today who are in possession of Cockren's remedies; if there are, I only wish they would contact me.

Where did the GD derive its alchemical teaching? Mainly from the Zoharic treatise, *Aesch Metzareph* (= Purifying Fire) which forms part of von Rosenroth's *Kabbalah Denudata* though it was not included in Mathers' translation. The two versions of an alchemical Tree of Life which figure in *Liber 777*, and where planetary sigils represent the corresponding metals, derive from its first chapter. The earliest translation into English was made in 1714 by "A Lover of Philalethes". Dr. Wynn Westcott published an edition in 1894; it was he who contributed more than Mathers to the Order's alchemical knowledge in its early days, William Ayton being his most devoted pupil. I have heard that some of Ayton's papers survive in the possession of a descendant and again, I can only ask that if this is so he will contact me.

Though a Ritual for Transmutation formed part of the GD magical *corpus* and was intended for practical working, Mathers did not attempt to include the fugitive symbols of the Art in *The Book of the Concourse of the Forces.* No doubt he wished to be sure of his own understanding before passing it on to students and it was not until after a profound study of Jacob Boehme's *Mysterium Magnum* and of the treatises in Salomon Trismosin's *Splendor Solis* that he grasped the full import of the subject. So highly did he also come to value Kirchweger's *Aurea Catena Homeri* (1722) (=Homer's Golden Chain), believing it to enshrine powerful cosmic secrets, that he allowed no adept below the grade of 7°=4° to study it. He had previously soaked himself in the thought of Boehme, who takes over much of the alchemical world-view and develops it into his own mystical system.

What of the Elixir of Life? A suggestion of Mathers having discovered it, a Faustian aura, hovers around him throughout his life, from the time when, among his early pupils, it was rumoured that he had sought and found it like Zanoni in Bulwer-Lytton's novel. Later he identified himself in some sort with King James IV of Scotland, about whom the tradition of immortality lingers. Apart from this, the air of mystery surrounding his death and the lack of detail regarding his burial, there is little to substantiate such beliefs. Yet he was an enigma—a man who influenced his generation and those succeeding it, yet himself left hardly a trace beyond his few published works; who used a title, yet was not a member of any discoverable chivalric Order; who specialised in military matters, yet never joined a regular army; who established himself as a scholar without evidence of higher education. Was he of the race of the Comte de Saint Germain, of those immortals who (as esoteric tradition avers) appear and disappear at will, taking on a temporary humanity for an unknown purpose?

Boehme inspired Kirchweger; compare his "Seven Qualities of God" with some of the 'links' of the *Catena*. Kirchweger posits corresponding qualities, naming his first three the Earthly Ternary: this consists of Chaos or the Wrath of God, which he contrasts with Light or the Love of God. The contrary action of these two qualities or forces generates Rotation—Boehme's *Kreutzrad* (= Cross-Wheel)—as third term. Boehme calls the two antecedent qualities Uncreated Will, Seed or Contraction—and Will, giving rise to duality: otherwise, he speaks of Salt, Mercury and Sulphur in that order, thus transposing the more usual sequence (adopted by Kirchweger) which makes Sulphur and Salt the opposing forces and Mercury their combined rotation. It is easy to recognise here an Occidental and literary equivalent of the well-known Taoist diagram of Yin-with-Yang. In the "Chain" the *Kreutzrad* appears but does not immediately follow the first two "links".

I find myself drawn to the *Aurea Catena* more strongly than to any other alchemic text, to me it is inspiring for three reasons: first, I have discovered that exciting relationships with the Tree of Life and the colour-scales of the GD's *Minutum Mundum* develop spontaneously in the "Chain" when one makes sketches of it. Then, I find it depicts the identity of Nirvana and Samsara by its use of an identical sigil for the last link at either end of the Chain, both the "lowest" and the "highest". One sigil is upright and the reversed—but which is which? By inverting the usual order, suggestive relationships emerge. "As above, so below" is the Hermetic equivalent; the Qabalistic, "Kether is in Malkuth and Malkuth is in Kether, but after another manner". Thirdly, the *Catena* sets out with clarity a Yin-Yang metaphysic under the names of the two basic alchemical qualities:

Sulphur	*Salt*
Acid	Alcali
Spirit	Body
Father	Mother
Male Seed	Female Seed
Universal Active Principle	Universal Passive Principle
Heaven	Earth
Air	Water
Steel	Magnet
Hammer	Anvil
Subtle	Coarse
Clear	Dark
Volatile	Fixed

Other authors assign the qualities differently, the Fixed becoming Male and the Volatile, Female; but most are "Tantrik" in so far as they insist on the antinomy and its resolution.

The sexual content of alchemical literature is obvious and some alchemical terms bear a physiological analogy:

Alembic: the uterus.
Bath of Venus: the vagina, or possibly the amniotic sac.
Moderate Fire: (sexual) heat of the body.
Aqua Vitae: fluid secretions in general, female secretions in particular, of which eighteen are listed in Tantrik texts.
Seminal Viscosity: semen or rather its subtle counterpart, the Sanskrit *bindou.*
Sperm of the Philosophers: spermatozoa, male secretions.
Medicina Catholica: the quested essence; in particular, the feminine principle, perhaps the *anima* of Analytical Psychology, most alchemical literature being written from a masculine viewpoint.

It is interesting to compare my list with one in a diary kept by W. B. Yeats in 1889 (Nat. Lib. of Ireland, 13570) where he records the following:

Simon Magus says:
Eden = universal womb.
Rivers of = umbilical cord.
Streams of = 2 veins and 2 arteries.
Embryo = point cosmic [?]
Vital fluid = [?] Amnium = Akasa.
Womb = Ether of space, photo [--------?] manas.
Umbilical cord = Elementals, comets,
dream-content of [----------?] Kama Rupa.

His handwriting is difficult to decipher, but this brief note indicates that his association of ideas was following a similar direction. Some of the instructions for the OTO higher degrees are couched in an alchemical code, where

athanor = penis.
serpent / blood of the red Lion = semen.
retort / cucurbite = vagina.
menstruum of the Gluten = vaginal secretions.
First Matter = vaginal secretions mixed with semen.
Amrita / Elixir = First Matter transmuted.

If one consults still other alchemists, one finds three principles called the Three Serpents or the Triangle: these sometimes represent Soul, *Spiritus Mundi* (= Soul of the World) and the Solvent. At others, Mercury, Sulphur and Salt are almost equivalent to the *Gounas* of Hinduism, whose names may be translated as the serene, the aggressive and the sluggish tendencies in Nature. Turning again to the *Aurea Catena*, *Spiritus Mundi* is subdivided into three: *Volatilis Incorporeus*, (= Volatile Unbodied), contrasted with *Acidus Corporeus* (= Acid Corporeal) or Sulphur, and *Fixus Alcalinus* (Fixed Alkaline) or Salt. Sulphur and Salt, their antinomy resolved, come together as Double Salt, the *Prima Materia* (= First Matter). A diagram clarifies this:

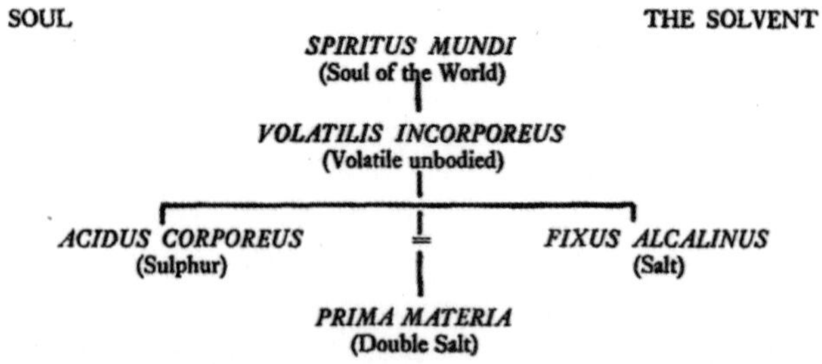

Offshoots of the GD have tried to carry on the alchemical tradition: Francis King's *Ritual Magic in England* reproduces an experiment worked by the Hermanoubis Lodge, Bristol, in this field. While other evidence suggests that its active period was less recent than Mr. King implies and may date back some forty years, its alchemical work seems to have had a practical application and the resulting medicines are reported efficacious when taken in small "homeopathic" doses, like Cockren's metallic oils. Such efforts, with those of Caro in the Midi, would seem to carry on the genuine line of Rosicrucian therapy.

In *The Monolith* for Spring, 1967, Robert Turner, then Co-Chief of the Order of the Cubic Stone, in a brief essay related the alchemical processes to the diagram of the Tree of Life. This gave no sign that he or any member of his Order had engaged in practical alchemy and I am not convinced that his interpretation of the Lions (Black, Red and White) and their riders is valid: he leaves out the (most usual) Green Lion and alters the generally-accepted colour-sequence of black/white/red. He borrows three out of the Four Horsemen of the Apocalypse and mounts them instead on Lions. He ignores the alchemical Trees of *Aesch Metzareph* and *Liber 777* and assigns the metals according to their respective planetary spheres. Thus, following the planets, he identifies only seven processes; his interpretation is no more than an exercise in comparative symbology, shedding little light on the basics of alchemical discipline.

I have no space here to analyse Edward Garstin's two unpublished essays on *Alchemy and Astrology* but I will try to examine in some detail another work left by him, *A Glossary of Alchemical Terms.* I prefer all these to his *Theurgy* (1930) and *The Secret Fire* (1932)—though the former is soon to appear in a French translation—because they get down to (alchemical) brass tacks more than either of the published works. Edward disclaimed any practice in physical transmutations but admitted, if pressed, that he had attempted what he called "spiritual alchemy". I do not know exactly what he meant by this term, but too often the phrase indicates a merely-academic knowledge or some theory about the nature of the Great Work. Sometimes it covers no more than pious allegorising along the lines of "purging the soul of its mortal dross to reveal the true spiritual gold", and so forth; or the equation of heat with love in a vein of sentimental religiosity. Where a hint of such attitudes occurs in Edward's published works they fail to touch the profundities of his subject. Judging by *A Glossary*, he may have known more than he was willing, or perhaps able, to say.

Besides Cockren, the *Aesch Metzareph* and the *Aurea Catena*, his sources include Thomas Vaughan's works, *The Ordinall of Alchemy* by Thomas Norton, pupil of Ripley, Trismosin's *Splendor Solis, A Suggestive Inquiry* by Mrs. Atwood (1850), Dr. John Dee's *The Hieroglyphic Monad* and the *Clavis Chimicus* from *The Rosicrucian Secrets* (unpublished), with *The Alchemical Writings of Edward Kelley* (1894), *The New Pearl of Great Price* by Peter Bonus (1546) and *The Triumphal Chariot of Antimony* of Basil Valentine. Edward emphasises the work of past alchemists in Britain and shows no interest in those on the Continent at the present day. I base the following summary on his anthology of definitions because in elucidating the symbolic language of alchemical literature it also gives an idea of how certain GD students approached this recondite subject.

SUBSTANCES. Alchemy postulates a bodiless state which subsists both "below" and "above" that of the universe manifested to humanity as matter. (The use of such spatial imagery in order to hint at types of being outside the space-time continuum as ordinarily cognised is awkward and even misleading, but inevitable since language is limited by human perception.) This incorporeal state is the *Primum Ens* (= First Essence) by which its embodied counterpart, the *Prima Materia* (= First Matter) is bounded. Viewed as most dense in its "central" manifestation, this *Prima Materia* operates a scale of changes both "upward" and "downward"; and it is with these extremities—"the confines where matter ends" in the words of *The Chaldaean Oracles*—that alchemy deals. Aristotle called it "the Spagyric (i.e., separative) Art" because it consists largely in dividing the *Primum Ens* from the *Prima Materia* or *Corpus* which acts as its vehicle in the physical universe, "separating the Volatile from the Fixed". In an imagery which is remarkably constant across the boundaries of culture and epoch, the Eagle and sometimes other birds and winged beasts stand for the Volatile—also for the female, and Mercury when this is used for the feminine half in the alchemical equivalent of a Yin-Yang concept. The Lion and other beasts represent the fixed, also the male and Sulphur. The Gluten of the Eagle, otherwise called *Lac Virginis* (= Virgin's Milk), must be mixed with the Blood of the Lion to effectuate the combining of Yin with Yang. The imagery in other contexts for these polar opposites may be: White Woman and Red Man, Venus ♀ and Mars ♂, the Moon and the Sun, Silver and Gold and the Queen and King.

The partition of the universe into the *Primum Ens* and *Prima Materia*—more or less equivalent to the *Pourousha* and *Prakriti* of Vedantic thought—is diagrammatic since reality is structured rather as a series of scales or degrees. In a recent and in some respects horrifying book, *The Beginning was the End*, Oscar Maerth employs a four-fold cosmic division—spirit, half-spirit, half-matter and matter—which he learned during his stay in a Chinese Buddhist monastery and which applies both macrocosmically and microcosmically. In a similar sense, when alchemists speak of "three Mercuries" or "three Sulphurs" they are calling attention to the varied forms and functions of substances at different levels of being, and indicate by this particular subdivision just three of those several levels.

Comparatively few physical substances seem to be used in alchemical experiment but in its literature—of whose vast scope, extending throughout history and into all cultures, the ordinary educated person has no idea—each goes under a diversity of pseudonyms. Wherever the Art is found, its practitioners seem to be doing—and even saying—the same basic things. Some of their variants refer to a given substance at a particular stage of the Great Work or at a particular cosmic "level"; but the problem of decipherment is complicated by the use in some texts of the same name for distinct substances. One cannot understand an alchemical text by trying to translate it into everyday language: its challenge is more than that of a de-coding job and needs some faculty analogous to poetic appreciation. It is strange that the literature of alchemy has been neglected as an art-form—which it is, among much; beyond my own immature article in *The Quest*, I know of little except Claude d'Ygé's *Anthologie de la poésie hermetique*. The engraved illustrations which enliven many alchemical texts or, like *The Book of Lambspring* and the *Mutus Liber*, stand in their place, also await aesthetic assessment; as far as I know, the only attempt in this direction is Van Lennep's *Art et Alchimie*.

M. Caro tells me that today, should the aim be to experiment alchemically with physical substances, it is most difficult to obtain materials of the right quality through ordinary channels. The products available commercially are almost always "doctored" chemically to facilitate packing, storage or transport; or indeed, brutally vitiated with a view to larger profits. To the alchemist they are therefore useless and he must place special orders or undertake other *démarches* to obtain what he needs.

ELEMENTS. There are four forms of the spirit (the incorporeal state) related to the (corporeal) Elements: *Azoth* is its watery form, *Kibric* its airy, *Alocohoph* or *Alicosoph* its earthy and *Sandarace* its fiery form. These are the Elements' subtle counterpart and the animals that figure prominently in alchemical texts and their illustrations are often emblematic of these Elements: whales or fish, of Water; the eagle, of Air; the lion or the ox, of Earth and the salamander or the dragon, of Fire.

Paracelsus (1493-1541) concocted an elaborate personal terminology which gives *Iliades* or *Ileidus* as a collective name for the incorporeal Elements, Chaos, which he calls *Iliaster* and which is, like the

Elements, four-fold. Macrocosmically, it is the Chaos of Earth, Water, Air and Fire which reflects itself into man as microcosm and is there known as *Iliaster Primus, Secundus, Tertius* and *Quartus* or *Magnus*. To go deeper, these *Iliastri* are concerned with the Elixir of Immortality and in this sense are extended by certain epithets or phrases. The *Iliaster Primus* (Earth) is called the Life-Force, Balsam of Nature and Balsam of Life. The *Secundus* (Water) can give conditional immortality through the four corporeal Elements. The *Tertius* (Air) is the Astral Power, to be obtained through the Quintessence or Fifth Element. The *Quartus* or *Magnus* (Fire) is called the immortality of Enoch or of Elias, brought about by a "translation" of the dense body—which implies a re-arrangement of the particles composing it.

STAGES. In the course of the Great Work—the production of the Elixir of Life and/or the Philosophers' Stone—the chosen basic substance, whatever it may be, goes through three main stages called after the colours that occur when it is heated: Black, White, Red. These are further differentiated by some authors, thus:

Black
    Blue or Grey
White
    Saffron
Red
    Purple

In Dom A. J. Pernety's *The Great Art* (1786), the colours which mark the stages of the work are arranged with their planetary and attributions thus:

Black	*Grey*	*Peacock's Tail*	*White*	*Yellow*	*Red*	*Purple*
♄ lead	♃ tin	☿ mercury	☽ silver	♀ copper	♂ iron	☉ gold

More fully-tabulated, the stages can be related to season and Zodiac in this way:

Putrefaction or Dissolution	*Black*	*White*	*Red*
Winter Capricornus Aquarius Pisces	Spring Aries Taurus Gemini	Summer Cancer Leo Virgo	Autumn Libra Scorpio Sagittarius

The mention of colour reminds one of a passage in *The Alchemist* where the house-boy, Face, complains:

> ...these bleared eyes
> Have wak'd to read your several colours, sir,
> Of the pale citron, the green lion, the crow,
> The peacock's tail, the plumed swan.

Here the order of the colours and the stages they signify is confused, but the lines show how symbolic birds and beasts sustain a pictorial element in alchemical writing. Sir Epicure has already drawn attention to a special interpretation of Classical myths:

> I have a piece of Jason's fleece, too
> Which was no other than a book of alchemy
> ....
> And all that fable of Medaea's charms,
> The manner of our work; the bulls, our furnace,
> Still breathing fire; our argent vive, the dragon;
> The dragon's teeth, mercury sublimate,
> That keeps the whiteness, hardness and the biting;
> And they are gathered into Jason's helm,
> The alembic, and then sowed in Mars his field,
> And thence sublimed so often till they're fixed.

The *Atalanta Fugiens* (1618) of Michael Maier extends the technical use of mythology to alchemical ends.

SECRET FIRE. With the consideration of heat, the actual processes of alchemy come in question. There are said to be four grades of Fire related to Zodiacal signs and known as Sun of Aries, Sun of Taurus (Black Stage), of Gemini (White Stage) and of Leo (Red Stage), respectively. Or there may be a division into three grades instead: those of Aries, Leo and Sagittarius, the signs composing the Fiery Triplicity of the Zodiac, and further described as natural, unnatural and contra-natural. I suggest that the first of these three refers to the natural warmth of things—perhaps also to the utilisation of dung as a heating agent in some experiments; or a method of breaking up metals by proximity to a swiftly-turning disk of steel, without direct contact and without heat or oxydisation. In alchemical terms, this "melting" is operated through the action of hidden (Elemental) Fire. The second may indicate the direct use of sunlight, and the attraction of lightning in the production of alchemical results sometimes associated with the Dry Way using crucible in place of Philosopher's Egg. The third may allude to "the Puffers" excessive application of heat in the athanor. The grades of Fire are sometimes more simply classified as Internal and External, or natural and applied heat.

PROCESSES. The processes leading up to the accomplishment of the Great Work are numbered in one text as four. These are: Solution of the chosen substance in mercurial water, Preparation of the Philosophical Mercury, its Corruption and the Generation from it of the Philosophical Mercury, its Corruption and the Generation from it of the Philosophical Sulphur. They are otherwise given as Solution, Ablution, Reduction and Fixation.

Most authors, however, posit a greater number of processes; the *Aurea Catena* has ten "links" but twelve is more usual, often related to the Labours of Hercules. Norton symbolises them as Twelve Gates, Basil Valentine as Twelve Keys; I adopted the latter's nomenclature as chapter-headings in my esoteric novel, *Goose of Hermogenes* (1961). *Le Livre des Feuillettes Hermétiques* (1763) of Kerdanek de Pornic describes twenty-two *Arcanes*, a number inevitably recalling the Major Arcana of the Taro. Here, in *Arcane XIII, La Floraison: "La Fleur des Sages croît sur la plante philosophique"*, and in *Arcane XIV, La Fructification: "...couleur du pavot des champs ou rouge vif du sang"*, exactly describe the "flower" in Cockren's laboratory, which must have reached a stage intermediate between these two when Edward saw it. This text was reproduced in *Initiation et Science*—famous for its articles on alchemical themes—No. 55 (1962) by Claude d'Ygé de Lablatinière, who died two years later. No. 63 (1965) of the same review contained an obituary by Serge Hutin and featured on the cover a photograph of d'Ygé which, strangely enough, bears a strong resemblance to Edward. Another text in French, *Le Pilote de l'Onde Vive* (1678) by Mathurin Eyquem, Sieur du Martineau, contains twenty-one "movements" and one "fixed point", the latter frankly equated with the Fool of the Taro.

MICROCOSM. Scattered through the writings of Paracelsus one can find much lore relating not only to the subtle counterpart of metals but to the subtle body of the human being. When alchemy is used therapeutically, it is to this vehicle or to one of its subdivisions that treatment is directed and through which the cure is thought to ensue. In the Paracelsian system, the parts of the soul—or, better to say, the scale of subtle bodies—compare neatly with the Hindu (and Theosophic) seven-fold scheme. In order of subtlety, beginning with the most incorporeal or volatile, these vehicles are:

Paracelsian System	*Hindu System*
Spiritus	Atma
Flesh of Christ	Buddhi
Flesh of Adam	Higher Manas
Archaeus	Lower Manas
Evestrum	Kama
Iliastri	Prana
Limbus	Linga Sharira
Corpus	Sthula Sharira

THE GREAT WORK proceeds in three stages: the first, Rebis, is the conjunction of Sulphur and Mercury, frequently depicted in illustrations by a hermaphrodite human figure, equivalent of the geometric Yin-Yang diagram. The second, the Elixir, is itself sub-divided into Elixir of Bodies, or "first rotation" proceeding to the Blue stage; there follow the Seven Imbibitions which lead to the White Stage or White Tincture and then to the Red Stage or Red Tincture. The third is called the Elixir of Spirits or Elixir of Fire and is brought about by "fermentation".

There are said to be two kinds of gold—White Gold which is "Our Mercury" and Red Gold, 'Our Sulphur'. The possessive pronoun indicates that common mercury and sulphur are not intended. It would seem to be just one more image for the concept of Yin-Yang polarity underlying alchemical thought.

I will conclude by stressing that the Elixir and the Stone are quested objects as agents of transmutation at all levels; and will quote one occasion, recorded in Thomas Vaughan's *Memoriae Sacrum* (1658), on which the Great Work was effected:

> ...on the same day my dear wife sickened; and on the Saturday following, which was the day she died on, I extracted it by the former practice so that on the same day, that proved the most sorrowful to me, whatever can be, God was pleased to confer upon me the greatest joy I can ever have in this world after her death.

Metallic transmutation, though to the achieved alchemist's end, is no more than a token of the Sage's profounder knowledge and wider powers. The toiling Hyperchemist may produce transmutations of a sort in his laboratory, but without the ability to manipulate forces on "the confines where matter ends" he is no Alchemist. †

Druidry (after 1975)

Colquhoun was involved in esoteric Druidry starting in the 1950s. In 1957 she joined a Druidic ritual at Stonehenge and by 1958 was a member of the Ancient Order of Druids, also known as the British Circle of the Universal Bond or the An Druidh Uileach Braithreachas (ADUB). Druidry was Colquhoun's first foray into what developed into Celtic Spirituality, and through her writings we can track the ways in which this many pronged and varied spiritual movement develops over the latter half of the twentieth century, as it engages with, reforms and also rejects Christianity in rather equal measure. Much of this text reflects a mythic history of modern Druidry, heavily influenced by the Welsh writer Edward Williams, (better known by his pen name Iolo Morganwg), aiming to show its continuity with pre-Christian traditions. It is likely that Colquhoun was not aware of the creative and inventive nature of Morganwg's *Barddas*, published in the nineteenth century after Morganwg's death, which was a key text for many Druids in the twentieth century. This essay is not historically accurate. It should be understood as Colquhoun's way of expressing her interpretation of Druidry as an important native spiritual tradition with key teachings and methods that persisted despite a Christian overlay. It is possible that this essay went through drafts in both the 1960s and 1970s, given the descriptions of events she describes as "current".

> Blessed Bran commanded his followers to cut off his head, and "Take my head," said he, "and bear it even unto the White Mound in London, and bury it there with the face towards France."

This quotation from the Welsh legend-cycle of the *Mabinogion*, translated into English by Lady Charlotte Guest, describes one of the numerous oracular heads of Celtic mythology, and links the Druidic tradition of these islands with that of our nearest Continental neighbour.

Though other Classical authors declare that Druidic influence stretched from Scandinavia to Spain, Julius Caesar states that the German tribes had no Druids. He tells us in some detail, however, about the Druids of Gaul—the European country where the Druidic system may first have developed—and about those of Britain where, in its hey-day, the most advanced centres of learning were established. At the time of Aed Mawr[1], who succeeded Hu Gadarn[2] as leader of the Cymri about 1000 BC, there were over thirty of these centres; the seats of the three Arch-Druids were London, York and Caerleon (S. Wales) and it is noteworthy that two of these are still the Sees of the Anglican Arch-Bishops.

It was in Britain that Druidry made its last stand against the Romans, when a remnant which had fled to the island of Anglesey was massacred. (The Ile de Sein, off the coast of Brittany, was the scene of similar carnage.) Did these butcheries—for such they certainly were, since Druids underwent no training in the use of arms and were forbidden even to defend themselves by force—mean the end? Or did their teaching "go underground", to re-appear in various places much later? There are several groups in existence today who to the latter question would answer, yes.

---

1 Also known as Addedomarus, a British king from the first century BCE who was mentioned in the Welsh Triads as one of the first kings of Britain.

2 Hu Gadarn, a minor figure from the French romances, was made legendary by Iolo Morganwg, in *Barddas*, and the figure was later popularised by Robert Graves. Morganwg portrayed Hu Gadarn as leader of the Britons and conflated him with Jesus, while Graves morphed him into a Brythonic solar deity and horned god.

Some Druids fled to Scotland, a country never subjugated by the Romans; many more took refuge in Eire, which these invaders never touched and where Bardic Schools survived at least until the seventeenth century. This is established in Daniel Corkery's book *The Hidden Ireland*, where we read of Bards training their pupils in those feats of memory characteristic of ancient Druidic method. They led them in a life of seclusion resembling that of a Tibetan hermit for months at a time, with the purpose of mind-training and poetic composition—all this at a date many centuries later than the absorption of Druids, as "Culdees", into Celtic Christianity. Traditional usages persist long after they are supposed to have died out; and it may be that even today, in spite of Roman (ecclesiastical) and Anglo-Saxon (political) tyranny, traces of active Druidry in Ireland could still be found.

In Wales, the *Eisteddfod* or Bardic Session has been from time immemorial a feature of local life; Welsh has persisted as a living language against pressures of many kinds, its complex verse-forms still in use. The country has never ceased to produce a succession of poets who, if they were appreciated at their true value, would rank with some of the finest in Europe. (Needless to say, a Saxon-cum-Latin slanted culture has done nothing to make them known, and they remain for the most part untranslated.)

In 1957 I visited Bob Owen[3], a Bard well-known for his wonderful library of books and manuscripts in the Welsh tongue. Every room of his house in the tiny village of Croesor (N. Wales) was stacked with books, some dealing with what he called "the Black Art". He read aloud to me the work of poets who lived this century and last, and whom he praised as equal to the greatest. Certainly, spoken in his voice they sounded so, though I understood (at conceptual level) little beyond their titles. When his death occurred about 1960[4], his treasures were left to the National Library of Wales.

---

3 Bob Owen was a Welsh antiquarian, local historian and book collector who wrote many essays for Welsh *eisteddfod* competitions, newspapers and periodicals.

4 1962.

The *Gorsedd* or Druidic Circle of Wales was re-organised in 1799 by the Bard Iolo Morganwg[5]—J. A. Williams ap Ithel—who translated and edited the *Barddas*[6] of Llewelyn Sion[7]—reviving the ancient categories of Druid (in white robes) for philosophers and mystics; Bards (in blue) for creative artists, historians, teachers, the intelligentsia in general; and Ovates (in green) for land-workers, doctors, applied scientists, practical people in general. The National Eisteddfod was officially inaugurated in 1896, and the Gorsedd holds its annual public gathering on this occasion. But besides this public Gorsedd, regional or family Druidic groups still exist, wherein various poetic and psychic gifts, notably "second-sight", passed from parent to child are fostered by practice. I cannot help thinking that the mystical poet Henry Vaughan (1622-95) belonged to such a group, and that his cognomen, "the Silurist", refers to this. His twin-brother Thomas, who was none other than the alchemist "Eugenius Philalethes", called himself Silurist also.

The Gorsedd[8] of Brittany takes its succession from that of Wales, and follows it in according the three ancient categories of membership. There must, however, have been more or less organised groups of Druids in Brittany long before the present century, since Breton delegates attended the meeting convened at the Apple Tree Tavern, London, in 1717, which I shall later describe. It is certain that the Breton Gorsedd is not the only Druidic group working at present in France; there is, for instance, the Gaulish circle led by M. Paul Bouchet[9] which admits the one category of Druids only, if I am not

5 Morganwg was a key figure in Modern Welsh history as an antiquarian, poet, Unitarian and promoter of Welsh language and history. He is recognised as the founder of the modern Gorseddau and helped drive the eighteenth century revival of the *Eisteddfod*.

6 Barddas was published after Williams' death in two volumes in 1868 and 1872 by Welsh antiquarian John Williams. The text was wildly popular and promoted the idea of a continuous history of Druidry. His ritual format was central to the establishment of both cultural and esoteric Druidry, and is still used today even though the work is widely known as a literary forgery. Nevertheless, it had a huge impact of the development of contemporary British Paganism.

7 Llywelyn Siôn was an actual sixteenth century Welsh poet to whom Morganwg attributed *Barddas*.

8 In Breton *Goursez Vreizh*.

9 Paul Bouchet was a French Grand Druid, artist and author.

mistaken. About other groups in France I cannot write, having no first-hand information beyond the fact of their existence. But there is a London-based group, the Golden Section Order[10], established in 1975 and derived from the Gaulish Druids at Drancy.

Britain has Druid-groups, one of which, the Ancient and Archeological Order of Druids, is open to Freemasons only. It was founded last century by Dr. Wentworth Little, who was also concerned with the founders of the Hermetic Order of the Golden Dawn, made famous (in spite of its secrecy) through its distinguished membership. Then there is a Druidic Order among the fraternal societies known as "poor man's Masonry", which draw their membership chiefly from the workers.

The Gorsedd of Cornwall[11] also derives from Wales, but consists of Bards only. It was revived in 1928 when, for the first time after a lapse of a thousand years at least, the gathering was held publicly on Cornish soil. It is significant to recall that in earlier times "the three Gorsedds of Britain" took place at Boscawen-un (W. Cornwall), Brynn Gwyddon (Wales) and Stonehenge (Wiltshire) respectively[12].

The Druid Order, *An Druidh Uileach Braithreachas* (ADUB), now based in London and admitting only Druids, antedates any other organised Druidic Circle now operating in these islands, as will be seen by the following summary of its origins[13].

Before the Norman Conquest, a circle of Druids, Bards and Ovates flourished at Oxford, then considered—no doubt for good "telluric" reasons—to be the centre of England. Before the founding of the

10 The Golden Section Order was a group devoted to developing a Pan-Celtic mystical tradition based in mythology and earth mysteries, but was also infused with the agenda of a Pan-Celtic nationalism. Colquhoun was very involved with Colin Murray's Golden Section Order, and remained an affiliate until about 1986.

11 In Cornish *Gorseth Kernow.*

12 This is likely from Morganwg's eighteenth century *Triads*, not medieval Welsh literature.

13 The following section needs to be read as a mythic ancestral history of the Ancient Order of Druids. There is no evidence that any of these people were a part of a Druid order.

University there, a confraternity deriving from the Grove of Cor Emrys which survived in Snowdonia and which guarded the mysteries of Ceridwen, the Earth-Mother, was active. By the time Haymo of Faversham was its Chosen Chief, it was known as *Celli-y-Henafiaeth*, the Grove (or Lodge) of Antiquity. After Haymo's death, this circle was revived (about 1245) by Philip Brydydd, a Bard of Siluria, under the name of Mount Haemus, recalling the Classical home of the Four Winds in Thrace. The aim was

> to claim and assert the dignity of the Druids, and to ridicule many popular errors

and there is still need to implement this purpose. Though gaps in the history are many, it is known that in 1643 John Aubrey, the antiquarian, unified various other Druidic bodies with Oxford's Mount Haemus.

In 1717 John Toland, of Londonderry (N. Ireland), made a further effort towards unification; and on Primrose Hill, London, at the Autumn Equinox the same year it was announced that an assembly of the existing Druidic Circles would take place at the Apple Tree Tavern, Covent Garden. This was attended by delegates from London, Oxford, York, Wales, the Isles of Man and of Anglesey, Scotland, Ireland and Brittany. From this list it seems that Druidry was not confined to the Celtic fringe at this date, but had again spread itself throughout Britain. Toland was elected Chief and he inaugurated the Mother Grove of London, *An Tigh Geata Gairdeachas*. Since then, the succession of Chiefs has been uninterrupted and can boast of several celebrated names, including that of the poet William Blake.

Some years later, the ceremony of the Autumn Equinox on Primrose Hill was again to mark a turning-point in the history of the Order: in 1792[14] a proclamation was made to the effect that

14 Iolo Morganwg instituted the Gorsedd of the Isle of Britain with a number of Welsh activists in London on Primrose Hill on the Summer Solstice in 1792.

> The English language is now for the first time opened and proclaimed a Bardic language, to be used in future for ever as well as the Ancient British or Welsh

and odes were recited in English during the Gorsedd. No doubt the intention was to settle finally the disputes between English and Welsh Druids which had previously arisen over the language-question. Such quarrels are understandable enough in view of the official hostility with which the Welsh language—as also the Breton—has been treated; but it must also be remembered that the so-called Anglo-Saxon tongue has a firm Celtic basis.

Let us go back to the White Mound. This was one of a series of hills in old London—partly natural, partly the work of man—which included Barrow Hill, The Tot Hill, the Penton, the Lun Dun and Mount Llud. They were arranged, as was the more famous Stonehenge, to form a star-clock. Time was thus measured by the rising of certain heavenly bodies, and the moment marked for sowing, reaping and other agricultural activities. To quote Dr. R. MacGregor Reid, a recent chosen Chief of the Order:

> A people's calendar has always been the vertebral column of its organised culture.

In the popular mind, a change of calendar is associated (often justifiably) with a change of religion, and this explains why it meets with unconsciously-motivated resistance. Perhaps the same applies to measurement of all kinds, and explains some of the reluctance felt in this country to the adoption of the decimal system. Our own system comes down to us from the ancient Druids and, utilitarian considerations aside, it seems a shame to abolish anything that makes for differentiation in this standardised age[15]!

The Lun Dun, which gave its name to the Metropolis, still stands on the edge of Hampstead Heath but is now called Parliament Hill,

15 Obviously this is not historically accurate but it paints a picture of Colquhoun's political leanings and her nativism during the later years of her life.

reminding us that all these London hills were places of common assembly and free speech for the people. The Tot Hill has long been levelled and is untraceable except in the name Tothill Street, Westminster; but is it merely a coincidence that for years the Druid Order met every month at the nearby Caxton Hall for its public lectures? Mount Llud is Ludgate Hill, the site of St. Paul's Cathedral—Llud was a deity of the Cymric Afterworld. The Penton and Barrow Hill have been converted into reservoirs, but adjoining the latter is Primrose Hill, once crowned by a stone-circle and still the scene of the Autumn Equinox celebration. To quote the same Chosen Chief:

> Long before Hyde Park, Primrose Hill was a Speakers' Corner.

Brynn Gwynn, the White Mound, now covered by the Tower of London, is the legendary burial-place not only of the demigod Bran but of the first British King Dynwal Moelmud, c. 430 BC[16], who built the so-called "Roman" roads. He codified the laws, later taken over by the Saxon King Alfred as the Laws of Molmutius. The original mound may have been covered with pebbles of white quartz, as were many similar structures, for instance the tumulus of New Grange in Ireland. At noon on the day of the Vernal Equinox, "at the time of equal day and night", the Druid Order customarily repairs to a paved garden between Tower Hill and the Church of All Hallows, Barking-by-the Tower, which itself contains a pillar-base from the Druidic temple marked on the map of Roman London.

Having assembled, the Companions of the Order walk in procession across Tower Green led by the Sword-Bearer and form the circle, each officer taking up his appointed station. The Herald advances to the centre and sounds a call on the horn to the four quarters, summoning the living and the dead. The Sword-Bearer presents the sword to the Chief, who unsheaths it only a little (since it is a symbol of peace) as he turns to the four quarters asking at each, "Is it peace?" All answer, "Peace". The Druid Prayer follows; then the Lady and her attendants are bidden to enter the circle. She represents Ceridwen, the Earth-goddess, and she offers the chief Druids the Horn of Plenty containing

16 Likely sixth century CE.

mead or ale, and a basket of token seeds. A commemoration is then made for departed members of the Order, their names being read aloud by the Scribe. The Chief gives a short address and the Companions join hands in the circle, renewing their vow of solidarity. This is followed by a thanks-giving; and the ceremony closes with the Cry of Peace, the four Companions at the cardinal points turning outwards from the circle to proclaim it.

At the Autumn Equinox on Primrose Hill, the same ritual is used except for slight modifications appropriate to the season. Ideally, the Lady should be represented by a young girl in the Spring, a young woman at Midsummer and a mature woman in the Autumn. The Companions wear a simple white robe and head-dress, identical for men and women; the Chiefs of the Order wear also on the forehead a gold badge, /|\ , called *Awen* (the *Tribann* of the Breton Gorsedd) signifying the three pillars of light which are Universal Majesty, Verity and Love Infinite. (This device is used by the British Government on property that it wishes to mark as its own!) The banner of Mount Haemus Grove is still carried, representing the nine steps of perfection, the scales of Justice and the powers of the Sun and Moon.

Better known than either the Spring Equinox festival, *Alban Eilir*, or the Autumn one, *Alban Elfed*, is the Summer Solstice assembly at Stonehenge. The Order has from time to time been obliged to fight to keep this ancient temple as its meeting place, notably in 1928 when Sir Oliver Lodge gave it strong support. Through no fault of the Companions, proceedings have not always been orderly; in the recent past, before matters were regulated by the Office of Works, they were an ordeal for the participants, who had to force their way through the crowd of about four thousand spectators that always gathers overnight "to see the sun rise at mid-summer". Groups of "beat" musicians used sometimes to interrupt, and young soldiers from the military camps on Salisbury Plain could not refrain from "taking the mickey". Fire-crackers were thrown and on at least one occasion a Druid's robe was set alight. Persistence, concentration and even courage were necessary in order to carry out the ceremonies.

The first of these takes place on the midnight before the longest day, when an informal procession follows one of the "old straight tracks"—which preceded Roman roads—to a mound some distance south of Stonehenge itself. A circle is formed and past Companions linked to the Druid succession are commemorated; the Covenant of fidelity is renewed. The circle is then enlarged to include spectators and all join hands, while one of the Order's chief members gives a short address. All then return along the dark and rutty trackway.

Stonehenge was called The Dance of the Giants—*Cathoir Ghall* in Gaelic, *Chorea Gigantum* in Latin—which suggests that it was always associated with ritual movement. Before dawn, symbols of the Four Elements are placed outside its circle at the cardinal points—a rose for Air in the east, incense to burn in the south, bread and salt for Earth in the west and Water in the north. The Companions assemble and prepare for the ceremony; the Chief speaks the invocation and the Companions in procession collect the Elements and visit the Sun Stone (also called the Hele Stone and the Gnomen), symbol of Fatherhood, and the Recumbent Stone, symbol of Motherhood. The procession enters the circle from the east through one of the great trilithons and the elements are placed in the centre. The horn is sounded to the four quarters, the rising sun is hailed, the Words of Gold and the Words of Wisdom are spoken; then follows the Druid Prayer, and the rite closes with the Benediction.

At High Noon on the longest day begins the third ceremony, usually in windy sunlight, a welcome contrast to the darkness and misty cold of the previous two. The Elements are borne in procession and a sword is drawn from the Sun Stone; there is the Cry of Peace to the four quarters, the reception of the Lady and her attendants and the crowning with a wreath of oak-leaves of the Presider who is not a member of the Order but an honoured guest. The wreath is then placed on the head of each Companion in turn, the Covenant is renewed and departed Druids commemorated. The symbolic feast of Wine, Bread and Salt is shared among the Companions and any spectators who wish to join in. The Druid prayer is recited, and all leave the circle by the southern arch.

Yn ngwyneb haul a llygad goleuni, "in the face of the sun and the eye of day": so are the public solemnities of the year conducted, except of course the one midnight vigil. In 1963, all were accompanied by music on the *clarsach* and recorders, which added greatly to their impact. Other ceremonies are private and nothing can be said of these, except that they are conducted by the Groves—groups of Companions within the Order which have each their own special character and aim. It is at a Grove that The Gatehouse, the rite of initiation, takes place; and later, the rituals that advance the candidate to higher degrees.

The ancient Druids were prophets, priests, healers, teachers and lawgivers; they recognised the equality of men and women, and frequently lived in communities. They were treated with deference on all occasions, and had the right to speak first and last at meetings. They were exempt from military service and taxation, and were always present at religious rites and festivals. Druids of the present day remember these things and continue them where possible, in the hope that the once-universal respect of the Western world will again be accorded to them, and deserved by them. †

Taro as Colour (1977)

Colquhoun's Taro has been referred to as one of her surrealist masterworks, the pinnacle of her merging of occultism and surrealism. This was the essay that accompanied the exhibition of her taro cards at the Newlyn Gallery in 1977.

This design for a taro-pack is both personal and traditional. It renders the essence of each card by the non-figurative means of pure colour, applied automatically in the manner of psycho-morphological movement in surrealism.

The pack is traditional in following instructions drawn from the texts of the Hermetic Order of the Golden Dawn. It is, however, distinct from the figurative pack evolved in the Order's early days by MacGregor Mathers and his wife Moïna for the use of their students. The more advanced among the latter received the initiated titles of the cards which illustrate their character as meditation-glyphs. The title acts as Mantra to the design's Yantra. The employment of the Taro in divination and, still more, in commercial fortune-telling is thus seen as decadence.

The 22 Major Arcana are inseparable from the rest of the pack, i.e., from the four Court Cards and the nine Decanate Cards in each of the four suits. Basic to all is the concept of the Four Elements:

Air (Swords, pale yellow)
Water (Cups, deep blue)

Fire (Wands, scarlet)
Earth (Disks, indigo)

Four family groups appear, each dependent from one of the Aces or Roots of Power. Each Ace attracts to itself one card from among the Major Arcana as its *Shakti* or formative energy to co-operate with it in manifestation.

For example, the Ace of Swords (central colour, pale yellow) is entitled the "Root of the Powers of Air" and captures The Fool, entitled "Spirit of Aether", the Air-card of the Major Arcana. Together they produce the Court-Cards: the Prince of Swords (central colour, pale yellow), the Queen (deep blue), the King (scarlet), and the Princess (indigo). These represent respectively Air-of-Air, Water-of-Air, Fire-of-Air and Earth-of-Air. The Decanate Cards depend in their turn from the Court Cards—the numbers 6 and 9 of Swords from the Prince, the 3, 5 and 8 from the Queen and the 2, 4 and 7 from the King. Only the number 10, the Earth-number, depends upon the Princess. Number 1 is identical with the Ace, partaking of the nature of both Court Cards and Decanate Cards.

The same scheme applies in the other three suits, the Ace of Cups—Root of the Power of Water—capturing The Hanged Man (the Water Arcanum), the Ace of Wands capturing The Angel (the Fire Arcanum) and the Ace of Disks The World (the Earth Arcanum). The remaining eighteen Major Arcana arrange themselves according to their occult titles into four groups which seem to have Elemental affinities:

1. The Four Magi: The Juggler, The Priestess, The Hierophant and The Hermit with the Princesses (Earth).
2. The Five Daughters: The Empress, Strength, Justice, Temperance and The Star with the Queens (Water).
3. The Five Lords: The Emperor, The Wheel, The Devil, The Tower and The Sun with the Kings (Fire).
4. The Four Children: The Lovers, The Chariot, Death and The Moon with the Princes (Air).

After I had completed the pack I saw some slides showing nebulas in outer space and the birth of stars. These recalled my designs and confirmed my conviction of their cosmographic function. †

Essays from the *Hermetic Journal* (1979)

The Zodiac and the Flashing Colours (1979)

The next three essays in this collection were published in Adam McClean's wonderful *Hermetic Journal* that ran from 1978 to 1992. These essays were concerned with the use of colour in magic, which was a clear preoccupation for Colquhoun during this time in which she was creating some of her most significant automatic magical enamel paintings. In 1977 she completed her abstract Taro deck and from 1978-1979 she was working on the *Decad of Intelligence*, her colour study of the four worlds of the Sephiroth. It is evident that she was deeply immersed in the role of colour in shaping consciousness and in serving as portals to other dimensions. This first essay goes into great detail about the Golden Dawn practice of Flashing Colours, placing opposing colours together, to create changes in consciousness.

Basic to much that was taught in the Order of the Golden Dawn is the doctrine that colour applied to certain objects and allied with certain mental praxes may be the instrument of a change in consciousness. Though nowhere definitively stated in its instruction papers, this teaching is nevertheless implicit in their contents. According to it, colour provides an avenue into "worlds" or spheres-of-being other than that recognised by everyday perception.

The Golden Dawn (or rather its unknown superiors) evolved from the spectrum a rather elaborate colour scale, of which a design, the Rose of Twenty-Two petals, manifests the completed symbol. The following list of Zodiacal attributions is drawn from this design:

1. Red	♂
2. Red-Orange	♇
3. Orange	☉
4. Amber	⛢
5. Lemon Yellow	☿
6. Apple Green	(Isis?)
7. Emerald Green	♀
8. Peacock Blue	(?)
9. Blue	☽
10. Indigo	♄
11. Violet	♃
12. Magenta	♆

For the last, the Order's decree was Crimson, but Allan Bennett, one of its more advanced members, in a note entitled "Of Flashing Sounds" (*The Monolith* Vol I, No 2) replaced this with the more apposite Magenta[1]. I adopt this and the terms Lemon Yellow instead of Greenish Yellow, Apple Green for Yellowish Green, Peacock Blue for Green-Blue, being more vivid.

The sigils of the Zodiacal signs should be painted in its appropriate colour upon a background of its spectral opposite. Thus, Aries is bright red on a ground of emerald. The pigments must be luminous but not transparent and must be evenly applied. The exact shade of each must be found so as to make a complete contrast with its opposite. Order papers suggest that enamel paints be used or coloured paper to give the required tone-intensity and evenness of surface. So it came about that a magical order was advocating the methods of *collage* and op-art[2] more than fifty years before such procedures filtered through to the art-circles of Europe.

---

1 This may explain why Colquhoun used a colour much closer to magenta rather than crimson to represent Binah in the King Scale, see Hale 2024. Colquhoun would opt for colour changes that produced the greater effects when required.

2 An abstract style popular in the 1960s and early 1970s that produced optical illusions using patterns, often to produce a sense of movement.

Having made a sigil according to these instructions, look fixedly at it for a few moments and its two colours will seem to "flash" one against the other as if with a life of their own. In fact, it constitutes what the Order called a "flashing tablet", sending a signal from the material world to the world of formation. That the practice of gazing at such a tablet would today be designated a mild form of self-hypnosis is not significant: if pursued, it may involve the inquirer in unanswerable questions about the validity of subjective impressions. What is important is that the process may initiate a change in consciousness.

A set of Zodiacal Signs thus represented forms a helpful item of equipment in a personal temple or sanctum. Meditation on each Sign in turn can prove a fruitful source of knowledge, and will at least stimulate speculation. Meantime, even a cursory glance at the completed set demonstrates some suggestive parallels in symbolism.

It is at once obvious that the series divides naturally into two halves at Libra which, being represented by an emerald sigil on a red ground, inverts the "flashing colours" of its Zodiacal opposite, Aries. Similarly, Scorpio inverts those of Taurus, and so on. In this way opposite Signs are both linked and distinguished.

The colours of the sigils move from Aries to Pisces through spectral gradations, from bright red to magenta. The same colours in their grounds from Libra to Virgo.

Arranged as in a clock face, the Zodiac forms an elegant diagram, that stresses the inherent polarity of its constituents. Aries is placed at the zenith, and twelve o'clock, Libra at the nadir and six, Cancer at three and Capricorn at nine. Taurus at one o'clock faces Scorpio at seven, Gemini (appropriately!) at two faces Sagittarius at eight, with Leo at four and Aquarius at ten, Virgo at five and Pisces at eleven.

The colours of the four elements being red (Fire), yellow (Air), blue (Water) and indigo (Earth)—with their flashing opposites of green, violet, orange and amber—it would seem by the colours attributed to them that Aries and Libra, respectively Cardinal Fire and Cardinal Air, have a special overall affinity with elemental Fire. Leo and Aquarius, respectively again Kerubic Fire and Kerubic Air, have a corresponding affinity with elemental Air, as do Sagittarius and Gemini, Mutable Fire and Mutable Air, with the element of water. Again, Capricorn (Cardinal Earth) and Cancer (Cardinal Water) correspond with elemental Earth.

All these links are stressed by the colour and ground-colour of each sigil, but it must be noted that according to the Rose[3], the colours assigned to the Elements are not identical to those of any sign in the Zodiac. Air is described as "bright pale yellow", Water not as the blue of Sagittarius but as 'deep blue', Fire as 'glowing orange-scarlet' and Earth as a group of four colours difficult to represent diagrammatically. However, as a near approximation, the reds may be aligned with Fire, the yellows with Air, and the blues with Water. As for the attribution of indigo to Earth, it is the colour attributed to the 32nd path of Ietzirah and Earth is also attributed to this same path.

To the Signs of the fiery triplicity belong the primary colours—red, yellow, and blue; to those of the airy triplicity the secondary, orange, green and violet. But the triplicity of Earth seems to fall outside this sequence with red-orange, apple green and indigo instead of the tertiaries, russet, citrine and olive, which would result from a simple mixing of two of each of the secondaries. No more can the watery triplicity with amber, peacock blue and magenta, take its place in this classification.

The planets may be paired in the same way as the Signs, by referring to their flashing colours:

Red	E	Emerald Green	D
Red-Orange	J	Peacock Blue	(?)
Orange	A	Blue	B
Amber	H	Indigo	G
Yellow	C	Violet	F
Apple Green	(Isis?)	Magenta	I

3 Here Colquhoun is referring to the centre of the Rose Cross.

The Golden Dawn colour scales included the five traditional planets with the Sun and the Moon, but now the more recently studied Uranus, Neptune and Pluto may be added. The Late Dr. W. B Crow suggested tawney (which approaches amber) for Uranus and magenta, already attributed to Pisces, for Neptune. Red-orange seems suitable for Pluto, but as the trans-Plutonian planet Isis is still astronomically half-discovered, the ascription to it of apple green is guess-work. However, if Madame Blavatsky was right to claim in *The Secret Doctrine* that our solar system contains ten planets besides the Sun and the Moon there is still another to be revealed and may prove to be suited to the remaining peacock-blue.

While the foregoing considerations should be given due weight when judging a natal map, the best use of a Zodiacal or planetary "flashing tablet" will always be a meditation glyph. †

Colour and the Two Sigils (1979)

In this short piece Colquhoun advocates for the colouring of the *Sigillum Dei Aemeth*, which she notes is most commonly seen in black and white. She comments that colouring the sigil might help to reveal its meaning.

It is reported that *The Sworn Book of Honorius* gives directions for colouring its most important sigil, on which Dr. Dee's famous *Sigillum Dei Aemeth* is based. If those directions are followed and both diagrams are coloured accordingly, the result will be a revelation of force and beauty. It is noticeable that the Honorius Seal is visually the more striking.

This one appears primarily as a sun-wheel, the outer circles being yellow or gold, and on this a green circle is superimposed. In fact, green predominates in the design, which is appropriate since this colour, like the number 7, represents the influence of Venus. The outer heptagon or first line of defense is ascribed to Mercury (purple) and the heptagram, indicating the operation of the magician, to Sol (yellow). The inner heptagram protection is azure or Jupiter, the other benefic planet with Venus. The red pentagram in the centre stands for the Martian energy of the magician himself: his centre being sun-coloured shows the link between macrocosm and microcosm.

The sigil therefore would seem to symbolise a Venusian operation within the regency of Sol, making use of the protective powers of Mercury and Jupiter and the activity of Mars.

To grasp the meaning of these tinctures is the first step towards understanding the two sigils. To me, a sigil does not begin to live until it is represented in colour. As MacGregor Mathers notes in the preface to his edition of the *Key of Solomon*, some of the MSS he consulted in the British Library are illustrated with coloured diagrams and in some of these, gold and silver are also employed. I believe the use of colour must originally have been universal in such designs. Oriental equivalents are always coloured. I would go further and add that expert craftsmanship is concomitant with esoteric knowledge; poor craftsmanship is an indication of distortion or deficiency in such knowledge. It is possible that in the West the use of tinctures may have been kept secret or have lapsed in course of time; as far as I know, Dee did not use colour. His seals which are (or were) on view in the British Museum, were in black or sepia line on off-white wax.

The two sigils are printed on separate enclosed sheets of paper in order that readers who wish to may colour them according to the indications.

TECHNICAL NOTES

Transparent pigments are useful for colouring lettered diagrams as they can be applied so as not to obscure the lettering. Acrylic pigments are more suitable than water colours since, being quick drying, they can be put on thinly in successive layers, and are also more permanent. It is important to aim for maximum contrast in adjacent colour areas in order to obtain a "flashing" effect.

Yellow : Lemon yellow
Green : Viridian
Azure: Cobalt Blue
Red : Vermillion
Purple : Crimson Madder over Ultramarine

(Purple is seldom supplied in ordinary colour boxes and though red and blue make purple in the spectrum, to mix them as pigments usually results in mud. The above method is a compromise).†

Note on the Colouring of Homer's Golden Chain Diagram (1979)

This is an interesting short piece where Colquhoun demonstrates a colour scheme of the Homer's Chain Diagram as theorised in her cousin Edward Garstin's *Glossary of Alchemical Terms*.

A coloured version of Joseph Kirchweger's famous diagram precedes the entry on the *Aurea Catena Homeri* (1722) in the unpublished *Glossary of Alchemical Terms* by E. J. L. Garstin, but no authority is cited to explain the choice of colours. Garstin's diagram, though neatly drawn, is very roughly tinted with coloured chalks. In my copy of it I have used acrylic colours instead.

I have replaced his yellow and grey with respectively, gold and silver paint, though I am not sure that this is justified. At the third "link" in the Chain, I have assumed that his mixture of red and blue strokes was a substitute for purple. In his above-mentioned entry on the *Aurea Catena* he refers to his MS copy of the *Manual Operation of the Philosopher of Leyden*[1]. I myself have not seen this MS of Garstin's and I fear it must be lost. It might possibly throw some light on this colour scheme for the various "links".

Since two constituents, the circle and the straight line, compose each "Link", I have called the former Venus and the latter Mars, as Western equivalents of Yin and Yang. Employing these, the poem which ensues may serve as a *memoria technica* for the colour sequence. A natural caesura occurs at the fifth "link", after which red is always assigned to the Mars-element. It seems that this is the only instance of a connection in these colours with those traditionally ascribed to the planets or the Zodiacal signs. If analysis by colour helps to unveil the secrets of this most recondite of texts, analysis by form also may do so. The Venus-element, the circle, remains constant throughout the Chain, but the Mars-element, the straight line or lines, varies as to position in each

1 This appears to be in reference to the letter of Actum Leyden dated 27 March 1662 which gives a procedure for creating a tincture that is the Philosopher's Stone. It was published in Manly P. Hall's 1928 *Secret Teachings of All Ages.*

"link". Most striking is the identity in form of the figure which begins the Chain at number one, with the figure which ends it at number ten, the difference being that the former is upright and the latter reversed. As I noted in the *Sword of Wisdom*, I see this as a Western apprehension of the dictum "Nirvana is Samsara".

Cannot some maker of esoteric jewellery, embody the diagram in an actual chain of gold, with the colours in gems or enamel?

AURA CATENA HOMERI

Venus blue-and-gold
    Mars blue
Venus blue
    Mars green
Venus green
    Mars red
Venus green
    Mars gold
Venus silver
    Mars gold-and-red
Venus gold
    Mars red
Venus green
    Mars red
Venus purple
    Mars red
Venus silver
    Mars red
Venus red-and-gold
    Mars red

Pilgrimage (1979)

Colquhoun loved travel and engaging with the spirits of place, and she gravitated to places where the magnetic power of the earth could flow and be experienced through caves, springs, and stone monuments. This essay has a lovely psychogeographic sentiment to it, suggesting that one must intuitively attune oneself to their surroundings to understand the natural energetic rhythms in a location. Of course, she notes that understanding the effects of the motions of the planets on the energy of a location will enhance its magic. This short piece was published in *Sangreal* in 1979.

Most of the "great" religions and the esoteric groups that echo them state that the ultimate ground of being is One: for mono-theists there is "one God," for adherents of more esoteric associations, 'the One.' Usually, no reason is given for these assertions, as though they stated a truism needing no support. Yet observable fact would seem to contradict them: multiplicity is more in evidence than any fancied unity and for proof one has only to look around (or indeed, within).

Illumination is therefore contingent on being in one of the many right places at the right time. This necessitates pilgrimage: ideally the devotee becomes a perpetual pilgrim, a "noble voyageur" without permanent base.

Over the earth's surface are to be found localities which the ancients called "Fountains out of Hecate." To tap these chthonic power-centres it is essential to be near them at the times when they erupt as geysers of energy. Certain places have an affinity with certain times—of the day, of the week, of the year, of the cycle. Many of these are still to be discovered, or rediscovered; mythology and folklore provide clues, calendrical observances being especially useful. One's own hunches about the atmosphere of certain places are often worth following up. Short of becoming a wandering "venerable", it is important to live (or at least occasionally to stay) near one of these "Fountains". In this way one can gradually come to know the seasons when its stream of power wells up most strongly. One can immerse oneself in it, even if one lacks the knowledge to direct it to other purposes.

I am aware of centres whose power can be classified under elemental Water and Earth (to use Rosicrucian terms)—and here the power seems to "rise." Probably there are others situated some distance above the ground which are allied to Fire and Air and whose power "showers down." Earth-centres often mediate their force through caves—sometimes artificial—and subterranean "faults"; Water-centres through underground streams, blind-springs, holy wells, haunted rivers and lakes.

The power of any centre varies with the seasons, and these in turn are influenced by the positions of Sun and Moon, the Zodiac, the Planets and the Fixed Stars—a lore needing much research. The earth's surface and the atmosphere above it can be envisaged as a chequer-pattern: the Places, demarcated by horizontal lines, being "fixed" while the Times, represented by verticals, are in a state of perpetual motion following the dance of the heavenly bodies. When a cross is formed by its appropriate vertical passing over a particular horizontal, this marks the moment when the pilgrim should aim to be present. One might call it a shuttle service which indicates both the origin of calendars and their necessity. Incidentally, it shows why any arbitrary change in a calendar, however "reasonable," often encounters popular resistance stemming from the collective unconscious.

What does the pilgrim do, once arrived? Perhaps nothing, beyond holding himself in a state of expectancy; but anything that produces a state of readiness to absorb the forces presenting themselves will be a help. Ritual—ancient or modern, traditional or self-devised—may do this but entire passivity may be equally effective. What is likely to be of no effect at all are the meetings in unconsecrated places and at (esoterically speaking) haphazard times, which some of the churches are now offering as an alternative to traditional ceremony. †

Bibliography

Documents housed in the Tate Archives are detailed in the notes with their Tate Gallery Archives (TGA) reference number. In some cases, manuscripts used were kindly provided to me from private collections. Some of these essays have been republished in Nichols (2007), Shillitoe and Morrisson (2014) and Shillitoe (2019).

To date, Richard Shillitoe has compiled the most complete catalogue of Colquhoun's work, and has also compiled a list of all Colquhoun's published works which can be found in the highly recommended collection *Medea's Charms.*

"The Quest of the Divine: A paper read before members of the Quest Society, in criticism of an address by the Rev. Ethelbert Goodchild" TGA 929/2/3/1

"The Connection Between Mysticism and Blasphemy" TGA 929/2/3/2

"Prose of Alchemy" *The Quest* (vol. 21, no 3), pp. 294-303, 1930.

"Explanation of a Design for a Painting on Silk" TGA 929/2/1/23

"Dance of the Nine Opals" TGA 929/2/1/17

"The Divine Marquis and the Myth of Liberty" TGA 929/2/1/22

"The Water Stone of the Wise" in Alex Comfort and John Bayliss (eds.) *New Road 1943.* Essex: Grey Walls Press, 1943.

"The Night Side of Nature" in *The Glass* No. 8, pp. 8-12,1953.

"Children of the Mantic Stain" *Athene* 5 No. 2, pp. 29-34, 1951.

Untitled Heaven and Earth Column, Profile of Gerald Gardner *The London Broadsheet* No. 1, p. 4,1954.

"Divination up-to-date" *The London Broadsheet* No. 2, p. 4, 1955.

"Portrait of a Magician: Austin Osman Spare" *The London Broadsheet* No 3, p. 4, 1955.

"The Dying-Kick of the Dying-God" *The London Broadsheet* No. 4, p. 6, 1955.

"Unidentified Flying Objects" *The London Broadsheet* No. 5. p. 4, 1955.

"The Qabalah" *Prediction*, Vol. 24, pp. 39-41, May 1958.

"The Ten Sephiroth" *Prediction* Vol. 24. pp. 36-37, June 1958.

"The Twenty-Two Paths" *Prediction* Vol. 24. pp. 39-41, July 1958.

"The 400 Desirable Worlds" *Prediction* Vol. 24. pp. 37-40, August 1958.

"An Analysis of the Rose Cross Symbol related to the Spectrum" TGA 929/5/12/1/26

"Dimensional Interrelation: A Meditation on the Platonic Solids" TGA 929/2/1/21

"Lights In The Air" TGA 929/2/1/34

"Surrealism and Hermetic Poetry" TGA 929/2/1/60

"Meditation Begins at Home" *Prediction* Vol. 35, No. 8, pp. 9-10, 1968.

"The Thirteen Treasures of the Isle of Britain" *Prediction* Vol. 35. No 6, pp. 12-14, 1968.

"The Tree Alphabet and the Tree of Life" TGA 929/2/1/66

"The Infernal Worlds of The Qabalah" TGA 929/2/1/32

"The Openings of the Body" *Quest* No. 4, pp. 26-27, 1970.

"Wisdom Tradition of The Gael; Part One: The Green Diamond" *Prediction* Vol. 36. No. 4, pp. 20-22, 1970.

"Wisdom Tradition of The Gael; Part Two: The Danaan Tree Of Life" *Prediction* Vol. 36. No pp. 20-22, 1970.

"The Order of the Sun and The Moon, Nicaragua" TGA 929/2/1/43

"Banners from the Sky" *Prediction* vol. 39 no1 pp.23-24, 1973.

"Pilgrimage" *Sangreal* Vol. 2. No. 1, pp. 29-31, 1979.

"Surrealism and Hermetic Poetry" TGA 929/2/1/60

"Aspects of Graal Symbolism" TGA 929/2/1/3

"Paganism" (after 1973) TGA 929 2/1/46

The Sword of Wisdom: MacGregor Mathers and the Golden Dawn. London: G.P. Putnam's Sons, 1975.

"Druidry" (after 1975) (private collection mss.)

"Taro as Colour" *Sangreal* Vol. 1 No. 2 pp. 31-33, 1978. 1977.

"The Zodiac and the Flashing Colours" *The Hermetic Journal* No. 4, pp. 5-7, 1979.

"Colour and the Two Sigils" *The Hermetic Journal* No. 4, pp. 8-9, 1979.

"Note on the Colouring of Homer's Golden Chain Diagram" *The Hermetic Journal* No. 6 pp. 15-17, 1979.

Additional Reading

Ferentinou, Victoria. "Ithell Colquhoun, Surrealism and the Occult." *Papers of Surrealism* 9 http://www.surrealismcentre.ac.uk/papersofsurrealism/journal9/index.htm, pp. 1-24, 2011.

Ferentinou, Victoria. "The Iconography of Coniunctio Oppositorum: Visual and Verbal Dialogues in Ithell Colquhoun's Oeuvre." in Peter Forshaw (ed.) *Lux in Tenebris: The Visual and the Symbolic in Western Esotericism*, pp. 363-96, 2016.

Ferentinou, Victoria. "The Quest for the Goddess: Matriarchy, Surrealism and Gender Politics in the Work of Ithell Colquhoun and Leonora Carrington" in Tessel Bauduin, Victoria Ferentinou and Daniel Zamani (eds). *Surrealism, Occultism and Politics: In Search of the Marvellous*, London: Routledge, 2017. (Kindle edition)

Greer, Mary K. *Women of the Golden Dawn: Rebels and Priestesses*. Rochester: Park Street Press, 1995.

Hale, Amy. *Ithell Colquhoun: Genius of the Fern Loved Gully*. London: Strange Attractor, 2020.

Hale, Amy (ed.) *Women in Western Esotericism: Beyond Seeresses and Sea Priestesses*. London: Palgrave, 2022.

Hale, Amy. *Sex Magic: Diagrams of Love, Ithell Colquhoun*. London: Tate Publishing, 2024.

White, Manon Hedenborg. *The Eloquent Blood: The Goddess Babalon and the Construction of Femininities in Western Esotericism*. New York: Oxford University Press, 2020.

Mahon, Alyce. *The Marquis de Sade and the Avant-Garde*. New Jersey: Princeton University Press, 2020.

Morrisson, Mark. S. "The Periodical Culture of the Occult Revival: Esoteric, Wisdom, Modernity and Counter-Public Spheres." *Journal of Modern Literature*, Vol. 31, (No. 2), pp. 1-22, Winter 2008.

Nichols, Steve. *The Magical Writings of Ithell Colquhoun*. Raleigh, North Carolina: Lulu Enterprises, 2007.

Noble, Judith, Craig, Tilly and Ferentinou, Victoria. *The Dance of Moon and Sun: Ithell Colquhoun, British Women and Surrealism*. Somerset: Fulgur Press, 2023.

Owen, Alex. *The Place of Enchantment: British Occultism and the Culture of the Modern*. Chicago: University of Chicago Press, 2004.

Shillitoe, Richard. *Ithell Colquhoun: Magician Born of Nature*. Raleigh, North Carolina: Lulu Enterprises. 2010.

Shillitoe, Richard and Morrisson, Mark (eds). I *Saw Water: An Occult Novel and Other Selected Writings*. University Park: Penn State University Press, 2014.

Shillitoe, Richard (ed). *Medea's Charms: Selected Shorter Writings of Ithell Colquhoun*. London: Peter Owen, 2019.

Kontou, Tatiana. (ed.) *Women and the Victorian Occult*. Abingdon: Routledge, 2011.

Speculative Bibliography

This bibliography has been added to provide the reader with access to some texts which Colquhoun very likely would have read and which may have provided some of the resources Colquhoun used in writing these essays. This is not comprehensive and where a modern edition of a text exists for the reader to consult, that has been provided as it will be of the most use to readers who are interested in looking at Colquhoun's sources. Colquhoun had an extensive library, much of which remains in the Tate Archives. However, as these essays indicate, she also consumed a lot of occult and esoteric publications and small poetry magazines which are lost to time, or, such as *The Monolith* from the Order of the Cubic Stone, occasionally emerge as edited collections. I would direct the interested reader to The International Association for the Preservation of Spiritualist and Occult Periodicals which maintains an online archive of scans some of these important publications and which is often updated. http://iapsop.com/

Baird, Robert. *Miguel de Molinos: The Spiritual Guide.* New Jersey: Paulist Press, 2010.

Blake, William. *The Marriage of Heaven and Hell.* Boston: John W. Luce and Company, 1906.

Brotchie, Alastair and Galletti, Marina (eds). *Georges Bataille: The Sacred Conspiracy: The Internal Papers of the Secret Society of Acéphale and Lectures to the College of Sociology*. London: Atlas Press, 2018.

Breton, André. *Surrealism and Painting.* Boston: MFA Publications, 2002.

Crowe, Catherine. *The Night Side of Nature or Ghosts and Ghost Seers.* London: TC Newby, 1848.

Crowley, Aleister. "The Blue Equinox". *The Equinox.* III (1). Detroit: Universal Publishing Co. 1919.

Erdman, David V. *The Complete Poetry and Prose of William Blake*. New York: Doubleday, 1988.

Finneran, Richard J. *The Collected Poems of W. B. Yeats*. New York: Scribner, 1996.

Fortune, Dion. *Avalon of the Heart*. London: Aquarian Press, 1971 [1934].

Gardner, Gerald. *Witchcraft Today*. London: Rider and Co, 1954.

Garstin, Edward Langford. *Theurgy or the Hermetic Practice: A Treatise on Spiritual Alchemy*. London: Rider and Co, 1930.

Garstin, Edward Langford. *The Secret Fire: An Alchemical Study*. London: Search Publishing, 1932.

Glover, Edward. *The Technique of Psycho-Analysis*. London: Ballière, Tindall and Sons, 1928.

Graves, Robert. *The White Goddess*. London: Faber and Faber, 1948.

Guénon, René. *Symbolism of the Cross*. Ghent, NY: Sophia Perennis et Universalis, 2004 (1931) accessed from https://archive.org/stream/reneGuénon/1931%20-%20Symbolism%20of%20the%20Cross_djvu.txt

Guénon, René. *The Multiple States of The Being*. (English trans. Fohr, Henry D.) Hillsdale: Sophia Perennis, 2001 (1932) accessed from https://archive.org/stream/reneGuénon/1932%20-%20The%20Multiple%20States%20of%20the%20Being_djvu.txt

Hall, Manly P. *The Secret Teachings of All Ages, Unabridged*. New York, Discovery Publisher, 2020 [1928].

Haycock, Marged (ed and trans). *Legendary Poems from the Book of Taliesin*. Aberystwyth: CMCS Publications, 2007 (2nd Revised edition 2015).

Hegel, Georg Wilhelm Friedrich. *The Phenomenology of Spirit. Cambridge Hegel Translations*. Cambridge: Cambridge University Press, 2019.

Hudleston, Roger (ed). Julian of Norwich. *Revelations of Divine Love*. Mineola, New York: Dover Press, 2006.

Kirnan, Alvin B. (ed.) Ben Jonson. *The Alchemist*. New Haven: Yale University Press, 1974 [1610].

Levi, Eliphas. *Transcendental Magic: Its Doctrine and Ritual*. Trans. A. E. Waite. London: William Rider & Son, Ltd., 1923 [1896].

Macpherson, James. *Ossian's Fingal: An Ancient Epic Poem, in Six Books*. Trans. George Harvey. London: Cadell and Davies, 1814 [1762].

Mathers, S. L. MacGregor (Samuel Liddell MacGregor), 1854-1918, and Christian Knorr von Rosenroth. *The Kabbalah Unveiled: Containing the Following Books of the Zohar: The Book of Concealed Mystery; The Greater Holy Assembly; The Lesser Holy Assembly*. London: Routledge K. Paul, 1962 [1887].

McMorran, Will, and Wynn, Thomas (eds and trans) *Marquis de Sade: 120 Days of Sodom*. New York: Penguin Classics, 2016.

Mead, G. R. S. *Quests Old and New*. London: G. Bell & Sons, Ltd., 1913.

Maier, Michael. *Atalanta Fugiens: An Edition of the Fugues, Emblems, and Epigrams*. Grand Rapids: Phanes Press, 1989 [1617].

Morganwg, Iolo (Edward Williams) *Barddas*. Trans: Rev. J. Williams Ab Ithel. London: Long Ian & Co., 1862.

Péret, Benjamin. *La Parole est à Péret*. New York: Éditions Surréalistes, 1943.

Philalethes, Eirenaeus (George Starkey). *An Open Entrance to the Closed Palace of the King*. Seattle: Amazon Digital Services, 2010 [1667].

Philalethes, Eirenaeus. *The Three Treatises Of Philalethes: The Metamorphosis Of Metals; The Celestial Ruby; The Fountain Of Chemical Truth*. Montana: Kessenger Publishing, 2010.

Poe, Edgar Allan. "Al Aaraaf". *The Complete Works of Edgar Allan Poe, Vol. 2 : Al Aaraaf, Tamerlane, and Minor Poems*. Hastings: Delphi Classics, 2017 [1829].

Praz, Mario. *The Romantic Agony*. London: Oxford University Press, H. Milford, 1933.

Rolleston, T. W. *Myths and Legends of the Celtic Race*. London: Constable, 1911.

Regardie, Israel. *The Golden Dawn: The Original Account of the Teachings, Rites & Ceremonies of the Hermetic Order*. St. Paul MN: Llewellyn Publishing, 1989 [1937].

Riemann, Bernhard. *On the Hypotheses Which Lie at the Bases of Geometry*. Germany: Springer International Publishing, 2016 [1873].

Seaver, Richard and Lane, Helen R. (trans.) *Andre Breton: Manifestoes of Surrealism*. Ann Arbor: University of Michigan Press, 1969.

Spengler, Oswald. *The Decline of the West: Form and Actuality*. Trans. Charles Francis Atkinson. New York: Alfred A. Knopf, 1926.

Symons, Arthur. *Images of Good and Evil*. London: William Heinemann, 1899.

Underhill, Evelyn. *A Book of Contemplation: The which is Called The Cloud of Unknowing, in the which a Soul is Oned with God*. London: J. M. Watkins, 1922.

Comte de Villiers de L'Isle-Adam, Auguste. *Tomorrow's Eve*. Champaign: University of Illinois Press, 1982 [1886].

Waite, Arthur Edward. *The Hermetic Museum, Restored and Enlarged: Most Faithfully Instructing All Disciples of the Sopho-spagyric Art how that Greatest and Truest Medicine of the Philosopher's Stone May be Found and Held*. Boston: Red Wheel/Weiser, 1999 [1893].

Waite, Arthur Edward (ed). *Works of Thomas Vaughan: Eugenius Philalethes*. London: Theosophical Society, 1919.

Watkins, Alfred. *The Old Straight Track*. London: Abacus, 1974 [1925].

Westcott, W. Wynn. *Collectanea Hermetica*. Boston: Red Wheel/Weiser, 1998.

Weston, Jessie L. *From Ritual to Romance*. Cambridge: Cambridge University Press, 1920.

Yeats, W. B. *Ideas of Good and Evil*. Stratford: AH Bullen Press, 1907.

Yeats, W. B. and Yeats, George. *A Vision: An Explanation of Life Founded upon the Writings of Giraldus and upon certain Doctrines attributed to Kusta Ben Luka*. London: T. Werner Laurie, 1925.

A

B

D

E

Acknowledgments

I would like to the following for their generous assistance in providing me with manuscripts, scans, and copies of Colquhoun's work: Clive Harper, Barbara Cormack, Richard Shillitoe, Marcus Williamson, Julia Phillips, and Tony Hutchins. This project started about fifteen years ago, and I would like to thank everyone from the Tate Archives who assisted in this project over the years, most importantly the stellar Victoria Jenkins without whom I would simply be lost. I am grateful to Barry William Hale, Emma Sharples, and Richard Shillitoe for continuing magical and Colquhoun collegiality and for providing insight and commentary on this material. I would like to thank Steven Cline and Hazel Cline for their early assistance with this manuscript, and especially Dr. Robert Puckett for expert help in putting this together. I could not have completed this without his tenacity, patience and expertise. I would also like to extend my deepest and most profound appreciation to Richard Bancroft who deftly and thoroughly edited this challenging, quirky set of texts with care and precision. Thank you to Jamie Sutcliffe and Mark Pilkington of Strange Attractor Press for continuing to believe in Colquhoun's wonderful weirdness and also mine. Last but never least, thank you to Rhett Kit Aultman for all the things over all the years.

STRANGE ATTRACTOR PRESS 2026